Approaches to Theological Ethics

Approaches to Theological Ethics

Sources, Traditions, Visions

Maureen Junker-Kenny

t&tclark

LONDON · NEW YORK · OXFORD · NEW DELHI · SYDNEY

T&T CLARK
Bloomsbury Publishing Plc
50 Bedford Square, London, WC1B 3DP, UK
1385 Broadway, New York, NY 10018, USA

BLOOMSBURY, T&T CLARK and the T&T Clark logo are
trademarks of Bloomsbury Publishing Plc

First published in Great Britain 2019

Cover design: Terry Woodley
Cover image: *The Calling of Saint Matthew* c.1599 by Michelangelo Merisi da Caravaggio
(1571–1610). Contarelli Chapel, Church of San Luigi dei Francesi, Rome

A catalogue record for this book is available from the British Library.

A catalog record for this book is available from the Library of Congress.

ISBN: HB: 978-0-5676-8296-3
       PB: 978-0-5676-8295-6
       ePDF: 978-0-5676-8297-0
       ePUB: 978-0-5676-8298-7

Typeset by RefineCatch Limited, Bungay, Suffolk
Printed and bound in Great Britain

To find out more about our authors and books visit www.bloomsbury.com
and sign up for our newsletters.

To the students of the BA in World Religions and Theology whose engagement with the themes of this book in the past 25 years has been instructive and motivating, and to my colleagues in the Department of Religions & Theology, in gratitude for their commitment and friendship.

Contents

Preface

I am dedicating this book to the students of the BA in World Religions and Theology whose questions and essays over the past 25 years of teaching this course have been insightful, probing and motivating. It is equally dedicated to my colleagues in Trinity College's previous Department of Religions & Theology (1980–2018), which has now been absorbed into its new School of Religion: Alexandra Grieser, Daniele Pevarello, Cathriona Russell and Jane Welch. Specific thanks are due to them for looking after my administrative tasks during the sabbatical in which this book was written. Their professional perspectives and their commitment have made work in the Department over the past years enjoyable and exciting.

Fiona Kenny is to be thanked for willingly and thoroughly taking on the expert tasks of formatting, proofreading and copyediting the manuscript. Her precision and good spirits have graced the final weeks of completion. Peter is owed thanks for his learned comments and all his help in sourcing books, Kilian for computer installation and maintenance, and all of my family for their support, humour and patience.

The feast of the Epiphany is a good date to complete a comparative study of approaches to theological ethics. The journey of the Magi, gentiles from the 'East', to a newborn child relevant for all cultures of the world, is a biblical story that has shaped imaginations and visions, perceptions and horizons of expectation. It exemplifies the universalist scope of ethics to which the Bible gives rise from Genesis to Isaiah and the New Testament. Matthew's gospel draws on prophecies and parallels to the story of Moses which his community would have recognized, in order to show the incomparable significance of the birth of Jesus Christ. The scholars from the East following their star to Bethlehem are an arresting and diverse symbol of what theology identifies as the universal salvific will of God. One criterium by which the following approaches are judged is whether they do justice to this biblical essential.

Introduction

The title of the present study, *Approaches to Theological Ethics*, indicates two main interests. One is in the conversation of this theological discipline with philosophical schools of ethics. Using the label 'Christian ethics' in the title could have implied that the counterpart for specifying what makes it Christian are other religions. Choosing the heading 'theological ethics' is to situate it within theology as a systematic reflection on the Christian faith which has always engaged with the general consciousness of truth of different eras, as pursued by philosophy. The second interest is in analysing which traditions of thinking are being employed, resulting in the internal diversity of this discipline. To explore what unites Christian ethics would be a different enterprise, and other authors have carried this out in historical and thematic studies.[1]

In comparing the starting points and concepts of the different approaches, the aim is to shed a light on the intellectual and linguistic traditions that are operative in their argumentations. Who are their conversation partners, what are benchmarks for justification and how directly do realms of praxis figure in them? One major divide which this book sets out to bridge is linguistic. Continental theological authors normally only appear in Anglo-American debate when a book or article has been translated into English. It leaves the majority of the work done in German-speaking moral theology and social ethics inaccessible, as well as its continental philosophical backdrop. This imbalance is worth remedying.[2] Together with these ethicists, some philosophers will be introduced who figure in their work as much as fellow theological

---

[1] For example, J. Philip Wogaman, *Christian Ethics: A Historical Introduction* (Louisville: Westminster/ John Knox, 1993, 2nd enlarged edn 2011); Victor Lee Austin, *Christian Ethics: A Guide for the Perplexed* (London: T & T Clark, 2013).
[2] Translations from sources in German are my own.

ethicists do.[3] How the same classical positions (such as Aristotle, Aquinas and Kant) are treated in continental and theological ethics is an important point of enquiry. For example, a different take on 'virtue' in philosophical and theological ethics from the English-speaking sphere will emerge. Elucidating the unbroken significance of the autonomy tradition may also allow its crucial role in systematic theology to be better understood. For their North American and British counterparts, virtue ethics and revisionist natural law are key approaches. This variety in the frameworks chosen calls for comparison and analysis: from their use of the Bible and its theological and cultural histories of reception, to their attitudes to modernity and its different concepts of reason, to their understanding of church and of engagement in the public sphere.

The book is structured into three parts: sources; approaches; and visions. The first part, on 'sources', leads straight into the interdisciplinary task of theological ethics. It has to accommodate under its roof widely differing types and methods of enquiry. This variety of commentators with characteristic attitudes gives their host the task to understand their brief as well as introduce them to each other, and to direct them into fruitful conversations. From these, conclusions are drawn under the normative perspective of the chosen approaches to ethics that convert them into directions for travel with routes compared, burdens assessed, checkpoints highlighted and horizons scrutinized.

The cross-disciplinary task is not confined to the two sources from reason, analysed in Chapters 3 and 4: the 'normatively human', as elucidated in philosophy, and individual disciplines in the sciences and the humanities relevant for the subject matters at hand, such as biology, psychology or economics. Also, the two sources from revelation, namely the Bible (Chapter 1), and 'tradition' as its history of reception and normative interpretation (Chapter 2), are subject to analysis by secular sciences, such as history, sociology and textual criticism. From the start, it becomes clear that theological ethics is a '*res mixta*', a mixed matter, not based solely on revelation but also on the enquiries of individual disciplines with their changing paradigms and refinement of methods. How to define 'objectivity' in this search for truth has been a disputed theme in philosophy and in feminist theory with conclusions relevant for theological ethics.

---

[3] In *An Introduction to Christian Ethics: Goals, Duties, and Virtues* (Nashville: Abingdon Press, 2011), Robin W. Lovin also deals with philosophical background traditions and their theological reception and critique, under the headings of 'Goals', 'Duties', and 'Virtues', after a first part on origins of ethics and varieties of Christian 'stances'.

In Part 2, 'approaches', some of the schools of philosophical ethics treated under the third source, 'normative accounts of the human person', are examined in greater detail. They are regarded as internally coherent 'thought forms' that use categories of ethics such as 'justice', 'practical reasoning' and 'will' in a way that is consistent with the horizon of its system. This may be teleological or deontological, an analysis of 'power', or a structured combination. One of the critical questions to the approaches is how they accommodate within their terms the Christian message of creation, redemption and human agency in its response.[4]

Like the individual disciplines which can be preceded by stern or colourful reputations, the approaches to theological ethics and the major schools in the history of Western thinking to which they relate are not nondescript characters. They come with pre-understandings attached to them that for some fellow ethicists make it undesirable to meet them. My hope is that on closer acquaintance some of the dubious renown they are held in may be replaced with an understanding of what drives them, why they draw red lines where others don't, and why their company is needed also on behalf of those who are not in the room and cannot make their voices heard. The first one, to be introduced in Chapter 5, is virtue ethics. Different angles and interests have been involved in the rediscovery of this type and in the ways in which thinking in virtue terms affects the interpretation of Christian origins and of faithful agency. The second candidate, examined in Chapter 6, specifies worship as the foundation of Christian ethics and anchors virtue in the liturgical gathering of the community. The third member of the group is natural law, treated in Chapter 7 both in a classical and a revisionist appearance. Moving on universalist grounds, the distinction from the mainly polis-based context of the two previous ones is evident, though it does not prohibit a visit. Chapter 8 on autonomous ethics in a Christian faith perspective welcomes a continental character to the gathering who has sought the company of Kant and considers his deontological model of ethics to be compatible with a Christian understanding of freedom and love. Chapter 9 sees a group joining the conversation that differs internally in their vantage points: feminist natural law, care ethics and autonomy; but they are united in their practical interests of counteracting gender-based discrimination and of examining the history and present stage of thinking of their discipline for its undeclared androcentrism.

---

[4] This 'thought form analysis' is taken over from the systematic theological approach of Thomas Pröpper. Cf. *Dogma und Denkform. Strittiges in der Grundlegung von Offenbarungsbegriff und Gottesgedanke*, ed. Klaus Müller and Magnus Striet (Regensburg: Pustet, 2005), with reference to Thomas Pröpper, *Erlösungsglaube und Freiheitsgeschichte. Eine Skizze zur Soteriologie* (Munich: Kösel, 3rd edn 1991).

Part 3 compares 'visions' that motivate and direct different versions of the discipline: the ecclesiocentric vision of radical orthodoxy; a praxis-oriented conception; and a theory-focused third vision that spells out the theoretical work to be done in the three constituencies David Tracy has identified with their methods and perspectives: university, society and church.

The conclusion first sums up each part through one core theme. It then relates the task of theological ethics to the recent discourses about sources of civic solidarity and cohesion, and to the question of how to participate in public debate: with 'unfiltered' theological standpoints,[5] or with contributions justified internally as possible interpretations of the Christian core and translated into concepts of reason, such as dignity, that are accessible from all quarters in a pluralist democracy?

The aims of this book do not include being comprehensive. There are much-debated approaches and authors in English- and German-speaking theological ethics that do not appear. The key concern has been to build up a framework in which students can locate the specific use of core ethical concepts and argumentations in each school. What they need in addition to facts and information on theories, access to which is at their disposal in a digital age, is the reflective ability to compare intellectual frameworks and methods. Getting to know the history of reflection and debates about key turning points in the eras subsequent to the biblical age should help them establish some foundations for their own thoughtful agency.

---

[5] Saskia Wendel, 'Religiös motiviert – autonom legitimiert – politisch engagiert. Zur Zukunftsfähigkeit politischer Theologie angesichts der Debatte um den öffentlichen Status religiöser Überzeugungen', in *Religion – Öffentlichkeit – Moderne. Transdisziplinäre Perspektiven*, ed. Judith Könemann and S. Wendel (Bielefeld: Transcript, 2016), 298.

Part 1

Introduction: The sources of theological ethics

1   **The Bible as a source of theological ethics**
2   **The second source: Tradition as *norma normans normata***
3   **The third source: Normative accounts of the human person**
4   **The fourth source: The individual human sciences**

As a discipline, theological ethics straddles and seeks to integrate four distinct sources, each with their own methods, normative standards and histories of debate: (1) the Bible; (2) tradition; (3) philosophical accounts of the human; and (4) the individual human sciences.[1] Theological ethics is thus a *res mixta*; it draws on and relates divine revelation and human reason to each other. The first two sources deal with revelation, the latter two with

---

[1] The proposal of its 'quadrilateral' composition enjoys considerable agreement across denominations in English-speaking theological ethics. Cf., for example, the brief description by Lisa S. Cahill, *Between the Sexes* (Philadelphia: Fortress Press, 1985), 4–8, 12–13, with references to its author John Wesley, as well as to James M. Gustafson and Robert J. Daly.

reason in its different forms and capacities to examine human experience. The ways in which these four sources are integrated in order to arrive at ethical judgements and make decisions vary in the five approaches to be examined in Part 2.

Each of these sources comes with its own set of hermeneutical questions and controversies on starting points and premises, alternative frameworks and concepts, and relationships to other sources. This is also the case in philosophical ethics. What gives an additional normative edge to theological ethics is that it understands itself as a response to the prior initiative of God as Creator and Redeemer. God's self-revelation is the context out of which theological ethics develops alongside systematic theology which reflects on the theoretical implications of faith in God. How this distinctive horizon shapes and modifies the normative expectations to agents is outlined with different accentuations by each approach. The fact that theological ethics arises from a distinctive, positive, historical foundation endows it with a normative task not paralleled in schools of philosophical ethics. The scriptures require a discipline of their own, biblical studies, to investigate the historical origins of this religion in the life and destiny, proclamation and praxis of its founder, the person of Jesus. Naming him Christ means to accept him as the saviour, the 'anointed one' expected in the Jewish tradition.

Before beginning to examine the contribution of each of the four sources and their possible integration, the whole analysis needs to be put under a qualification: neither end of the interpretive process is clear-cut. At the contemporary end, what would be necessary to establish cannot be completely delivered: an account of the premises of the era and culture that shape one's current understanding. Regarding the biblical end, also this pole does not constitute a self-contained message. It offers interpretations of God by reflecting on God's action in the history of Israel and of Jesus. Thus, for the task at hand an 'information' model based on univocity from beginning to end is inadequate. It ignores the interpretive effort needed at both points, which has to be laid out and justified. In his introduction to *Reading the Sacred Scriptures*, the Irish theologian and theorist of education Fiachra Long points out the difference of the actual hermeneutical task from the impression conveyed by the myth of the messenger god Hermes:

> The Greek god, Hermes, who may have been fleet of foot and hugely competent in his essential work of communicating the wishes of Zeus to humankind, is not a very good model to explain the more ambiguous context of human meaning-making, not to mention the more complicated process of reading and re-reading the scriptures. Homer models his idea of message

transfer on a linear logic, invoking a general asymmetry between the gods and humankind where the message, originating in a separate domain (Mount Olympus), is then communicated without distortion to a messenger (Hermes), before being translated by means of Hermes's consummate skill into the mind of a human recipient . . . In such a case, the translation is doubly certain, untouched by human misunderstanding on two counts, it being perfectly clear in itself and second perfectly translated. The listener, as a result, has no desire to do anything else but to be patently enlightened by the message handed over . . . To add to our difficulties, our receivers are not only technically imperfect listeners but are often prejudiced and closed to the message communicated because of their own learning ... A historical vulnerability seems to be built in to this process of engagement between creator and receiver.[2]

It was on behalf of the readers of the Bible that Luther defended its immediate accessibility with no need for intervention or explanation by church authorities. Yet the claimed perspicuity of scripture, which is seen as *sui ipsius interpres*, has to be qualified not for ecclesial, but for theological reasons. The Bible itself witnesses to and already interprets God's revelation, and is thus not identical with it. It gives meaning to prior events by reading them as actions and responses of God. Its various text forms and books document a history of development in the understanding of God. Also, regarding the readers, the ever-changing situations of reception introduce uncertainty into the process of delivery and rule out a model where the recipients are seen as merely passive. For the practical task of discovering ethical guidelines, this insight implies that submitting the biblical writings to 'norm-hunting'[3] is especially inadequate: this reading strategy is not open to unexpected insights from the biblical text. It has a prior selective agenda and assumes the priority of the current horizon in defining concerns. A hermeneutical mode of enquiry aware of the role of pre-understandings will question the idea of a neutral condition of listening on the human side, uncomplicated by symbolic frameworks and other presuppositions influencing personal and collective attentiveness. To safeguard the normative standing of the Bible, its otherness has to be protected from premature claims, the mediated nature of God's revelation acknowledged, and the

---

[2] Fiachra Long, 'The Hermeneutic Task', in *Reading the Sacred Scriptures: From Oral Tradition to Written Documents and Their Reception*, ed. Fiachra Long and Siobhán Dowling Long (Abingdon: Routledge, 2017), 2.

[3] Tom Deidun, 'The Bible and Christian Ethics', in *Christian Ethics: An Introduction*, ed. Bernard Hoose (London: Cassell, 1998), 22.

authority of the Bible interpreted on this basis. Collapsing the two, God's Word, and the human words in which it is expressed, prevents such careful discernment and fails to justify the choice of the guiding perspective which a reader will inevitably make. The task to lay open one's premises also relates to the two sources of reason: normative accounts of the human and research in the individual human sciences. But it appears with even greater urgency in relation to the renewed efforts of each age to interpret God's self through the communication contained in scripture. The active role exercised first by the biblical writers and then by the readers calls for a theological framework that allows to put forth revelation in terms of a divine–human encounter, not as a divine communiqué complete in itself, which does not require any effort to be understood. For the latter view, called 'extrinsicist', the authority of God's message depends on discounting any role of the addressees in interpreting God's revelation. However, just as systematic theology reflects on the questions and capabilities of the human recipients that correspond to God's self-revelation, the discipline of theological ethics has to explore the human subjectivity that is called to respond to God's offer. This is spelt out especially in the two sources called 'the normatively human' and the 'human sciences'.

Distinguishing four sources already implies that they are compatible in principle. But their argumentations are on different levels, with separate criteria of normativity; this allows for argued steps of integration into a specific judgement, requiring a process of assessment that keeps the limits of their methods in mind. With these preliminary indications of the independent standing of each source and their inherent boundaries that make precisely defined enquiries possible, the following chapter on the first source opens the dialogue with scholars of the texts and contexts of the Bible.

1

The Bible as a source of theological ethics

While Chapters 1 and 2 will analyse the Bible and 'tradition' separately, since different questions arise from each for their use for contemporary issues, it needs to be stated at the beginning that both sources are internally related. The only available access to the foundational writings of Christianity is through their history of reception, which includes the process of canon formation completed after new cultural challenges had been encountered. Regarding their ranking, they are distinguished as *norma normans non normata*, recognizing the Bible as the originating, authoritative document, and as *norma normans normata*. The normative value of tradition, consisting of the sequence of the understandings created by the efforts to relate the message of God's self-revelation in Jesus Christ to new intellectual contexts, is derived from the primary source, the Bible. The achievement of these early theological interpretations is to give direction to the subsequent understandings of the Christian message: the communities and intellectual streams they spoke to, the creeds and Council decisions on debates on how the person and work of Jesus Christ could be expressed most adequately. Summarized as *norma normans normata*, this body of writings is acknowledged as providing an ongoing normative standard: the theological decisions they contain on conflicting appropriations of its core retain their validity. A memory of theological milestones develops: when a new dispute arises, it is possible to ascertain how a previous definitive statement of the church was arrived at. Marcion's relegation of the Old Testament out of the not yet completed canon of the Christian Bible, and his selection of parts of the New Testament as constituting what he regarded as Gospel were rejected, safeguarding the priority of the foundational documents to later appropriations in new contexts.

Thus, the readings and apologetic achievements of the Early Christian centuries have set standards for the subsequent eras of Christianity. How these are to be related to the third source, the normatively human, will be a question for the end of the second chapter. Yet source one, the Bible, owes its final shape to source two, 'tradition'. So does closer inspection of the process by which they were made part of Sacred Scripture reveal that the primary position assigned to the Bible does not equate to the status of an absolute beginning, but in fact hides the real origin which is owed to the church?

Exactly what standing is given to scripture if it is designated as *norma normans non normata*, in distinction from all subsequent developments and decisions on its behalf? Can the process of canon formation carried out by the church of the first centuries be seen as the cause of its validity? But where does that leave its understanding as the 'unnormed', that is, the originating, norm, if the church is prior to what from then on counts as 'Holy Scriptures' (1)? Is starting with an understanding of the Bible as the authoritative 'Word of God' a better alternative, giving it a different status from subsequent appropriations by the church (2)? Or is the reason for the unsurpassable place of scripture the fact that the witnesses contained in it are historically closest to the events understood as God's self-revelation (3)? Finally, what questions need to be pursued into the following chapter on tradition as the second source, and what consequences do these debates have for argumentations in Christian ethics on how to justify criteria for action (4)?

The problems debated in systematic theology about cause and effect, about the ground and the content of attributing the primary normative role to the Bible, are relevant for Christian ethics; they aim to clarify the logic of argumentation and highlight shortcuts and pitfalls to be avoided. Besides analysing standpoints and criteria within Christian ethics, the first chapter thus has to take on board also systematic theological reflections on the structure and direction of the scripture–church relationship, and on the criteria that govern the interpretation of the foundational documents of the Christian faith tradition.

1. Scripture as a creation of the church

For some Christian ethicists, the special normative standing of the Bible is linked with its canonicity. At the same time, this result of a process of selection within the first centuries is not just regarded as a historical feature of the corpus of biblical writings, but as equally presupposing a contemporary church which bases its life on it. The immediate link to its current interpretation and activity becomes evident in an explanation of the status of the Epistles by the New Testament scholar Stephen Barton: 'from the viewpoint of Christian faith the epistles are not just ancient texts. They are also constituent parts of the canon of scripture, the appropriate context for the interpretation of which is *the ongoing life of the Church in its participation in the life of God in the world.*'[1]

The significance of the canonical standing of these texts can be elucidated in different ways. The hermeneutical awareness of the need to identify the premises of one's own reading of such ancient texts can be specified, as Stephen Barton does, as belonging to the same community and being able to avail of a living link to the past. The hopes attached to the 'canonical turn' as one approach to biblical studies include the normativity of these writings also for ethical reflection. The German exegete Georg Steins sees the continuity in the 'narrative structure', as distinct from the assumption of an identical message. He summarizes with reference to authors such as Brevard Childs and Andrew T. Lincoln that while 'the differences are not harmonized' between the writings from different periods, the unity to be found in its overall narrative structure consists in projecting a 'world' in which one can situate oneself:

> Who is God, how can he be found, how should one live and understand one's relation to God, humankind and the world – all these questions are the subject of the canon. Canon and religious community mutually constitute each other, the canon exists because the church exists – and the church knows what it is, where it comes from, where it goes and what to do underway because of the canon ... the patient and accurate listening/reading becomes

---

[1] Barton, Stephen C., 'The epistles and Christian ethics', in *The Cambridge Companion to Christian Ethics*, ed. Robin Gill (Cambridge: CUP, 2001), 68. He elucidates what is implied in the term 'context' which is usually taken as a descriptive, historical reference; here, it ties the validating role to the horizon of the contemporary church: 'In other words, the context for interpreting the epistles is *the present* ... It is only as the church "performs" the epistles in the ongoing context of its sharing in the life of the Holy Trinity that such performances will contribute to the shaping of a holy people.'

a fundamental ethical act ... Thus, a horizon of meaning is constituted in which concrete actions can be composed into a coherent whole. Narratives, exempla and symbols are hereby decoded as prerequisites for coherent, meaningful, fair and good action.[2]

By providing diverse material for identity formation with its 'larger-than-life figures who challenge us to make a position statement', the writings of the biblical canon provoke current engagement. Like Stephen Barton, Georg Steins locates the validating function in the present community: 'The canon is thus not normative by itself, but only becomes so in the creative process of meaning-making and appropriation, which presupposes and involves the freedom of the hearers.'[3]

While Steins includes the historical-critical and the literary turns into the methods of biblical interpretation, his similar emphasis that 'Canon and religious community mutually constitute each other', and that creative readings are called for today gives rise to a question. Is it conceivable in this model that gaps and discrepancies occur between the Bible and the church of specific eras? Is the thesis of 'mutual constitution' perhaps true only at a level which abstracts from conflicts over concrete interpretations, where churches of the same or of different ages disagree on what the foundational texts signify and demand? A counter-argument against a circular, mutually reinforcing relationship between canonical scriptures and church is put forward by the British New Testament scholar Tom Deidun. With reference to a university and a church using 'biblical grounds' for exclusions such as apartheid he comments that a

> caveat must apply to those who insist that 'the believing community' is the indispensable context for the appropriation of the Bible in Christian ethics ... 'the importance of the believing community as the context for the authority and appropriation of biblical materials seems to be part of a developing consensus'. But which believing community?[4]

Invoking the idea of 'church' in such a general theological sense that controversies about limits of membership do not appear, is in danger of offering an idealized or spiritualized concept from which concrete judgements

---

[2] Marianne Heimbach-Steins and Georg Steins, '"Canon and Community". On the Social-Ethical Relevance of Scripture', in 'The Soul of Theology'. On the Role of Scripture in Theology, ed. Pierre Van Hecke, Conference Proceedings, Leuven, September 17–20, 2015, 164.

[3] Marianne Heimbach-Steins and Georg Steins, '"Canon and Community"', 163.

[4] Deidun, Tom, 'The Bible and Christian Ethics', 45, n. 68, quoting Allen Verhey, in The Use of Scripture in Moral Theology (Readings in Moral Theology No. 4), ed. Charles E. Curran and Richard A. McCormick (Ramsey, NJ: Paulist Press, 1984), 216.

on ethical issues cannot be derived. One methodological conclusion from comparing statements from these three exegetical authors on canonicity must be that in each case, the respective concept of 'church' merits special scrutiny. Deidun points to the fact that the variety of churches and ecclesial self-understandings which can be found empirically in World Christianity will yield such diverse evidence on contested issues that it is inoperable as a basis for valid conclusions. But not only because of the visible variety of Christian groupings, with each claiming to propose an authentic reading of the Gospel for the issues under debate, a more principled basis for evaluating the scripture–church relationship has to be established. Since the relations and dependencies between treatises and core themes in Christian dogmatics are at stake, a thorough-going reflection on the basis of the validity of judgements is needed. Instead of privileging current appropriations by church communities and validating them in advance as 'participation in the life of God in the world', as Stephen Barton does, the historical distance is to be appreciated and exegetical disputes are to be recognized.

The role of historical reason in examining the origins of the Gospels is highlighted by Walter Kasper, validating its irreplaceable function for interpreting the content of the Christian message. As a systematic theologian interested in argumentations that are accessible also from other subject areas and disciplines in the university, he takes account of the 'new debate on the historical Jesus' which was launched by Ernst Käsemann in 1953 against Rudolf Bultmann's historical scepticism, and identifies four causes that need to be defended. It is of paramount importance to emphasize the real historical basis of the church's kerygma, its message of Jesus Christ as saviour, in order to avoid several pitfalls:

Firstly, it is a question of the rejection of myth. The eschatological event ... happens once and for all. This historical contingency reflects the freedom of God's agency. It also grounds the new *kairos*, the new historical possibility of our decision. Secondly, it is a question of the rejection of Docetism and of the conviction that the revelation occurs 'in the flesh'. Therefore everything depends on the identity of the exalted Lord with the earthly Jesus. It is a question of the reality of the Incarnation and of the salvific meaning of the true humanity of Jesus. Thirdly, it is a question of the rejection of enthusiasm and of a purely presentist understanding of salvation. Reference must be made to 'the *extra nos* of salvation as the given basis (*Vorgegebenheit*) of faith'. A faith which refers only to the kerygma becomes in the end faith in the Church as bearer of the kerygma. In the quest of the historical Jesus, on the other hand, what has to be emphasized is 'the undisposability (*Unverfügbarkeit*) of salvation, the *prae* of Christ before his own, the *extra nos* of proclamation, the necessity of the exodus of the faithful from themselves'. It is a question of the primacy of Christ before and over the Church . . . The historical however serves as a criterium of the kerygma and of faith.[5]

Prioritizing the church over the Bible, as some theological readings of canonicity do, is thus a problematic endeavour because the enquiry remains at one level: the faith of the church, based on the canon generated by the same church. What is needed instead for systematic theology is to recognize the limits of its own domain and take on board what can only be researched by historical reason in the real world within which the New Testament originated; the findings that historical research alone can produce are of great 'theological relevance'. What must be rejected is a position that ends up prioritizing the church over the foundational documents themselves. Fellow dogmatic theologian Wolfgang Beinert clearly shares this ordering of Kasper's when he states:

> The reason for the validity of the canon is thus neither the ecclesial magisterium (which would then be the supreme norm of faith instead of the Bible) nor an inner-biblical 'centre of the Bible' (which would then have to be justified as such), but the authority of Christ which is experienced in the primitive church (*Urkirche*) as divine authority.[6]

The significance of the concrete decisions on which writings to include into the canon has to be elaborated in view of the arguments made under the historical circumstances of the challenge of Gnosticism. 'Canonicity' as a theological claim that takes the unity of the epistles, the four gospels, Acts and Revelation for granted is problematic; it minimizes the differences between today's church and the first century and replaces detailed historical work with an overarching connection. Tom Deidun warns against the consequences of such a monolithic assumption for ethics: 'For if canonicity renders the Bible normative, it must render *all* of it normative, even when elements within it stand in tension to each other or are mutually exclusive.'[7]

The dangers of an approach that subordinates the Bible to the church relate first of all to Christology, but also to the whole reconstruction of God's

---

[5] Walter Kasper, *Jesus the Christ*, trans. V. Green (London: Burns & Oates/New York: Paulist Press, 1976), 33–4, translation amended. The sentence quoted as final here is missing in the translation. Kasper's quotes, n. 42, p. 39, refer to Ernst Käsemann, 'Sackgassen im Streit um den historischen Jesus', in *Exegetische Versuche und Besinnungen II* (Göttingen: Vandenhoeck & Ruprecht, 3rd edn, 1970), 67.
[6] Wolfgang Beinert, 'Kanon', in *Handbuch der katholischen Dogmatik*, ed. W. Beinert (Freiburg: Herder, 1987), 301.
[7] Deidun, 'The Bible and Christian Ethics', 9.

relationship to humanity as that part of God's creation which can understand and respond to God's initiative: first, the '*extra nos*' of God's revelation is negated if Scripture is seen as a product of humans who remain finite interpreters even when they are ecclesially united in a church. Secondly, the independent standing of the Bible from subsequent generations is denied when it is delivered over to the church and 'domesticated', that is, reduced from its universal salvific scope to the confines of contemporary forms of church.

These two warnings relate to the human side, the institutional and individual interests in owning a message that due to its divine origin extends with necessity beyond human confinement. What other starting point than the church can be used, then, to ensure the abiding *extra nos* origin of the biblical message? Is the opposite end more promising, to begin with its provenance as the Word of God?

2. The Bible as the authoritative word of God

In comparison with the previous embedding of the Bible in the church of the first centuries, with its danger of subordinating the Bible to a concept of church, its designation as God's Word highlights its origin in the initiative of God and safeguards its nature as divine gift. Some argumentations see it as unproblematic to link both approaches and view the two bases of validation as consonant. But in terms of justification, the second approach makes it clear that the 'authority' lies in its provenance from God. For this position, the Bible itself is the 'supreme tangible sacred reality'.[8] The understanding that God is its author does not merely refer to its truth as given by God, and not constructed or established by humans. It means the document itself as a whole and in each sentence is revealed and therefore inerrant. If only one element was to be shown as factually wrong, it would affect the authority and credibility of the whole written revelation of God as the foundation of faith. Thus, the divergences discovered, for example, when comparing the passion stories in the four gospels in historical-critical

---

[8] James Barr, *Fundamentalism* (London: SCM Press, 1977), 36, quoted in Veronika Hoffmann, *Vermittelte Offenbarung. Paul Ricoeurs Philosophie als Herausforderung der Theologie* (Mainz: Grünewald, 2007), 20. I am drawing on her analysis of the first two forms in her useful heuristic classification of three forms of negating the mediated character of revelation: objectivist, subjectivist and pluralist.

exegesis, have to be explained in other ways. Key features of this objectivist understanding of revelation as recorded in the Bible are: (1) God is the revealer and is seen in terms of authority; (2) revelation is understood as cognitive-propositional; (3) the human addressee is taken as a passive recipient; and (4) the person of Jesus is approached as a teacher of divine truths.

The reasons for the difference in kind of this message to other cognitive contents that can be assimilated by humans is its origin in God. This assures that it is a document *sui generis*, incomparable to human modes of communication. Its singular standing is evident and does not need to be established via the detour of the church. The Bible itself is the revelation of God's will to humankind; its impact is immediate and reflection on the media of its transmission is not needed. An unintended side effect is that here, too, the human person of Jesus has little relevance. A different standing would result for Jesus if his historical existence was taken as the contingent beginning of a proclamation of God and God's kingdom that 'once and for all' disclosed God's unconditional love for each human being. In effect, the unique significance of Jesus' life and death does not come into view since the content he discloses is a truth in the theoretical sense, which, being supernatural, is beyond human understanding. Mediation is negated, and the message taken in terms of a body of information to be accepted without any involvement in grasping it.

Two more points arise from realizing where an objectivist account of revelation locates its key value. First, the ethical capability of reflection in the process of coming to moral judgements is affected when the hearer of the revelation is deemed to be passive. The model of morality is deontological, marked by obligation, but heteronomous for the human side. And since key questions of interpretation that have moved the history of theological thinking over millennia – such as the relationship between creation and redemption, between God's mercy and justice, human freedom and sin – are not debated, it is also the self-understanding of the human agent which is affected. Questions such as the following should be legitimate: What is the reason for following God's will: gratitude, or fear, or hope? Does the believer have to reckon with a *Deus absconditus* who can appear in divine wrath at any time from behind the proclamation of Jesus who set his life on a God of abundant love and mercy? How is Jesus' death to be spelt out: as atonement for the sin of Adam, which was needed as the voluntary act of the one sinless human being in order to restore the injured order of creation, as in Anselm's philosophical explanation of why God became human? If these systematic theological debates cannot be taken up, human action in response to God's Word is hard to specify. It would require imagination to discover similarities between their contemporary lifeworld and the situations that are vividly portrayed in Jesus' parables, sayings and symbolic actions. It downplays the role of free response, of being attracted and motivated to follow this example. Isolating the authoritative standing of God's Word from the human capabilities of reception and response risks calling forth authoritarian concepts, divisions and fears of punishment in those addressed. Decisive debates cannot take place, such as, which image of God to choose as the guiding one in the two parts of the Bible, and what view of the end of history is being envisaged. There must be space for dealing with the alternative interpretations contained in the New Testament. They are clearly admitted in Jürgen Moltmann's analysis, relating here to the relationship of justice and mercy as attributes of God: 'The different biblical traditions of judgement day cannot be harmonised, one has to decide on the basis of theological arguments.'[9]

Biblical ethics needs systematic theological reflection on the implications of the radical statements the Bible contains which have had enormous histories of reception, before it can evaluate courses of action. What also seems to be underestimated in the Word of God approach is the weight of the subsequent theological schools of thinking and their key concepts, and church practices, including those in relation to groups considered heretic. Hermeneutically, it is clear that there is no possibility for contemporary readers to access the Bible without the impact of its subsequent interpretations: in the organizational forms of the Christian churches, the diverse depictions in Christian art, the memory of wars in the name of God, rules for daily life, or the interaction of theology with forms of piety. The pure Word of God is concretely available only through these mediations, which need to be compared, explained in their internal connections, and personally reflected in order to get to the message itself. While the theological qualification of the Bible as *norma normans non normata* is crucial to capture its position as the counterpart to all ecclesial appropriations, it does not mean that each new generation has an entirely fresh access that is independent of the previous histories of reception. The emphasis of the Word of God approach on God's action prior to the human reception of the Bible is necessary and valid as a

---

[9] Moltmann, Jürgen, *Sonne der Gerechtigkeit* (Gütersloh: Gütersloher Verlagshaus, 2008), 136, quoted in Ansorge, Dirk, *Gerechtigkeit und Barmherzigkeit Gottes. Die Dramatik von Vergebung und Versöhnung in bibeltheologischer, theologiegeschichtlicher und philosophiegeschichtlicher Perspektive* (Freiburg: Herder, 2009), 53.

correction of an understanding of canon that collapses the two, scripture and church. Yet the problems incurred by insisting on an objectivizing understanding of revelation include: turning the content into a cognitive proposition which humans had to be taught; making the separate task of the recipients disappear; and letting a response other than obedience appear as deficient – with revealed norms, no judgement of one's own is needed. Above all, however, it sidelines the life and actual proclamation of Jesus by identifying the theological concept of the Word of God with potentially every verse in the Bible. The concrete actualization of the Word of God in the human person of Jesus is of little interest, risking a docetic understanding in which only his divinity is accepted.[10] An ethics inspired by the Gospel is then only possible at one remove, filtered first through what is interpreted as being the will of God as laid down in scripture. It is necessary to insist on the mediated character of revelation, as these two systematic theologians do: Veronika Hoffmann characterizes the 'objectivist' approach as one 'in which revelation is conceived of primarily as doctrine that reaches us almost as verbatim minutes of the divine will.'[11] Jürgen Werbick comments on the role of the recipient in the Word of God approach: There is an 'immediate accessibility of truth because the creator of the facts disclosed immediate access to humans … they are not required as 'decipherers' who actively seek a path towards truth but as people perceiving it and submitting to it.'[12] Accepting every verse as equally validated by divine authority makes it impossible to distinguish between a core message and time-bound, surpassable expressions, in order to 'decipher' and decide on justifiable courses of action. This position can also not account for developments within the Bible towards understanding God as creator in universalist terms.

But what is the alternative? With the first approach that traces the Bible back to the church, it is possible to avoid these problems by locating the authorizing ground not in its biblical origin but in the interpretive action of the community.[13] Yet, the price of shifting the validating authority to the church or its congregations is that the question of criteria is not posed. Past and contemporary church history reveals contradictory and misguided

---

[10] Hoffmann points out the link Jürgen Werbick establishes between an objectivist understanding of revelation and a docetic Christology, in *Vermittelte Offenbarung*, 28.

[11] Cf. Hoffmann, *Vermittelte Offenbarung*, 13–14.

[12] Werbick, Jürgen, 'Einleitung', in *Offenbarungsanspruch und fundamentalistische Versuchung*, ed. J. Werbick (Freiburg: Herder, 1991), 21, quoted in Hoffmann, *Vermittelte Offenbarung*, 17.

[13] Apart from the biblical scholars quoted previously in 1.1, also Stanley Hauerwas takes this route, as Jeffrey Siker and Gareth Jones observe, and as will be discussed in Chapters 5 and 6.

performances which cannot all be equally true. The search for the Bible's prerogative as 'unnormed norm', that is, as more directly linked to God than to church interpretation, must be continued on a different level, one that takes the link of the Bible to historical events and persons seriously. Some of them, like Israel's exile, can be verified independently of the biblical texts. Others, such as the Last Supper, are not accessible without the passion narratives, but are not entirely reducible to them. Investigating what is recounted in the New Testament for its historical core continues to be necessary, in line with the new phase of research into the Historical Jesus after Bultmann's questioning.

3. The New Testament as the earliest testimony to God's self-revelation in the person of Jesus

Understanding the biblical text itself as the Word of God, taken down faithfully by humans as God's scribes, does secure its standing as *norma normans non normata*. As Gareth Jones sums up this 'normative understanding of biblical authority': the 'traditional view of the Bible straightforwardly as the Word of God' makes it 'normative for all church teaching'.[14] But it is evident that the cost of this version of the Bible's supreme authority is high. Despite its intention of valuing all parts and verses of the Bible equally, it is affected by the deficits Lucas Chan points out for current uses that do not distinguish between the original and the contemporary settings. Invoking the Bible as the standard for making decisions in specific cases inevitably subjects it to readings that prioritize some sections over others. Its 'limitations are a (1) selective use of Scripture, and (2) a less than satisfactory interaction with biblical scholarship. They are still concerned more with interpreting the text's meaning for the contemporary world than with first examining its original meaning to see whether the text can be rightly employed.'[15]

The Bible's standing as the norm for all church teaching has to be argued for on grounds other than the sheer authority of God. Accepting the

---

[14] Gareth Jones, 'The Authority of Scripture and Christian Ethics', in *The Cambridge Companion to Christian Ethics*, ed. Robin Gill (Cambridge: CUP, 2001), 22.

[15] Yiu Sing Lucas Chan, 'Biblical Ethics: 3D', in *The Bible and Catholic Theological Ethics*, ed. Y. S. L. Chan, James Keenan and Ronaldo Zacharias (Maryknoll, NY: Orbis, 2017), 20, in a highly insightful survey of the Catholic and Protestant English-speaking discussion especially from the 1990s.

mediated nature of revelation in the Bible allows to distinguish between a core understanding of the Creator's universal salvific will, and time-bound biblical expressions that may be surpassable. The Bible owes its standing to the fact that it is the one source that gives access to the life and destiny of Jesus Christ and to his own faith tradition of Jewish monotheism. Thomas Pröpper elucidates the internal connection between the unique status of the New Testament, the need to validate one's own hermeneutical premises, and the indispensable role of the Hebrew Bible and Jesus' contemporaries:

> Why do theologies of every age have to legitimate themselves in relation to the earliest testimonies of the Christian faith? And why do they have to enquire about the historical foundation of faith that these witness to? This connection . . . originates from an internal necessity . . . that the core content of faith is tied to the form of being freely given and is only true if . . . God has indeed, as the writings of the New Testament testify, revealed God's self, and when this remains recognized in faith . . . the whole of the life and destiny of Jesus Christ has to be encompassed . . . since in all these events . . . God's salvific action took its ultimate shape . . . The expectations of the Old Testament and of his contemporaries . . . are to be protected from being lost, both against a spiritualization, and because they form the original horizon of meaning which allows an appropriate understanding of Jesus and of the New Testament confession in the first place.[16]

What this foundation of the Bible's unique position implies will be outlined in three points which theological ethics needs to take on board in relation to its first source. They are, first, the distinction between, and priority of, exegesis to personal appropriation (a); second, a theological proposal responding to the question about the theological significance of biblical, especially New Testament pluralism (b); and third, a guiding perspective for Christian ethics (c).

(a) Exegesis before appropriation

Tom Deidun's programmatic conclusion from his exegetical survey of problematic forays of ethicists into the biblical domain clarifies the methodological alternatives: 'Christian ethicists intent on "using" the Bible in their discipline must consider the two steps of exegesis and appropriation.'[17]

---

[16] Pröpper, *Erlösungsglaube und Freiheitsgeschichte*, 38–40.
[17] Deidun, 'The Bible and Christian Ethics', 20.

Neglecting the difference between those two modes of relating to the Bible is in danger of offering projections of current concerns onto issues that should be reconstructed first in the lifeworlds of the original communities. While 'appropriation' is an essential final element of any hermeneutical effort, it is based on a synthesizing movement resulting in the adoption of a specific meaning where several readings could be argued for. Exegetical research offers conjectures and an array of likely interpretations, but the decision to go for one specific option among those that can be reasonably defended is on a different level. The need for hermeneutical reflection and ultimately decision arises from being confronted with a number of literary forms and with not only 'polyphonic', but contrasting and at times contradictory statements which need to be resolved and integrated into one consistent understanding.[18] The biblical text itself consists of different poetic genres and does not come in the mode of a speculative, conceptual or existential discourse. To ignore this difference is to fail to acknowledge the otherness of the text. The tasks arising for incursions into a world with many unknown features include reconstructing ancient eras with differences that have not yet been accounted for. What needs to be investigated first are the questions New Testament communities were facing to which those texts respond. The task is to elucidate what is only implied in New Testament debates, 'the unrecorded side of the interchange'.[19] Deidun treats the example of the view on marriage espoused by some community members in Corinth that St Paul was arguing against in his First Letter to the Corinthians.[20] To become aware of a counter-position which is only indirectly accessible qualifies the understanding of the text preserved. Unlike an argument from silence, which is inadmissible to decide historical questions, Paul's letters originated as responses to existing controversies in the first Christian communities. They can only be appreciated in their exact argumentation if their backgrounds and changes in the groups

---

[18] Wayne Meeks argues convincingly for the 'polyphonic' nature of St. Paul's ethics and for a 'polyphonic ethics' with 'at least the following voices: . . . scripture, including the history of its effects . . . tradition, in all its multiplicity, but with all its weight of communities past. The voice of the suppressed – the quiet, those deprived of a voice, those injured by the tradition. The voice of the outsider, the critic, the worldly wise, the great secular traditions as well as the great non-Christian religious traditions.' Meeks, 'The Christian Beginnings and Christian Ethics: The Hermeneutical Challenge', in *Bulletin European Theology* 9 (1998): 181. He sees the problem of bringing these voices together. For ethics, the term 'polyphony' can insinuate a compatibility also in cases that have to be contested and decided on the basis of a hermeneutical decision, such as prioritizing a God of love over one of punishment. The interpretation of concepts such as nature, grace, election, or judgement will differ accordingly, as will conclusions for concrete life forms and political structures.

[19] Deidun, 'The Bible and Christian Ethics', 13.

[20] Deidun, 'The Bible and Christian Ethics', 16.

addressed, for example between the First and the Second Letter to the Corinthians, are included. Shortcuts using biblical texts for today's needs without requiring the competence of the exegetes to assess them in their original settings will result in historically naïve and misleading conclusions. Though sayings and stories from scripture, similar to models offered in literary fiction, have a timeless appeal by being immediately evident, the believers' own interest should extend to understanding the original setting, given that the Bible contains theologized history and not merely fiction.

(b) The theological significance of New Testament pluralism

The historical, philological and literary scholarship required will yield first of all disparate evidence, and will leave different possibilities open. Why is it important to respect this inconclusiveness on key questions explored in the different gospels, such as how Jesus understood the growing probability of a violent death? The reason is that it is the unique life and practice of the person of Jesus which is the basis of all claims to his being the saviour sent by God. This means that all clues have to be pursued in order to be able to defend with reasons the interpretation espoused after weighing up all the evidence. The *quaestiones facti* need the expertise of biblical scholars to be resolved, and their answers to be respected. Do they judge the status of enquiry on specific questions to be suitable to be investigated, or to be inaccessible? It is not just a speculative religious claim that Jesus Christ is the self-revelation of God, but a thesis within a specific, researchable religious belief system and life form of which the key factors can be identified. While the appropriation of this claim is a personal religious response, the elements relevant for Jesus' understanding of God – as creator of a fertile earth, as Lord over history critical of human power structures, as forgiving to humans in their freedom – can be described with some accuracy. The variety of the Gospel accounts is thus to be valued as an enrichment, not a draw-back or an irritation of what seemed to be certain before. The exegetes intend their debates to lead to clarifications of what can and cannot be established with historical reasons. The outcomes can guide believers in their imagination of the reality contained in the texts. Yet exegetes can only hope that theologians accept the task to make sense of the plurality of possible readings on theological grounds. An example for an answer from a systematic theologian to the accepted state of unending disputes among exegetes are the conclusions

Roger Haight draws after characterizing the five distinct Christologies expressed in the four Gospels and in the letters of Paul. The 'significance of the pluralism of New Testament Christologies' is found in their historical concreteness which each contain a dimension that transcends their specificity; each of them uses the images and concepts available to them, yet they do not completely describe the identity of Jesus. The categories given in his era are also moulded by him. For the contemporary age, this means the 'necessity' of Christological pluralism based on the same insight that each is a symbolic description which does not exhaust its subject. The thesis guiding Haight's interpretation thus is:

> these concepts that interpret Jesus are also interpreted by him. In every case, the categories do not fit his historical life perfectly; they do not completely sum him up. He changes the meaning of the categories. For example, the idea of the Messiah would have to take into account that he was crucified and thus died as a criminal.[21] ... Interpretations of Jesus Christ now risen cannot prescind from, but must be modified by, the concrete datum they interpret, namely Jesus ... Thus Jesus research provides a way of checking whether a christology has some realistic, historical connection with Jesus ... Thus in the development of christologies one can see displayed the principle that Jesus in his earthly life is a norm and criterion for what should be said about him.[22]

While each biblical portrait of Jesus is coherent in itself, their plurality is in keeping with the insight that the figure of Jesus also transcends them. This point is also an answer to the frank question put by Deidun to interpreters seeking to draw practical conclusions from the significance of Jesus' message: 'But who is doing the categorizing? It might just as well be maintained that *all* of Jesus' reported sayings are to be taken as hyperbole in the service of paradox (which seems a bit of an overkill); or that *all* of them are to be taken literally (which won't work).'[23]

Haight works with the assumption that each gospel has a consistent, particular perspective on Jesus. None is complete on its own in expressing the depth of this singular figure and his relation to God. This thought makes it possible to replace the alternative between having to accept 'all' sayings

---

[21] Roger Haight, *Jesus, Symbol of God* (Maryknoll, NY: Orbis, 1999), 178–9, and n.87, with reference to Joseph A. Fitzmyer, *The Gospel According to Luke. Introduction, Translation, and Notes* (Garden City, NY: Doubleday, 1981, 1985), 1565: 'The notion of a suffering Messiah is not found in the Old Testament or any text of pre-Christian Judaism.'

[22] Haight, *Jesus, Symbol of God*, 179.

[23] Deidun, 'The Bible and Christian Ethics', 19.

either literally or metaphorically with a different awareness. The portrayals in the various gospels have to be related to the trajectory of Jesus' life. It can never be captured completely, yet still with sufficient accuracy to rule out, for example, practices of non-inclusion and violence justified in his name. Unlike the first approach to the Bible as a church-bound source of Christian ethics, the third one allows the Bible to be a critical counterpart to current practices in church and society. Unlike the second approach for which every part of the whole body of scripture has equal relevance, it identifies with hermeneutical justification a guiding perspective: God's self-revelation as love in the historical person of Jesus. Walter Kasper's insistence on the genuine theological reasons for taking history seriously, ultimately against docetic and Gnostic denials of Jesus' humanity, is shared by Haight. He emphasizes the superabundant nature of the ultimate symbol of God that Jesus represents in his life. It made God's love accessible in a historical person but the interpretations remain disputed because their content – the necessarily symbolic character of God acting in history and revealing God's self in the person of Jesus – is inexhaustible. Instead of having to take all of the Bible as equally significant and expressive, the judgement can be made, based on Jesus' proclamation, that the guiding interpretive principle is God's love.

(c) Correspondence of form and content of God's self-revelation

The Bible owes its status *as norma normans non normata* to being the most immediate, closest available account of Jesus Christ's life and destiny. Achieving autonomy from its era of composition by the move from oral tradition to the written papyrus, the New Testament preserves the diverse traces of the communities' memories of the stories told about Jesus' proclamation, death and resurrection. From the perspective that the superabundant content of revelation, God's love, could only be delivered through the free response of a human being, it becomes especially clear that the sayings and acts of this person could only ever be symbolic, pointing to its excessive subject matter. The inadequacy of isolating specific quotes and the need for a thought-through and historically defensible interpretation become even more evident from this insight. This means that it is not possible to comb the New Testament for practical exhortations that can be grasped instantly, in the hope that they will shine a light on today's moral landscape. Tom Deidun's warning against having one's 'whole ethical vision narrowed down to scattered biblical prescriptions' is apposite: 'people who see the Bible as a repository of divine commands run the risk of trivializing the Bible by isolating elements of it at whim, or by arbitrarily privileging one particular mode of biblical discourse over all others ("norm reductionism") . . . typically accompanied by the conviction that the Bible is the sole authority in ethical matters'.[24]

To summarize the discussion of the reasons for recognizing the Bible as the standard-setting source also of theological ethics: as *norma normans non normata* it is the originary source from which the second one, tradition, is derived. In logical terms, it is prior, and the fact that the canon was decided through the interactions and argumentations of communities and theologians cannot reverse the sequence of the two theological sources. What the formation of the canon achieved in the early centuries was to preserve the identity of Christianity in the variety of the New Testament sources. They testify to the historical person of Jesus in his universal significance. 'While theology cannot justify in historical perspective alone the ultimate significance of Jesus, it can show the real anchorage of the post-Easter interpretation in Jesus' earthly demeanour (*Auftreten*)'.[25] What the canon achieved is now entrusted to historical research.

In addition to arguing for this interpretive perspective within the Christian community, there is a truth claim to be justified also outside the church. The understanding of Jesus as saviour is backed up by identifiable historical traces, and the personal option for this faith can be explained to a general consciousness of truth. Being able to link the post-Easter interpretations of Jesus as the saviour, as Son of God, as Messiah, to the features of his life also sets a standard for the very first outreach to new cultures which the early church undertook. The changing horizons of this new phase called 'tradition' are the subject of Chapter 2.

---

[24] Deidun, 'The Bible and Christian Ethics', 23.
[25] Pröpper, *Der Jesus der Philosophen und der Jesus des Glaubens. Ein theologisches Gespräch mit Jaspers – Bloch—Kolakowski – Gardavsky – Machovec – Fromm – Ben-Chorin* (Mainz: Grünewald, 1976), 124.

2

The second source

Tradition as *norma normans normata*

The previous chapter has argued that the reason for the Bible occupying the place of the first source – not alone for Christian ethics but generally for all subsequent developments in Christian thinking – is an internal theological one. There is no other way of justifying the truth claim of the Christian faith than by making the case based on historical research that in his life and death Jesus linked his message to God's self. This claim, backed by his whole existence, to have the authority to interpret God's will and act as God's representative, was confirmed by his resurrection. The existence of God and the reality of the resurrection cannot, of course, be demonstrated like an empirical fact; faith in God has the status of a practical option alongside other reflected understandings of life. The point of the first two sources dealing with the truth of Christianity is not to make the decision to believe appear as the only available cognitive possibility, or to 'prove' that the God proclaimed by Jesus both exists and abounds in love. It is presupposed here what would need to be argued for philosophically, that religious belief is 'not simply "irrational"'.[1] The task posed here is to relate the theological understandings which developed out of the New Testament witness back to this origin which remains its critical standard. So 'tradition' is answerable to the primary source, the Bible. Evaluating the failure of a previous stage of ecclesiastical thinking to accord it this standing, Walter Kasper describes the Neo-Scholastic ordering of the ranks of normativity:

> In Neo-Scholasticism, theology starts from the *norma proxima*, the authoritative statements of the magisterium; scripture and tradition are now only *normae remotae* which serve to justify magisterial propositions. Councils, church fathers, theologians, etc. become forms of testimony of tradition. Exegesis, the histories of dogma, church and theology become auxiliary sciences to dogmatics, practical theology becomes an applied science of dogmatics and moral theology.[2]

In contrast to the 'one-sided traditionalism of the magisterium', a different concept of tradition was developed also in Catholic theology, led by the hermeneutical principle that the '(h)istory of reception is part of the interpretation of the original text'.[3] It comprises more than intellectual history: 'The testimonies of the tradition encompass not only the theological writings of the church fathers and the magisterial documents, but also and especially the testimony of liturgy, of ecclesial art, indeed, the entire life of the church throughout history and in the present era.'[4]

This encompassing view will turn out to be especially significant for appreciating the symbolic worlds generated by the biblical message which are as relevant for theological ethics as the argumentations of theologians, councils and church officeholders are. But the latter are key for tracing continuities and transformations in the understanding of human reason, will and agency in relation to God's self-revelation which are important for defining and

---

[1] Jürgen Habermas, *Between Naturalism and Religion*, trans. Ciaran Cronin (Cambridge: Polity, 2008), 112: 'the expectation that the disagreement between faith and knowledge will persist deserves the title "reasonable" only if religious convictions are also accorded an epistemic status as not simply "irrational" (*nicht a priori irrational*) from the perspective of secular knowledge (*Weltwissen*).'

[2] Kasper, 'Die Wissenschaftspraxis der Theologie', in *Handbuch der Fundamentaltheologie, vol. 4, Traktat Theologische Erkenntnislehre*, ed. Walter Kern, Hermann J. Pottmeyer and Max Seckler (Freiburg: Herder, 1988), 254.

[3] Ibid., 263. The joint Protestant and Catholic work of New Testament commentaries EKK, currently 40 volumes, includes the history of reception and its controversies. *EKK – Evangelisch-Katholischer Kommentar zum NT* (first Neukirchen: Neukirchner Verlag/Einsiedeln: Benziger) (Göttingen: Vandenhoeck & Ruprecht /Düsseldorf: Patmos, 1975–).

[4] Kasper, 'Wissenschaftspraxis', 263.

integrating the four sources. Therefore, my emphasis will be on them as evidence of turns in theological thinking and as benchmarks for valid interpretations. In view of these changes, key points of this chapter on tradition as the *norma normans normata* will be to investigate the concept of tradition from the perspective of its members (2). This includes examining the question of how the core content of the Christian message of salvation can be identified within the processes of translation and transformation (3). But before reflecting on the challenges that post-biblical developments responded to, and on how the sequence of inculturations affects theological ethics (4), I want to return to the Neo-Scholastic mode of thinking which was swept away by a 'revolutionizing of the existing understanding of theology', as Kasper notes.[5] As will also be seen in Chapter 7 on classical and revisionist understandings of natural law, a mindset persists that identifies the truth of Christianity with a propositional understanding of revelation. Similar in its insistence on the eternal nature of this truth, as distinct from a historically conscious understanding, the classical approach seeks the validating authority not in the biblical text itself but in the teaching office of the Roman Catholic Church (1).

1. Traditionalist views of tradition

In her outline of the second form, an 'objectivist' understanding of revelation, Veronika Hoffmann points out its similarity to the Biblicist form in its cognitive-propositional view of supernatural truths communicated by God to a receptive humanity. The difference is that now tradition takes the place of the Bible as the highest symbol of authority. Mediation is not ruled out completely, as the former model did based on the principle that it would subject God's Word to a level typical of inter-human communication; but it is sidelined for a different reason. In the traditionalist understanding of revelation, the form of the subsequent transmission is separated from its content to a degree that mediation is 'marginalized' and effectively disappears.[6] The argument is that its contents are not accessible to reason and that to presume the involvement of human reason is taken as attempting to 'stand in judgement over revelation'.[7] The basis for verifying the inspired nature of scripture are judgements by the church. Hoffmann summarizes:

---

[5] Ibid., 254.
[6] Hoffmann, *Vermittelte Offenbarung*, 29–38, 29.
[7] Ibid., 30.

'The authority of the self-revealing God is not encountered in the book of the Bible, but in the ecclesial magisterium (supported by tradition).'[8] This position is clearly the opposite of trusting in the perspicuity of the biblical text. It prioritizes the form of delivery which is 'authorized' to the contents which are taken to be supernatural, inaccessible divine truths; faith consists in intellectual consent. The believers' own relation to the Bible and to its history of effects, both church-internal – including ecclesial forms of celebration, teaching, in- and exclusion – and external in culture, society and self-understandings, is ignored. In this institutional version of a 'container' model of communication, the faithful come into play as its passive recipients. What they receive is not even the Word of God, but the word of the teaching church with an exclusive claim to elucidate its content.

> 'Thus not scripture decides between authentic and inauthentic doctrine, but the doctrine handed down decides about authentic and inauthentic scripture.' Therefore the *church*, proprietor (*Inhaberin*) of the oral tradition, remains older than scripture and *is called to give witness before and beside scripture* about its beginnings and its character.[9]

For neo-Scholastic theology, in line with a cognitive-propositional understanding of supernatural revelation, 'church' culminated in the teaching office of the Pope. The above citations from this school of theological thinking make it clearer why Walter Kasper has referred to the 'traditionalism of the magisterium' as 'one-sided'. In the argumentation quoted by Hoffmann the stage of the oral tradition preceding the fixation in writing is turned into an argument for the divinely installed church which is seen as prior to the New Testament writings. Instead of comprising the whole history of reception of the New Testament with its foundation in Jewish monotheism, tradition is channelled into the handing down of divine mysteries by the office-holders appointed in the Roman Catholic Church, itself promoted to be the 'owner' of the original oral tradition. The Christian and the Hebrew Bibles function more like an *aide-mémoire* for renewed acts of oral traditioning down the ages. They can no longer serve as a critical counterpart to subsequent eras of theological thinking and church practices.[10] The original language of the

---

[8] Ibid., 31.

[9] Hoffmann, *Vermittelte Offenbarung*, 31, with reference to Andreas Schill, *Theologische Prinzipienlehre. Lehrbuch der Apologetik*, 2nd edn revised by Oskar Witz (Paderborn: Schöningh, 1903), 299–300.

[10] As Hermann Josef Pottmeyer comments in his article on 'Tradition', in *Dictionary of Fundamental Theology*, ed. René Latourelle and Rino Fisichella (New York: Crossroad, 1994), 1123: 'Attention is scarcely given, however, to the critical function of Scripture in relation to postbiblical tradition.'

New Testament and the philological and historical research it invites are not of interest, either; reference is made instead to the Vulgate and its further translations.[11] It is only due to breaking with this model of giving the monopoly of the power to interpret the Bible to the magisterium that the enquiries to be treated in the following three sections were able to become matters of dialogue for theology with other subjects in the humanities.

2. Tradition as a general concept of culture and religion

An alternative starting point to the exclusive understanding of 'tradition' as governed by the magisterium is to begin with its general definition as a key factor in a culture, relating to the historical roots from which it has developed. Having established its conceptual origin and subsequent levels of use, its theological specification can be further determined. In a dictionary article on 'tradition', the New Testament scholar and historian of Jewish–Christian relations Rainer Kampling first analyses the linguistic history of the term. Philologically, it was originally a concept in private law denoting the handing over of a good; also in its metaphorical use in Christian theology, he points out that a legal element is still present in the idea of a 'rightful passing on, and thus of a proof of legitimacy'.[12] Secondly, as a communicative process it has both an active aspect, the act of passing on, and a passive one, the content that is being handed on. There is thus no process of tradition that is inert; it always includes an element of reflection and new accentuation:

> Tradition undergoes changes in a formal, a content-related, and a functional sense through the process of handing on, based on the adaptation of tradition to new circumstances … It follows that tradition is not an unquestioned entity for those passing it on and those receiving it; it contains a value for them which makes it meaningful for them to hand it on or to receive it.[13]

Kampling emphasizes the element of freedom in relation to a tradition based on the reflection required to select those of its strands that have

---

[11] B. Walde, 'Inspiration', in *Lexikon für Theologie und Kirche*, vol. 5 (Freiburg: Herder, 1st edn 1933), 426, quoted by Hoffmann, *Vermittelte Offenbarung*, 31.
[12] Rainer Kampling, 'Tradition', in *Neues Handbuch theologischer Grundbegriffe* vol. 4, ed. Peter Eicher (Munich: Kösel, 1985), 221–2. Regarding the 'freedom' important for 'dealing with a tradition' (223), he also refers to Habermas who argued for this aspect in his debate with Hans-Georg Gadamer.
[13] Ibid., 222–3.

resonance for these individuals. A view that extends the term and almost identifies it with 'socialization' is questioned by him since it veers towards a 'biological' category. Against such naturalizing assumptions, two functions are distinguished: first, the group-constituting one of handing on values; secondly, that of becoming aware of a historical nexus which links generations to a past that is still relevant. By insisting on the active, selective and meaning-creating character of appropriating a tradition founded in history, its internal credibility becomes a core element for opting to locate oneself in it. Kampling identifies this acceptance perceptively as the moment when a receptive member becomes a traditioning agent, someone who has taken a stance on what is valuable for him or her in a tradition and passes on their understanding of it. In other words, it amounts to a change of register when a heritage that had been unchosen now becomes a foundation that a person commits to, opening up a future for it. A similar point has been made by the philosopher Herta Nagl-Docekal when she captures the involvement of those electing to become active participants of a movement, social imaginary or religion. Critiquing a widespread static view of religions as unchanging systems of doctrine, she points out that also religious traditions 'can only persist through centuries if the believers manage – over and over again – to re-interpret the core convictions of their faith in a way that renders them accessible, and convincing, in view of their respective contemporary condition'.[14]

Treating key continuities and changes in the concept of tradition in Christianity in the second part of his article, Kampling points out the legitimating function already present in St. Paul's use of confessional formulas, sayings of the Lord and established practices to solve conflicts. Since in all religions, 'tradition' is the element linking the present time to the origin, the question of criteria for their continuity or correspondence inevitably arises.[15] The article concludes with a query that is already familiar from Tom Deidun's critical discussion of direct uses of the New Testament in a historically unexamined concept of church: 'It would be helpful for theological-ecclesial language to make it clear which tradition is meant when tradition is quoted as an argument of authority. If traditions are only habits, they have to be examined whether they serve the cause of Christ. They are not authorities in themselves.'[16]

---

[14] Herta Nagl-Docekal, '"Many Forms of Non-public Reason"? Religious Diversity in Liberal Democracies', in *Comparative and Intercultural Philosophy*, ed. Hans Lenk (Berlin/Münster: LIT, 2009), 85.
[15] Cf. Kampling, 'Tradition', 224–5.
[16] Kampling, 'Tradition', 233.

Highlighting the more difficult conditions for any type of tradition to be adopted in an individualized and consumer-oriented society, he makes the case that believers need to argue for the liberating potential of the Christian tradition as a critical contribution to civic debate.

With this claim, to offer a liberating alternative to contemporary incentives to buy into market-led self-understandings, a question has been raised that concerns also the history of effects of the New Testament message in theological ethics: the issue of criteria for identifying its core. How can one make the case that the memory of Jesus' person, proclamation and practice constitutes a unified, identifiable tradition through the last two millennia when it is equally clear that interpretations and doctrines, institutions, life forms and norms linked to this faith have undergone seminal changes?

3. How to verify what remains identical in processes of translation and transformation?

After discussing the principle of tradition as it was defined by Vincent of Lérins (a) and exemplifying the consequences for ethics of an even earlier controversy about the Christian understanding of God, creation and human freedom (b), I will outline the scale of enquiry posed by the question of the identity of Christianity (c). A new direction in the understanding of tradition will be proposed from the perspectives of the hermeneutics of Christian doctrine and fundamental theology (d).

(a) Vincent of Lérins's principle of tradition

In the midst of doctrinal controversies in Christology and theological anthropology, Vincent of Lérins, a French monk and critic of Augustine's doctrine of predestination, proposed a formula in 434 which appealed to three criteria: 'what everywhere (*quod ubique*), what always (*quod semper*), what has been believed by all (*quod ab omnibus creditum est*).'[17] As Rainer Kampling points out in his differentiated analysis of the *Commonitorium*,

---

[17] Ibid., 226, with reference to Vincent of Lérins, *Commonitorium* 2, 3; 29, 41.

these criteria, using and combining the widespread antique principles of consensus and anteriority, are also opened up to the faithful to be used individually as aids for deciding between true and false interpretations. The text ties tradition to scripture and seeks to safeguard a preserving, as distinct from an inventive, role of tradition. The judgement put forward by the Christian philosopher Theo Kobusch may relate less to Vincent's own argumentation than to its history of reception: 'By making the principle of tradition the criterium for distinguishing orthodoxy from heresy, the authority of the ecclesial magisterium is confirmed.'[18]

One would think that the three criteria formulated in the face of a major innovation, Augustine's doctrines of original sin and double predestination, which Vincent criticized, should have been successful in recalling how theologians already in the second century emphasized human freedom against deterministic philosophies. Jesus' practical premise that every human person is capable of *metanoia* to the God of love was thus spelt out in new intellectual contexts. But Vincent's formal rules do not decide on the content questions which had to be struggled with in theological disputes, such as those between Augustine, Pelagius and Julian of Eclanum: whether God's grace eclipses human agency, whether all human effort, with its beginning in human freedom, has to be discounted, or whether all lifestyles, including the monastic one, are equally neutral in relation to God's decision to elect or to condemn. In relation to the normative contents of any tradition – including legal ones regarding the interpretations of a constitution – the question arises how their core or identity can be specified in relation to new circumstances and cultural constellations. Should the Christian tradition be conceived as a continuous unfolding of the New Testament message, or does it consist of renewed attempts to reformulate core factors in the face of unprecedented challenges?

(b) An early test case for the core of the Jesus tradition: Marcion in the second century

To illustrate the newly emerging need for criteria of interpreting and explaining the Gospel in a new era to different linguistic and cultural traditions, a

---

[18] Theo Kobusch, *Christliche Philosophie. Die Entdeckung der Subjektivität* (Darmstadt: WBG, 2006), 248.

principled controversy which the earliest theological commentators engaged in with their fellow Christian opponents can serve as an example. A radically new situation that required an argued response arose when a new member of the Christian community in Rome, the naval merchant Marcion, proposed an understanding of salvation that rejected any continuity with the scriptures of the Hebrew Bible. The creator God reflected in it was assimilated to the demiurge of Gnostic provenance, and a dualism between the Old Testament God of justice to the Christian God of mercy established. In the struggle against Gnosticism, apologists like Justin and Irenaeus came up with reasons against isolating the Christian message from the first covenant and the God of creation from the God of redemption. Irenaeus – who worked in more than one cultural location of the church, having moved from Asia Minor to Gaul to become bishop of Lyons – developed a unified doctrine of God, a Christian anthropology of human free will and a first theology of history: Jesus Christ was conceived as the turning point in human history, 'recapitulating' what God had intended by creating humankind. The significance of the 'vigor with which . . . early Christian writings respond to that challenge' for the subsequent direction of the Christian religion is highlighted as a watershed by Philip Wogaman: Had the views that 'interpreted the world in essentially negative terms . . . been sustained in the early church', it

> would have had profound effects on all the church's moral teaching. Economic life would have become inconsequential. What importance could any longer be given to the plight of the poor or to teachings about stewardship? Everything material, having been dismissed as evil or unreal, would no longer count to a life lived in the spirit. Similarly, political questions . . . would lose moral relevance . . . These early voices sharply condemned, even ridiculed, the notion that the physical world is evil or that it has nothing to do with life in the spirit.[19]

Thus, it had practical consequences how the great mid-second-century disputes on how to identify the shared legacy of the different gospels took a stance on what was unrelinquishable. With Clement of Rome referring to the love of neighbour and Ignatius to the Sermon on the Mount, the

> early church, in fact, underscored the importance of the material world to God's purposes and human well-being by giving enormous attention to the relationships of rich and poor . . . The struggle with Marcionism was, in many ways, decisive in establishing whether the church would regard the created

---

[19] Wogaman, *Christian Ethics*, 25–6.

world as an expression of the divine spirit and love or somehow in opposition to the God of salvation. Mid-second-century Christian writers like Justin and Irenaeus specifically and vigorously condemned Marcion's ideas ... Irenaeus reasserted the connection between Jesus Christ and the God of the Old Testament who created the world ... their affirmation of the material realm as an expression of God's creative and redemptive purposes is fundamental to the whole structure of Christian moral teaching ... Without that connection ... between God and the physical universe ... the faith would have become irrelevant to the actual existence of people.[20]

As Wogaman analyses the crucial contribution of these theologians to the identity of Christianity, the fact that they argued against Gnosticism as a complete reversal of the biblical message has also constituted a condition of the possibility of developing Christian social ethics.

(c) 'Tradition' as a theme of Christian doctrine and its hermeneutics

The rules and reference points of interpretation that began to be developed one or two generations after the completion of the fourth gospel, well before Vincent of Lérins responded to new divisive understandings, comprised the following: the creed and baptismal formula, biblical interpretations by theologians, the concept of apostolic succession and finally the decision that the Christian canon would include the Old Testament.[21] Thus, reasons were given why the Gnostic and docetic interpretations were wrong and heretical. Confronting the issue in principle, however, and with the benefit of a long history of reception across different eras, leads to a conclusion that puts into question any theological or magisterial positivism. Winning the dispute with Gnosticism by endorsing the New Testament message of incarnation and bodily resurrection seems to be a clear-cut case. Yet the overall task of singling out the core of a tradition requires an awareness of methods and of the limits encountered by historical and normative thinking.

First, pursuing the search at a terminological level instead of a network of concepts will miss out on crucial dimensions. An example from ethics would be to trace the use or absence of the term 'dignity' in documents and conclude from the finding, for example, that Kant also speaks of the 'dignity' of

---

[20] Ibid., 28, 27.
[21] Dirk Ansorge, *Kleine Geschichte der christlichen Theologie. Epochen. Denker, Weichenstellungen* (Regensburg: Pustet 9, 2017), 29.

mathematics, that it is mistakenly overvalued in his ethics. Against such a terminological approach, the key to finding out about the significance of a concept like dignity is to equally include terms such as inviolability, singularity, unconditional respect, source of rights, protection or pricelessness. One can then assess the relevance of the whole field of meaning. Transposed to religion, if 'salvation' is seen as a core concept of the Christian faith, the net has to be cast wider than just this term. The history of effects of the Bible, however, poses a further problem, as Thomas Pröpper analyses: God's self-revelation is witnessed to in Scripture, where we encounter it in an already interpreted form. In order to establish the continuity of that faith in the changing forms of its ongoing reception, one needs to reconstruct the ways in which the question of salvation was posed in each era and culture. Instead of a steady process of linear unfolding, one has to reckon with processes of translation and transformation which one can only try to identify from the vantage point of the present faith of the church. Therefore, he concludes, the reconstruction of the tradition of Jesus and its critical contemporary appropriation go together.[22]

One insight into the hermeneutics of tradition is that becoming aware of the contingent starting points of the search for the identity of Christianity not only rules out an objectifying understanding, as if one could look back from an undisputed current position. It also requires taking a practical position that has to be borne out by its fruitfulness in unlocking the written, practical and institutional testimonies of the past. Communities of belief and new movements, theological arguments and council decisions that were marginalized are part of the evidence, and are to be reconsidered in the task outlined earlier, to reconstruct how the question of salvation was posed. Having compared different answers, Pröpper judges the question to be ultimately 'aporetic', with no conclusive answer possible 'within the limits of objectivizing knowledge'.[23] This admission of the limits of a theoretical definition of truth does not, of course, preclude, but rather encourages to opt for a vantage point from which the meaning of salvation, liberation or redemption is to be worked out; this working hypothesis has to be justified in relation to the origins of the tradition. Pröpper quotes the conclusion

---

[22] Cf. Pröpper, 'Exkurs 2: Ist das Identische der Tradition identifizierbar? Zur Aufgabe und Hauptschwierigkeit einer historischen Rekonstruktion der Überlieferungsgeschichte des christlichen Glaubens', in *Erlösungsglaube und Freiheitsgeschichte*, 230–35, with reference to Edward Schillebeeckx, *Jesus. An Experiment in Christology*, trans. Hubert Hoskins (New York: Seabury Press, 1979); and *Christ. The Experience of Jesus as Lord*, trans. John Bowden (New York: Seabury Press, 1980).
[23] Pröpper, *Erlösungsglaube und Freiheitsgeschichte*, 235.

offered by the Flemish biblical and hermeneutical theologian Edward Schillebeeckx to locate the continuity of the Christian faith in the Gospel-inspired practices of its communities; the common ground is thus sought in what different generations and eras made of their inherited faith, leading into the realm of ethics.

(d) From a propositional to a communicative understanding of tradition

With the realization that the quest to define the core of Christianity leads into diverse conditions of faith and culture in which the meaning of 'salvation' is each time determined anew, a *depositum* understanding of tradition has been left behind. Vincent of Lérins looked for a consensus that presupposed a propositional concept of revelation. How inadequate an instruction-theoretical interpretation is when the content to be mediated is God's self-revelation has already become clear in discussing cognitive and objectivist thought forms. As Pröpper summarizes, the 'entire New Testament agrees in the testimony that through Jesus Christ in whose history God's self acted and God's self was revealed as love, salvation has been opened up irrevocably for all human beings.'[24] This understanding of the content of revelation cannot be captured as supernatural truths imparted by God to receptive human creatures. It presupposes instead that while 'salvation is a gift', it 'does not, however, make the human being an uninvolved recipient.'[25]

Interpreting the encounter of God and humans in a way that respects their free response recalls the points made earlier about the active, selective and meaning-creating character of appropriating a tradition. Here, Jürgen Werbick marks out the decisive turns that have to be taken if the *norma normans normata* is not to be conceived as a package complete in itself. It is a process of reshaping, contesting, rediscovering and taking further in the face of new historical challenges; it is marked by inescapable conflict, and what it offers are not proven answers:

> The claim of continuity must repress the vivacity and plurality of tradition because only what has been handed on in an unfalsified way, with the same meaning that has always been valid, has legitimating power ... Discontinuity and individuality are what should not be, what should be eliminated. It is this

---

[24] Ibid., 60.
[25] Ibid.

trait that makes this concept of tradition incompatible with modernity. The fact that tradition manifests its richness and vigour exactly in enabling individuals to shape and *form it anew* is lost in an instruction-theoretical claim of continuity.[26]

Secondly, an unavoidable conflict of interpretations accompanies the re-actualization of the origins and their effective history: 'Especially in the tensions and conflicts that were not worked out one may be able to perceive what this process of tradition contains within itself: the not yet exhausted, indeed, repressed possibilities of being church and of ecclesial testimony that could be set free again if one dared sustain the memory.'[27]

And thirdly, an insight into how the early church proceeded in resolving disputes is the distinction between the demarcation of limits by negative definitions, like those of Chalcedon, and the space opened up for further thinking:

> In the decisive phases of formation of this concept of tradition and doctrine – for example, in the formulation of the Christological demarcations of the 4th and 5th century – one can observe that the guiding theological-christological concepts are *negatively* defined. They do not expound in the sense of a positively developed doctrine the way in which what has been defined must be understood, but state how not to understand it since it would be one-sided or reductive.[28]

For Werbick, an adequate image for the renewed attempts of positive exchanges on faith is that '(t)radition is not primarily a reservoir of answers but a space to remember ... not simply answers but testimonies of ... dealing with questions and challenges'.[29]

4. Consequences for the use of tradition as a source of theological ethics

Thus, tradition is not a matter of undisturbed continuity, but of innovative transformations of the foundational message in unprecedented historical

---

[26] Werbick, *Den Glauben verantworten. Eine Fundamentaltheologie* (Freiburg: Herder, 2000), 822.
[27] Ibid., 822–3.
[28] Ibid., 828.
[29] Ibid., 824.

circumstances. At the stage of the first transition into a new era in early Christianity, key contents were reaffirmed against religious competitors, such as Gnosticism, which determined the direction also for the practical understanding of the demands of the Christian faith. They include: (1) arising from their understanding of Jesus Christ as the incarnation of God, an appreciation of the bodily constitution of the human creature; (2) the development of an anthropology of human freedom; (3) a new world historical framework devised to capture the interaction of God and humans in their cooperation with God's will in history.

A concluding insight into the first two sources of theological ethics is that the excessive contents professed in this faith tradition – God's incarnation, Christ's resurrection – set a new process of theoretical and practical self-understanding in motion that called for changed categories of thinking and judging to be elaborated:

> Still, certain conceptions of God, of the human being and of history are so much connected to this faith in salvation that their mediation with the thought form of any era and culture had to cause change and initiate a process of transformation. This constitutes the particularly dramatic nature of the history of tradition of the Christian faith.[30]

What these new self-understandings mean in terms of shaping judgements and actions also beyond the Christian communities, will be looked at in the next chapter, normative concepts of the human.

---

[30] Pröpper, *Erlösungsglaube und Freiheitsgeschichte*, 40.

3

The third source
Normative accounts of
the human person

After the Bible and tradition as the theologically grounded sources, the two that are based on human reason are to be examined in this and the following chapter. Theological themes connecting the first two sources with the 'normatively human'[1] include creation, Christology and soteriology. Two capacities through which being made in the image of God have been defined in the dialogues of theologians with the intellectual streams of their time are freedom and reason. How do these distinctive features of humans appear in philosophical ethics?

The first section gives an overview of how schools of philosophical ethics differ in their anthropological starting points, in their key assumptions and in their relation to religion, and of the points of discussion between them (1). The aim of the second section is to compare what is implied in core

---

[1] This third source in the 'quadrilateral' test proposed by John Wesley is referred to by James Gustafson, for example in *Theology and Christian Ethics* (Philadelphia: Pilgrim Press, 1974).

terms, such as self and agency, relation to the 'other', to community and society (2). The impact of the reception of the New Testament through the work of Christian thinkers on the development of a key concept in European philosophy, the 'inner person', will be the theme of the third section. It concludes with a critique of the neglect of the conception of 'inner freedom' in contemporary philosophy (3).

1. Schools of philosophical ethics

The term 'ethics' is used for different dimensions which need to be distinguished in order to recognize at which level disputes arise and where agreement can be found.[2] At its origin, ethics is the human capacity to generate judgements of value, based on the ability of a self-reflective being to take a stance towards his or her thoughts and actions. All the diverse approaches to ethics presuppose this foundational faculty, although they explicate it in different terms. As the human capacity for evaluation, this faculty unites the plural worlds into which individuals are born and which they shape from within their own cultures and in their encounter with others.[3] Arising from this primary capacity for judgement come, secondly, the distinctive theories of ethics that are elaborated and repudiated, differentiated and specified; they will be briefly characterized in this section. A third level, not further explored here, are international, national and professional documents on ethics codes that have been achieved through the institutionalization of ethics in agreements at the level of the UN, the Council of Europe, in the European Union, between governments, and in professional bodies.

At the second level, the philosophical discipline of ethics includes the task of giving an account of the anthropological premises that carry the various schools of ethics. The following brief overview of three philosophical traditions with their key terms will elucidate how systems of ethics are connected to elementary anthropological assumptions, and will ask whether

---

[2] In the following overview, I am using and further specifying contents from a chapter, 'Recognising Traditions of Argumentation in Philosophical Ethics', in *Ethics for Graduate Researchers: A Cross-Disciplinary Approach*, ed. Cathriona Russell, Linda Hogan and Maureen Junker-Kenny (Oxford: Elsevier, 2013), 7–26.

[3] This instructive distinction of levels and of the originating source is proposed by Jean Greisch, 'Ethics and Lifeworlds', in *Questioning Ethics. Contemporary Debates in Philosophy*, ed. Richard Kearney and Mark Dooley (London/New York: Routledge, 1999), 56–9.

religion has a place in them. Concluding the first section, their mutual critiques will be identified for the conceptual and theological examinations of the second and third sections.

(a) Aristotelian ethics

The ethics developed by Aristotle (384–322 BCE) is based on a concept of the human being as an *animal rationale* that is social and political. It is therefore oriented towards a shared community or *polis* in which the individual can have a voice and where education in virtues takes place. In contrast to the understanding put forward in the dialogues of Plato that ethics belongs to the realm of ideas, Aristotle anchors it in an existing civic connectedness with its concrete values, and a mode of practical reasoning that argues about orders and priorities of values. Current Neo-Aristotelian and Neo-Hegelian proposals build on the internal resources of a community, the processes of recognition among its members and the ability of its ethos to provide what is necessary for their identity formation. Its basic framework is built on the human orientation towards a 'flourishing life', the wish for happiness or *eudaimonia*.[4] The human capacities aiding this goal are virtues as the stable dispositions and long-term orientations humans can make their own, enabling the individual to make context-sensitive, prudential decisions in a concrete socio-historical community. With its interest in formation, socialization and ethical growth in commitment to a community, it offers a hermeneutical starting point from a shared self-understanding to the realization of ethical values. The possibility of a rupture between the community and its members is not envisaged, and the eminently enabling properties of a shared culture and language are at the forefront. While rationality has a central status in this system since ethics is a matter of knowing what is right (a virtue), and wrong (a vice), the element of the human will is not an aspect discussed on its own. The striving for a fulfilling life occupies the place of what other approaches, both biblical and deontological, will elaborate as the prime candidate for scrutiny in ethics, the human will. The hermeneutical strengths of this view of ethics are evident in that the conception of self is closely tied to the values and paradigms provided in a culture. The social and political context is recognized

---

[4] Aristotle, *The Nicomachean Ethics*, trans. J. A. K. Thomson, rev. Hugh Tredennick, intro. Jonathan Barnes (London: Penguin, 1976), 73–4 (1097a15–b21).

as supplying decisive conditions for the training of character, in which the models of concrete lives can be seen and imitated as formative examples.

Regarding religion, while current theological adoptions of a virtue-ethical framework take over the community-based understanding of practical reasoning and replace the civic setting, the '*polis*', with a religious one, 'church', there is no internal necessity for such a move. It is just one other context of socialization in values; from the original view of the self in a social context, a religious dimension has no special significance for the realization of ethics.

(b) Utilitarianism

The next ethical system to be presented presupposes the move to modernity. Appearing just before the French Revolution, utilitarianism argues for prioritizing the needs of the majority. It sees human needs as foundational for ethics and measures the 'good' by the useful consequences of an action at the greatest possible scale. By taking 'needs' as its starting point, and concern for the number of people affected as a normative criterium, it offers an empirically based guide for action. For decision-making at this level, it is successful in making the case for sustaining conditions of living for future generations, for identifying global challenges such as food security, clean water and protection against climate change.

The four principles it uses for its evaluations have been reconstructed in the following sequence: first, the overarching criterium is to judge by the consequences, rather than by the original intention or the inherent quality of an act; second, the criterium to judge consequences is utility in regard to the good. These two principles give it its names, consequentialism or utilitarianism. The third principle defines what this good consists in; the criteria are empirical, namely experiencing pleasure and avoiding pain, thus, positive and negative utility. The question of how to determine the scale of utility leads to the fourth principle through the criterium of maximizing the good for those affected, the social principle.[5] As to the third principle by which utility or 'happiness' is defined substantially, Bentham's concept of pleasure is differentiated by John Stuart Mill (1806–1873), refining the underlying anthropology. Mill first distinguishes higher from lower pleasures, pointing, for example, to the pleasure of education, but then ultimately

---

[5] Cf. Arno Anzenbacher, *Einführung in die Ethik* (Düsseldorf: Patmos, 1992), 31–4, and Anzenbacher, *Einführung in die Philosophie* (Freiburg: Herder, 8th edn 2008), 323–6, with reference to Otfried Höffe (ed.), *Einführung in die utilitaristische Ethik* (Stuttgart: UTB, 1975).

retains the goal of maximum happiness both in quantitative and qualitative terms.[6] In comparison with antique virtue ethics, the concept of 'happiness' has changed. For Aristotle it was connected to a rationality that included virtue, existence in a well-governed *polis*, and time for *theoria* or contemplative reflection. Written during periods of major upheaval from the French Revolution to the Communist Manifesto, utilitarianism puts the right to have basic needs met first. In this regard, 'consequences' such as providing the ability to feed oneself, can be assessed.

In relation to religion, John Stuart Mill points out its compatibility with New Testament values at the practical level.[7] Yet for religion to have a place that can be justified against the critique of religion as illusory, the analysis would have to include more than basic needs for survival. The revision of the pleasure principle by distinguishing quality from quantity presupposes a dimension of reflection which would have to be elaborated in a much more principled way. Only then can the horizon of the question of meaning be reached where religion can be argued for as a possible answer. In comparison with the standards set by Aristotelian and Kantian ethics – the reasoned orders of priority necessary for a flourishing life, or the demands of the moral law in relation to happiness – a more differentiated analysis of the needs of the human person would be needed. They would have to include the desire for recognition and the hope for a life of meaning in which one's moral intentions do not mostly fail.

(c) Kant's deontological approach

The central insight that gives deontology its name is that in moral reflection the self discovers what 'ought' to be done, or rejected; it owes it to itself to do justice to this obligation. Thus, the starting point of Immanuel Kant's (1724–1804) conception of morality is the individual capability for moral reflection. It is an insight that cannot be proven or refuted from an objectivizing position

---

[6] 'It would be absurd that while, in estimating all other things, quality is considered as well as quantity, the estimation of pleasures should be supposed to depend on quantity alone ... According to the Greatest Happiness Principle ... the ultimate end, with reference to and for the sake of which all other things are desirable (whether we are considering our own good or that of other people), is an existence exempt as far as possible from pain, and as rich as possible in enjoyments, both in point of quantity and quality'. John Stuart Mill, *Utilitarianism, Liberty, Representative Government. Selections from Auguste Comte and Positivism*, ed. H. B. Acton (London: J. M. Dent & Sons, 1972), 11.
[7] 'In the golden rule of Jesus of Nazareth, we read the complete spirit of the ethics of utility. To do as you would be done by, and to love your neighbour as yourself, constitute the ideal perfection of utilitarian morality'. Ibid., 16.

and that can only become a reality through personal appropriation. Freedom could well be an illusion, as Kant admits, but it is equally impossible to prove by theoretical reason that we are totally determined. So, as the resolution (*Auflösung*) of the third antinomy states, 'causality through freedom is at least *not incompatible with* nature'.[8] The everyday consciousness of having been able to act differently reveals the reality of the moral experience. Kant argues that 'good will' is the foundational human capacity, despite a 'propensity for evil'.[9] 'Good will' is not to be confused with rationality or intelligence which are at the cognitive level of purposive reason (*Verstand*) and ultimately subject to the limits of pure reason (*Vernunft*), both theoretical and practical.

The three terms that profile this conception of ethics are 'autonomy', the 'categorical imperative' and 'human dignity'. To be autonomous means 'self-legislation' under the moral law; failing to do justice to the internal experience of obligation is 'heteronomy', that is, following the lead of other options for self-determination. The 'categorical imperative' – as distinct from 'hypothetical' imperatives regarding actions subordinate to specific, changing rationales – consists in recognizing the demand of the moral law in oneself and of the other person in her equally original freedom, forbidding instrumentalization. The 'humanistic' formulation of Kant's 'categorical imperative' is: 'Act in such a way that you always treat humanity, whether in your own person or in the person of any other, never simply as a means but always at the same time as an end.'[10] How demanding this account of morality is can be seen in the fact that this obligation holds regardless of whether or not the other person returns the recognition offered. Even if the relationship is not mutual, thus, including cases of silence or of enmity, morality demands of the self to continue to extend respect also when it remains one-sided. The third key term, 'human dignity', is defined as the capability for morality inherent in all humans which is the source of their rights. Current interpreters of Kant stress the internal connection between duties and rights, without which there would be no addressee for rights claims. Onora O'Neill points out that giving priority to the ability to deliver on the rights of others is more

---

[8] Kant, *Critique of Pure Reason* (1781), trans. Norman Kemp Smith (New York: St Martin's Press/ Toronto: Macmillan, 1965), 464–79. The possibility to think a causality from freedom is further developed in *Groundwork of the Metaphysic of Morals* (1785), trans. and analysed by H.J. Paton (New York: Harper, 1964), 114–31, and in the *Critique of Practical Reason* (1787).

[9] Kant begins his *Groundwork of the Metaphysic of Morals* with the statement: 'It is impossible to conceive anything at all in the world, or even out of it, which can be taken as good without qualification, except a *good will*' (61).

[10] Ibid., 96.

empowering than beginning with the rights owed to one's own person.[11] Herta Nagl-Docekal highlights the need to 'listen in a global dialogue'[12] that is implied in Kant's critique of paternalistic ways of supporting others. Other people's own analysis of needs and the ways they envision their happiness is crucial in this interaction. Drawing out the further implication of Kant's approach that a continuous deepening of sensitivity and attentiveness for moral matters like exclusion is required, she points to the need to spell out what 'moral literacy' entails, as Barbara Herman has done.[13]

In Kant's conception of practical reason, there is an internal link to religion, due to a decisive limit posed by a contradiction that humans in their finitude cannot reconcile: in the 'antinomy' evident in the fact that good moral action, without ulterior motives or tacit self-interest, and the happiness due to such a person, are not necessarily connected. People whose actions are led by justice are often the ones who suffer; no other philosopher, observes Ricoeur, has given as much weight to the role of hope[14] for being able to continue on a path that respects and supports the other as an end in herself or himself. There is no safety net for moral agents if this respect is not reciprocated. Offers of peace are turned down; anticipatory and generous invitations to others are exploited for self-interest. Against such experiences, Kant declares that it is in keeping with reason to base one's hope in the ultimate success of moral action on a God who has created a world open to unselfish initiative, and not ending in absurdity. Such 'subjective' reasonable (*vernünftig*) faith has the status of a 'postulate', not of knowledge.[15]

(d) Mutual critiques

Long-standing debates between these approaches include their starting points, the role of individuals in their dignity and vulnerability, and the status of ethics.

---

[11] Onora O'Neill, *Bounds of Justice* (Cambridge: CUP, 2000), 101: 'In short, the rhetoric of rights . . . is still a rhetoric of recipience rather than of action. It still takes the perspective of the claimant rather than of the contributor, of the consumer rather than of the producer, of the passive rather than of the active citizen.'

[12] Cf. Nagl-Docekal, *Innere Freiheit. Grenzen der nachmetaphysischen Moralkonzeptionen (Deutsche Zeitschrift für Philosophie Sonderband 36)* (Berlin/Boston: De Gruyter, 2014), 9. 92–102.

[13] Ibid.,101–2, with reference to Barbara Herman, *Moral Literacy* (Cambridge, MA: Harvard University Press, 2008).

[14] Ricoeur, 'Hope as a Structure of Philosophical Systems' [1970], in *Figuring the Sacred: Religion, Narrative, and Imagination*, ed. Mark I. Wallace, trans. D. Pellauer (Minneapolis: Fortress, 1995), 203–16.

[15] Kant, *Critique of Practical Reason*, trans. Lewis W. Beck (Indianapolis: The Library of Liberal Arts/Bobbs Merrill, 1980), 130. 128–36.

(1) Starting points

Both Aristotelian and Kantian ethics would regard it as misplaced to judge the goodness of an action, as utilitarianism does, by its consequences, rather than by its inherent quality or its original motivation. Insisting on the internal link of ethics to the agent is not possible in such a functional framework. Reflection and debates on priorities of virtues or duties are superfluous if success in reaching a defined practical outcome is the only measure. However, despite their agreement on goodness as relating to an act, disposition or the will behind it, the schools of Aristotle and Kant differ on how they conceptualize this 'good'. Kant's alternative to virtue ethics has been accused of 'formalism'. Instead of beginning with substantive and concrete contents, such as courage or compassion, the autonomy approach puts forward a formal rule of judgement and leaves it to the agent's conscience to decide. Subjective guidelines or 'maxims' of actions are judged by the principle of universalizability; the measure is whether everyone could do so, or whether the intended action is self-centred, claiming an exception just for oneself. However, labelling this type of judgement 'formalism' is misleading since it is the 'maxims' that supply the content.[16] The difference is that the measure for being 'good' is not the social expectation of a specific cultural context; such existing values are deemed as needing discernment on whether they pass the bar of respecting 'humanity' in the other and in oneself. The inherently critical glance at given social settings as well as at the purity of one's own motivations is an abiding source of disagreement between Kantian and Neo-Hegelian accounts of social and political ethics, the modern voice of Aristotelianism.

(2) Individuals in their dignity and vulnerability

The social principle of utilitarianism that prioritizes the basic needs of majorities can be shared by different schools of social thought. Differences on more controversial anthropological assumptions such as concepts of agency, self and intersubjectivity can be postponed in cases where the urgency of ensuring conditions for survival is paramount. For a modern approach, however, its lack of a principle of distribution is striking. The

---

[16] The example given by H. Nagl-Docekal is the maxim to do nothing that endangers one's health. It counteracts autonomy both in oneself and others since it binds the agent in advance and subordinates the categorical imperative by precluding risky actions that could protect others in need. *Innere Freiheit*, 80–1.

calculation of average happiness indicates that it is not the individual in her basic rights who is the measure for the justice of a system. No theoretical argument is available that establishes the just treatment of each individual as the standard by which consequences need to be judged. How is it possible, on the basis of which criteria, to distinguish between mere wishes, preferences or private interests which can be sacrificed, and basic individual rights, which cannot? The additive calculation of happiness until it meets the required average of a simple majority implies a 'sacrificial principle'.[17] This leaves utilitarianism open to the charge that the terms in which it has been developed at least originally do not allow for a categorical prohibition of instrumentalizing or violating fellow humans in the interests of a majority.[18] The modern concept of dignity, itself an achievement of monotheistic and philosophical reflection as well as of historical struggles, encapsulates this protection.

The Aristotelian framework also lacks a concept of inherent dignity. Through its substantial definition of goodness through virtues, the role of the wise agent in his phronesis is embedded in communal values. A radical critique by individual members in the name of human dignity is not envisaged in a framework that assumes a basic harmony between individual and community. While communal debate and mutual awareness-raising is part of the necessarily 'public' use of reason also for Kant, the capacity for principled moral judgement of her own maxims is located in the individual. Delegating it to the discourse of a group risks 'a heteronomous relation and a moral emptying of the subject'.[19]

(3) The status of ethics

Systems of ethics that begin with striving for a flourishing life or happiness are appealing. As Ricoeur explains, his attempt to combine Aristotle and Kant

---

[17] Ricoeur, *The Just*, trans. D. Pellauer (Chicago: University of Chicago Press, 2000), 52–3: 'It is one thing to say that an individual has to sacrifice an immediate and lesser pleasure in view of a subsequent, greater pleasure, and another to say that the sacrifice of a minority is required for the satisfaction of the majority.'

[18] Christoph Hübenthal discusses direct and indirect counter-arguments to utilitarianism in 'Teleologische Ansätze', in *Handbuch Ethik*, ed. Marcus Düwell, Christoph Hübenthal and Micha Werner (Stuttgart: Weimar, 2006 2nd edn), 61–8, and in 'Solidarität – Historische Erkundung und systematische Entfaltung', in *Solidarität und Gerechtigkeit. Die Gesellschaft von morgen gestalten*, ed. Dietmar Mieth, with cooperation by Katharina Eckstein (Stuttgart: Katholisches Bibelwerk, 2009), 77–8.

[19] Nagl-Docekal, *Innere Freiheit*, 84–5.

in an ethics defined by 'striving to live well, with and for others, in just institutions',[20] this orientation towards a good life 'begins as a wish before it is an imperative.'[21] In conceptions of ethics inspired by Aristotle the development of sustainable practices and virtues serves this aim; norms are natural explications of this understanding of self and community. However, the question that arises for a purely hermeneutical understanding of ethics is whether ethics can only explore the internal logic of a given ethos. Are moral judgements always situated elucidations of the self-understanding of a community and its agents? *Or* are context-independent principles possible? By opting for a deontological second level that submits the entry point of human striving subsequently to the test of the categorical imperative not to instrumentalize the other, Ricoeur affirms the latter position. Other philosophers, such as Herbert Schnädelbach formulate their criticism of a communitarian framework in terms of a fundamental choice: it is a '*phronesis* ideology' which is in danger of emphasizing the contingent, singular and contextualized nature of human action so much that no general evaluation according to recognized criteria is possible. The German philosopher clarifies in which political-intellectual neighbourhood he sees the renunciation to the 'strong normative claims' which Kant had put forward in principles like human dignity as the basis of critiquing undignified conditions and practices:

> If it is no longer possible to attach strong normative claims to an idea, a radical critique can also no longer be founded. Theoretical skepticism always favours the power of what is established ... The historically enlightened Neo-Aristotelian can in fact only be a skeptic ... leaving praxis – in equal distance both to a Kantian ethics of obligation and to a platonising ethics of value – to practical cleverness, and unburdening himself and us from normative challenges as far as possible.[22]

Thus, ethics needs some independence from the practices inherent in cultures, and this demand also affects its starting point and its view of agents in the diversity of their aims and purposes. How these controversies appear in the theological adaptations of some of these approaches, will be followed up in Part 2.

---

[20] Ricoeur, *Oneself as Another*, trans. Kathleen Blamey (Chicago: University of Chicago Press, 1992), 172.

[21] Ricoeur, *The Just*, XV.

[22] Herbert Schnädelbach, *Zur Rehabilitierung des animal rationale. Vorträge und Abhandlungen 2* (Frankfurt: Suhrkamp, 1992), 214.

2. Concepts of self, of the other and of the social framework

Three key concepts – the individual, the other and plurality as the structure of sociality – will be examined next as different aspects of the normatively human.

(a) Self and agency

In each approach, human agency is captured in different terms. In utilitarianism, before Mill's distinction between higher and lower pleasures, it appeared as a straightforward drive to satisfy both naturally given needs and pleasures. Mill introduced a reflective capacity of discernment, but the criterium for assessing an action still remained its consequence. Therefore, the link from the action back to the self as its author, which would be necessary if its inherent quality was being judged, is not spelt out.

While Aristotle's version of antique ethics locates the good in virtue-led action, the emphasis is on ends towards which we strive naturally. Virtues are reflected, ordered pathways organic to the community to realize these ends and purposes. With the modern removal of ethics from a prior substantialist framework, embedded in an objective metaphysics, the only property that can make an act good is the intention that guides it, the good will. One can see the influence of the heritage of biblical monotheism in Kant's repositioning of the good from the *cognitive* sphere of insight to which it was linked in Greek philosophy, to the quality of the *will*. Kant's insistence that acts need to be judged immanently, rather than by their external results, recognizes the decisive role of conscience and self-reflection that modern communitarianism and utilitarianism subordinate to historically or naturally given factors for different reasons. The ability to turn back on herself, and to halt an action that is not in keeping with the agent's view of herself, needs to be explained in its possibility. This is what the 'transcendental method' proposed by Kant does, seeking to uncover the 'conditions of the possibility' of knowing and acting within the self. In this metatheoretical move, one goes behind what is experienced – for instance, that there are actions that are done out of respect for the 'moral law' – to understand the condition of this possibility. The condition that one has to assume, but cannot prove empirically, is freedom. With this new paradigm – freedom as experienced by the agent in autonomous action that fulfils the categorical imperative of respect – the concept of 'happiness' has to be interpreted in terms of the quest for meaning, not of natural fulfilment. This quest for meaning or happiness is recognized in Kant's concept of the highest good that comprises both moral goodness and happiness; the priority is decisive in that the second has to be proportionate to the first. Morality is an order of its own, the two have to be distinguished, and their conflict leads to the antinomy of practical reason. The harmonious view of human striving as coinciding with what is good is not shared by Kant; the painful experience that good intentions can fail to reach their goal or be counteracted is acknowledged as a problem so serious that it puts into question the foundations of ethics. The question of motivation that was not a problem in Aristotelian and utilitarian concepts of agency here acquires a new urgency.

(b) The relation between self and other

Once the already existing historical connectedness to fellow members of a culture loses its relevance for the definition of morality, the relation to the other becomes a question. At the same time, the three approaches all share the view that human beings are not just antagonistic agents and that sociability is an inherent human feature. Even if utilitarianism does not pay the attention required to the basic human rights of individuals, its social principle belongs to an ethics of recognition. This assumption is denied in approaches in which the struggle for survival against hostile fellow humans is the basic starting point, as for Thomas Hobbes and later on for Nietzsche. These positions turn what is part of human ambivalence, the role of negativity in relation to others, into a single basic given, denying an equally observable orientation towards the other's well-being. They equally assume a vitalist basis for all human pursuits, a mere striving for material survival in a hostile nature and in the face of enemies. Instead, the struggle could be situated at the level of something foundational for humans, namely the recognition of who they are.[23]

How this recognition is conceived, however, differs. Ricoeur discovers a parallel to Kant's assumption of a 'good will' in the most comprehensive and leading virtue within Aristotle's outline, namely the capacity for justice.[24]

---

[23] Cf. Ricoeur, *The Course of Recognition*, trans. D. Pellauer (Cambridge, MA: Harvard University Press, 2005), 161–75.
[24] Ricoeur, 'Ethics and Human Capability: A Response,' in J. Wall, W. Schweiker and D. Hall (eds), *Paul Ricoeur and Contemporary Moral Thought* (London/New York: Routledge, 2002), 285–9.

There are four factors in utilitarianism that restrict a full account of responsibility for familiar and for anonymous others: (1) its calculation of average utility lacks the factor that is central for a modern theory of justice, namely a principle of distribution – be it happiness, basic goods or life chances; (2) the principle of consequences rather than a goodness immanent in agents or acts is an alternative to, and not compatible with, the internal assessment of the agents themselves which they can stand over in their conscience, even if they were unsuccessful in achieving the intended outcome; (3) the distinctness of the other is also lost when 'consequences' consist in the satisfaction of needs that they were not able to define themselves. It is impossible to assess consequences for anything but delivery on basic needs because the effect of actions on other persons is as unpredictable as their free responses are. This is why Kant criticizes benevolent, but still unacceptable paternalism in defining for others what the goals of their happiness should be.[25] Finally, regarding intersubjectivity, Mill's empirical view of 'autonomy' as independence from external influence can be read as taking the presence of others as a negative factor for self-determination. For Kant, 'heteronomy' is possible all by oneself, and a joint realization of one's freedom is no impediment to autonomy as self-legislation.

(c) The social framework: Community, society, world

Also in relation to how the structures of social life are envisaged, the three schools of ethics are based on different assumptions. These affect the types of relation under consideration, and the scope of ethics – whether its remit is global, such as justice on a cosmopolitan scale, or focused on one's native polity.

The *community* bonds highlighted by Aristotle as carrying substantive ethical commitments do not have to be seen as inherently conservative. In contrast to Schnädelbach, Onora O'Neill sees the main feature not in opting for a status quo or not wishing to develop one's ethos further, but in the restriction to 'insiders'. A critique like this is questioned by supporters of an Aristotelian view: from the perspective of the existing ethos of living communities, reserving the term 'moral' for something that can never be fully realized denies moral quality to ordinary relationships and social

---

[25] Nagl-Docekal, *Innere Freiheit*, 99–100.

bonds. For Kant, however, moral subjects owe recognition to others on account of their equally original freedom as humans, not because they are members of the same particular community. A different concern is raised by the political philosopher Otfried Höffe: it is an open question how far Aristotelian ethics, with its orientation towards continuity and a shared stock of communal values, can cope with either radical breaks in self-understanding or with a pluralism in which previously taken-for-granted standards are challenged.[26]

Regarding *society* which, unlike the antique *polis*, is made up by unknown others and is marked by segmentation and differentiation, pluralism is a key feature. It is in this context that confidence in the community's resources of goodness has been replaced by the idea of a contract. It operates at the legal level of reciprocity and takes only the external conduct of citizens into account, leaving them free in their internal motivations and priorities. Pluralism regarding different conceptions of the 'good' is protected, once the 'right' has been acceded to. The question this poses regarding a more demanding understanding of 'morality' as unconditional recognition, is what levels 'legality' and 'morality' are assigned to, and which of the two is foundational. A key concern from the Kantian perspective is not to collapse the two, and reduce the term 'moral' by taking 'legality' as the starting point of constructing morality. When the term 'moral' is applied, as in the expression 'moral subject' used by John Rawls, to the external realm of being fellow citizens, the meaning oscillates between the external legal sense and the internal commitment. When a concept is applied to cover both a previously precisely defined meaning (morality) and a new use that extends it to its former counterpart (law), the danger is that it becomes 'empty'.[27]

Regarding the *scope* of ethics, the alternatives between Aristotle, utilitarianism and Kant are: one's own polity, the majority of current or future fellow humans, or a worldwide scale. This scope is in keeping with the universalism of the Kantian foundation on the moral experience available to all human beings. In this most extensive scope of ethics, the cosmopolitan

---

[26] Cf. Höffe, 'Einführung in Rawls's Theorie der Gerechtigkeit', in *John Rawls – Eine Theorie der Gerechtigkeit*, ed. Höffe (Berlin: Akademie-Verlag, 1998), 25. I have discussed Schnädelbach's and Höffe's critiques in greater detail in 'Virtues and the God Who Makes Everything New', in *Recognising the Margins: Essays in Honour of Seán Freyne*, ed. Andrew Mayes, and Werner Jeanrond (Dublin: Columba Press, 2006), 298–320.
[27] Nagl-Docekal, *Innere Freiheit*, 88, with reference to John Rawls and the Frankfurt School, here Axel Honneth and Rainer Forst.

horizon of all of humanity, each individual member is entitled to respect and support. However, with such an encompassing perspective, the question arises of how it can be anchored in the motivation of agents.

3. Linking up with the Christian legacy in the development of European philosophy: The 'inner person'

The inspiration which antique philosophy received from the interactions of biblical and theological authors with its different schools is summed up by the Christian philosopher Theo Kobusch as the discovery of the 'inner person'. It has had profound effects on the paradigm of freedom which was developed in European philosophy (a). How it appears in contemporary philosophical approaches is analysed by the philosopher Herta Nagl-Docekal (b).

(a) Insights from the first centuries of reception

In his interpretation of Greek and Latin patristic authors Kobusch argues that the overarching perspective which links the otherwise 'heterogeneous philosophical world' of these thinkers over several centuries is their focus on the 'inner person'.[28] This is the theme that links Justin, Irenaeus, Clement of Alexandria, Origen, Didymus the Blind, the Cappadocians, Ambrose, John Chrysostom, Nemesius and Augustine. He clarifies the sense in which this is their 'discovery', elucidates crucial elements of their differentiated analyses of human freedom, and sums up its effects on the subsequent history of metaphysical thinking.

First, the achievement of the church fathers was to 'discover' the inner world of the person in its 'irreducibility'.[29] They elaborated a concept that could be found in Paul's Second Letter to the Corinthians and in the third chapter of Ephesians, but that had appeared before the origins of

---

[28] Kobusch, *Christliche Philosophie*, 21.
[29] Ibid., 18.

Christianity, in Plato's *Politeia*[30] and in Stoic thinking. This discovery became a 'comprehensive conception' with an 'impact' that was 'unforgettable' also in the general consciousness of the culture.[31] 'Interiority' is thought 'as a principle for the first time'.[32] The way in which Kobusch explains the discovery of 'subjectivity' or of the 'inner human being' makes it clear that a normative concept is being established:

> Western and Eastern patristics all agreed that the inner human being is the true *(eigentlich)* one … The independence *(Eigenständigkeit)* of the world of the phenomena of the internal life … relies on a specific relationship to oneself. Without the inner human being, there is none. This original idea of the foundational function of the inner human being is at the basis of all reference to her external behaviour.[33]

Elements which came to the fore in these controversies that deepened the sense of self included 'intention' and 'will', and a new status for 'regret' and 'forgiveness'. A 'decisive change in the image of the human being' took place when attention was given to the 'inner element that lies at the basis of shaping and developing the inner human being as its moving principle: the will and freedom as necessarily connected to it'.[34] The pivot point is the relationship to human 'nature' or 'essence' which had been the framework for Plato, for Aristotle, for the Stoics and very much for the Manichaeans. By assigning a 'constitutive function to the will in relation to action and, indeed, the whole conduct of life', Origen is the first to set the will as the determinating principle in a counter-position to nature. 'Freedom does not depend on essence, it determines essence itself. Rarely is the modernity of patristic thinking as immediately recognizable as it is here.'[35] This gives a new role to moral reflection on one's own free action. Even if Stoicism encouraged daily examinations of conscience, antique philosophy lacked 'a genuine theory of conscience'[36] which could now be developed on the basis of this distinction. Human nature 'is not what is absolutely given, but what has been shaped by

---

[30] Kobusch emphasizes the 'practical core' (64) of this concept in the ninth book of Plato's *Politeia* which is retained 'in all subsequent theories' of the inner person. *Politeia* 589 a) refers to the 'reason-endowed part of the soul' that together with courage can 'domesticate the many-headed animal of desire. It is instructive that it is the inner human being who experiences the benefit of the soul through justice.'

[31] Ibid., 18.

[32] Ibid., 69.

[33] Ibid., 21.

[34] Ibid., 106.

[35] Ibid.

[36] Ibid., 118–19.

the will'.[37] Reflecting on actions that have fallen short of the standard a person has committed to engenders moral feelings such as remorse. For Kobusch, there is 'no doubt that it was Christian philosophy which assigned the humane element of remorse into the context of a doctrine of human freedom'.[38] In sermons as well as in responses to debates with intellectual counterparts, remorse as the practical beginning of a change in life conduct, as well as forgiveness, were raised to a new standing.[39]

Patristic authors succeeded in making the concept of the 'inner person' which in Plato could be seen as part of an elitist philosophy, into a generally accessible consciousness.[40] The church fathers' critique of a 'theoretical type of metaphysics' and its re-conception as a 'spiritual exercise' matched, but also broadened, the antique pagan view of philosophy as a 'life form', focusing on the 'meaning of what is known for one's own life', in contrast to 'theoretical knowledge which is almost defined by its abstinence towards this question'.[41] This valuation of interior life extended beyond the world of monks to the ordinary people, as various patristic authors illustrate with conviction;[42] as Kobusch records them, the 'truth of Christianity is a truth that can be proposed (*zumutbar*) and be healing to all humans. It demolishes the limits of gender and occupation, language and estates', inviting 'old women, wool spinners, hand workers, seamstresses, servants, carriage drivers and gardeners' into this understanding of Christian life.[43]

The fact that Christianity, and not, for example, middle Platonism, took up the theme of the inner person, and, defending it against Gnosticism, made it into the 'genuine theme of (Christian) philosophy', was of 'seminal significance' for the Western history of thinking.[44] It undermined the idea of a given human nature[45] and countered the metaphysics of Aristotle 'with its orientation towards the realm of natural things' with a 'metaphysics of the inner human person'.[46] This epoch-changing history of effects was helped by

---

[37] Ibid., 67.
[38] Ibid., 114.
[39] Cf. ibid., 112–17 on 'Remorse and shame', with 204–6 for quotes on remorse as the positive possibility of self-distanciation and a new beginning, and 124–30 on forgiveness.
[40] Ibid., 64.
[41] Ibid., 22. Kobusch refers to Pierre Hadot, *Exercises spirituelles et philosophie antique* (Paris: Albin Michel, 3rd edn 1993).
[42] Kobusch quotes Nietzsche's diagnosis of Christianity as 'Platonism for the people' (41) as a somewhat perceptive judgement.
[43] Ibid., 49.
[44] Ibid., 64.
[45] Ibid., 68.
[46] Ibid., 15.

the inclusive understanding of Christian truth held by many patristic authors. They saw the Christian faith as taking up and completing directions that already existed in different philosophical schools, and that had to be defended with them against other movements, such as Gnosticism.[47]

In Kobusch's analysis, the break through from thinking in 'essences' that are unchangeable, to the will as the capacity for individual self-determination in response to God's call, is the major achievement of monotheism interacting with pagan anthropologies and ethics. It turned attention towards the internal basis of action, the will with its motivation, in the hope-oriented framework of the Christian faith in salvation. It emphasized human freedom over a given striving for a flourishing life in keeping with the typical features of human nature. This shift opened up the path to valuing the singularity of each human being in their potential to receive and take part in the message of salvation. The will in its changeability is the principle of individuality: 'The soul is the general nature of the human being, the factor through which she is human. The differences between human individuals are founded on their will, that is, their freedom.'[48] How does the legacy of this discovery of the 'inner person' inform current approaches to ethics?

(b) 'Inner freedom' in contemporary philosophical approaches

In Herta Nagl-Docekal's diagnosis, the new paradigm against which the experience of inner freedom is losing its previous foundational role is not an antique metaphysics of nature, but a slide to a legal, and therefore external, starting point. The individual's capacity of moral self-reflection is lost out of sight, and the reconstruction, remaining at the level of the 'citizen', can only judge external conduct. She provides a detailed analysis of the sequence of steps and levels of current approaches like those of John Rawls, Axel Honneth, Rainer Forst and Jürgen Habermas in comparison with two of the classic modern theories they draw from, Kant and Hegel. Identifying where differentiations are given up and the everyday consciousness of morality is not reached,[49] she draws attention to the need to examine key terms like

---

[47] The truth claim they put forward was not a divisive one that was a priori dismissive of others, but one that offered concrete criticisms of specific points. The critique that monotheistic truth claims as such imply violence is rejected by Kobusch (50).

[48] Ibid., 107.

[49] Nagl-Docekal, *Innere Freiheit*, for example, 9, 28, 62, 72, 79, 84, 90.

'reciprocity' and to keep levels of moral judgement distinct. When an analysis begins with actual conflicts between fellow citizens, instead of with the individual experience of a moral obligation to oneself and to others, it indicates the direction in which solutions are sought: they can be worked out in legal settlements. The language of expectation and entitlement also creeps into personal relationships when friendship, love, family and marriage are treated in terms of strict reciprocity. This misses the core of both primary and chosen relations where the 'logics of contract'[50] are not typical for either content or motivation. Collapsing the distinction between the civic and the personal, interior perspective leads to portraying citizens as being content with securing their rights in merely contractual exchanges; it would be equally possible for them to make a moral decision in a particular case to renounce to a right in favour of the other person in his or her singularity.[51] The internal touchpoint of moral reflection is also undermined when a judgement resulting from 'discourse' takes the place of individual validation, justifying itself through its intersubjective process. This externalizes the test of universalization demanded in Kant's concept of morality as self-legislation; it does not allow for the testing of one's own maxims which call for self-scrutiny, nor of obligations towards oneself, which to neglect can equally result in heteronomy. The oscillating use of 'autonomy' both in the sense of 'self-legislation' under the moral law, and of self-determination, self-formation and self-realization loses the specificity of moral reflection. Since it then covers both actions from self-interest and from morality, it is in danger of 'emptying' the moral subject.[52] She argues for keeping alive 'an option which is frequently not perceived and realized (*wahrgenommen . . . im zweifachen Sinn*): an attitude which assumes that it can be meaningful to orientate one's life by ideals, even if their realization presents itself as something that cannot be completed.'[53]

What is relevant for the next chapter and for discussing approaches in Part 2, is her observation that 'losing the inner dimension of morality out of sight results in an equal failure to illuminate the possible link between morality and religious faith'.[54] Spelling out citizens' ethics in the realm of socially given conventions and values risks falling prey to long-standing embedded

---

[50] Ibid., 9.
[51] Ibid., 21.
[52] Ibid., 10.
[53] Ibid., 12.
[54] Ibid.

structures of misrecognition. The only way out of this is to take seriously the individual capacity for moral judgement, discourse among those affected and listening by those with the power to initiate changes towards greater justice.[55] This starting point is jeopardized when the irreplaceable factor of inner freedom is sacrificed to purely external perspectives. To these belong values and structures of ethical life that constitute unnoticed barriers, a legal insistence on exact terms of exchange, and a muffling of questions of meaning that cannot be answered in a post-metaphysical framework. An example is the loss of a unique person who should not merely count as a habitual counterpart, but be mourned for their own sake.[56]

The different schools with their specific views of the 'normatively human' will play a role also in the next chapter on the need to include the individual human sciences. It will outline the differentiation of 'reason' into distinct disciplines and methods of enquiry which offer inductive insights relevant for the link between anthropology and ethics and for judgements in domain-specific ethics. It will become clear that the different schools are inescapable and that ethicists have to opt for a specific one, if they are to use terms like 'justice', 'autonomy' or 'action' consistently, with a definite, rather than a vague, generic or overlapping meaning. The distinctions and discussions of different conceptions of the normatively human will also play a role in Part 2.

---

[55] Ibid., 100, for example in relation to foreign aid and to terms of work contracts that many women are not in a position to refuse.
[56] Ibid., 57.

4

The fourth source
The individual human sciences

Chapter Outline

The fourth source of theological ethics is the array of distinct disciplines, encompassing both the natural sciences and the humanities, which conduct research into natural reality and fields of human practice. Guided by methodologies and models, they are both inductive and theory-led. Before examining their relevance for reaching ethical judgements (2), and the issues arising in the task of integrating the two sources from reason (3) as well as the four sources overall (4), the changed role of reason in the analyses of philosophy and in the individual sciences has to be explained (1).

1. Reason, rationality and scientism

It is evident that ethics cannot argue from conceptions of the normatively human alone and that it needs to seek information about human and natural reality. This is not just true for applied ethics, but already for these conceptions themselves which interpret human life. Philosophy, scientific enquiry and ethics are all bound to a real world that is given before they analyse it. The success of the individual sciences in producing such knowledge has affected the understanding of the role of philosophy (a). Two further aspects are the premises, limits and internal plurality of disciplines (b), and the question of the guiding ideal of knowledge and of ways of achieving 'objectivity' (c).

(a) Changes in the relationship between philosophy and the individual sciences

On the one hand, a reversal of the role of philosophy has taken place in that it no longer grounds the sciences or assigns them to areas based on its own classification, such as philosophy of nature, of history or political philosophy. The disciplines map their terrain themselves: 'Their structures, approaches, and functional laws can only be thematized on their own ground … Philosophers have to try to take their home in these sciences, that is, to grasp what is taking place within them.'[1]

On the other hand, since the renewal of the positivism dispute in the late 1960s, the programme of submitting both sciences and humanities to a unitary approach has been contested; the specific difference between researching objects in nature, and in culture as a product and a productive capability of humans has been upheld. Both enquiries answer to criteria of reason; but the boundaries between the two in view of their research matter and methods need to be respected. A consciousness of the strengths and the limits of each has to be elaborated as part of the research projects, and the ability for transdisciplinary exchange developed on both sides.

These objectives are made more difficult by the increasing specialization within disciplines, resulting in greater detail but also a fragmentation of knowledge. Thorough knowledge of a field is required to offer competent contributions which can advance the debate. This demand leads to ever-deepening research into more factors. Such professionalization works against pursuing over-arching questions. It seems that one of the functions left for philosophy is to point out the lack of a connection back to everyday life where the problems to be solved by people arise. Already in the early

---

[1] Walter Schulz, *Philosophie in der veränderten Welt* (Pfullingen: Neske, 1972), 88.14.

1970s, in his summary of the changes to the position of philosophy wrought by the unfolding of the distinct rationalities of the various disciplines, Walter Schulz identified two tasks that a theory of science cannot fulfil. They are, first, the ability to compare premises with the conceptual precision of philosophy, in order to offer a reflective diagnostic grasp of the contemporary era; and secondly, an integrative response to the question of what it is to be human.[2]

One model developed in response to the empirical turn of reason towards research enterprises is Jürgen Habermas's reconceptualization of philosophy as 'stand-in' or 'placeholder' (*Platzhalter*) for universalistic questions, and as 'interpreter', both between scientific rationalities, and between them and the lifeworld.[3] Philosophy retains the function of being the 'guardian of rationality'. It is still the case that 'ideas like truth or the unconditional with their transcending power' are needed as 'a necessary condition of humane forms of collective life'.[4] However, its claim needs to become more modest (*ermäßigt*), offering reconstructive hypotheses for empirically observable competences.[5] It puts its 'strong universalistic claims' to work within the sciences, by relating, for example, 'cognitivist ethics and a psychology of moral development' to each other.[6]

The second role, interpreter, replaces an alleged previous role of judge. This mediating capacity is to counteract the segmentation and fragmentation and to renew the integrating function of philosophical thinking. This is needed both at the levels of the expert cultures, and of citizens within a lifeworld that is being colonized and 'impoverished' in its traditions by the economic and political systems. Philosophy is trusted to be able to 'overcome the isolation of science, morals, and art and their respective expert cultures', and establish 'a new balance between the separated moments of reason . . . in communicative everyday life'.[7]

This programmatic adjustment of the previously foundational role of reason to the diversification of rationality has been critiqued for aligning philosophy so much with empirical research that there is no critical power

---

[2] Ibid., 19.
[3] I have given a more detailed account in Chapter 4 of *Habermas and Theology* (London/New York: T & T Clark International, 2011), 67–80.
[4] Habermas, 'Philosophy as Stand-in and Interpreter', in *Moral Consciousness and Communicative Action*, trans. C. Lenhardt and S. Weber Nicholsen (Cambridge, MA: MIT Press, 1990), 3.
[5] Habermas, *Moral Consciousness*, 16.
[6] Ibid.
[7] Ibid., 19.

left.[8] In its merely accompanying, subservient role, it operates according to the parameters set by the sciences, and a method of its own is explicitly denied. In subsequent decades, Habermas has reconfirmed the unique capacity of self-reflection that philosophy brings to the table. What this proposal of the early 1980s shows, is the realization that philosophy retains a role within the concrete questions of the material sciences. No matter whether other capacities are still allocated to it, at the least it explicates the universal concepts contained in the sciences, and integrates the theoretical, practical and aesthetic uses of reason.

(b) Taking the premises and methodological choices of disciplines into account

The strength of each individual discipline – for example, sociology, economics, psychology, biology or physics – lies in its ability to focus on aspects of conscious life and nature that it has the methods to investigate. Yet this means straight away that its research is conducted through models, specific discourses and frameworks that do more than just represent what takes place in the everyday world. The methods used in their reconstructions give an account of the selection of aspects a discipline *can* research, and where its competence ends.

This regular feature becomes especially clear when one examines Habermas's examples for initiating research into questions that are 'at the same time empirical, yet universal' *(empirisch bearbeitbare, aber universalistische Fragestellung)*. Theorists like Freud, Durkheim, Mead, Max Weber, Piaget and Chomsky stand for this combination, having 'inserted a genuinely philosophical idea like a detonator into a particular context of research'.[9] The observation that theoretical assumptions guide the design of empirical enquiries can be illustrated with the example of a research-backed theory: the stages identified

---

[8] Karl-Otto Apel insisted that the justificatory function of philosophy had to be retained which is not possible if its own mode of enquiry is denied. The 'moment of unconditionality' that distinguishes its use of reason from that of the sciences has to be accounted for. It does not make sense to submit philosophy to the fallibility tests of the empirical sciences. Cf. Apel, 'Normatively grounding "critical theory" by recourse to the lifeworld? A transcendental-pragmatic attempt to think with Habermas against Habermas', in *Jürgen Habermas*, vols. I–IV (Sage Masters of Modern Thought), ed. David M. Rasmussen, and James Swindal (London: Sage, 2002), vol. III, 344–78.

[9] Habermas, *Moral Consciousness*, 4.

in Lawrence Kohlberg's enquiry into moral development. Any stage theory is designed from the ultimate level down to the beginning; the questionnaires are drawn up on the backdrop of theses that will be verified or falsified in the course of the investigation. Counter-theories, such as Carol Gilligan's challenge to Kohlberg's theory of moral development, correctly identify a pre-understanding, in this case, of a specific concept of justice, that influences the result.[10] As the subsequent debates in psychology, philosophical and political ethics have shown, the stages could have been conceived differently. Had the element of 'care' or the personal support of known others required from moral beings been included as belonging to 'justice', the labels 'conventional' and 'post-conventional' might have been replaced with more differentiated divisions. Attention to immediate others could be seen as part of an understanding of the moral self that also includes all fellow humans but is different in the perfect and imperfect duties owed to either. The history of debate on male and female types of orientation towards 'justice' makes it clear just how theory-imbued research projects are, and how much the prior assumptions are reflected in the results. Having sparked new directions and perspectives of research, their explanations are met by counter-models which anticipate different answers. Another example of this contest of models and methods can be found in the shifts in historiography to new methodologies and themes.

It is a consequence from the premise-led character of research which never just captures its object immediately that disciplines, for example, psychology or sociology, are also divided into schools. Like those in philosophy, they continue to question each other in their approaches and guiding terms. There is no settlement to be expected, and each can point to the productivity of their guiding assumptions which yield at least partial results.

(c) Disputes about the ideal of knowledge and 'objectivity'

What follows from the insight into the relevance of guiding perspectives is the need for a new concept of objectivity. On the one hand, this challenges the claim of 'scientism' to be able to produce unquestionably valid results. A careful

---

[10] Chapter 9 on Feminist ethics will take up some of the questions raised by Carol Gilligan, *In a Different Voice: Psychological Theory and Women's Development* (Cambridge, MA: Harvard University Press, 1982); Lawrence Kohlberg, *Stages in the Development of Moral Thought and Action* (New York: Holt, Rinehart & Winston, 1969); idem, *Essays on Moral Development*, vols 1 and 2 ((San Francisco: Harper & Row, 1981, 1984).

account of procedures would show that the data collected confirm a specific hypothesis, sometimes only provisionally, as the history of paradigm changes in science has shown. On the other hand, claims that all research is utterly bound by the perspective of the researcher and that 'reality' is entirely constructed in line with dominant power structures can equally be shown to be based on premises, in this case Nietzschean. It overdraws the results of the debate on how standpoint-bound enquiries are and proposes a conclusion that is self-defeating: the thesis itself is subject to the same suspicion of not being 'true', but to be an expression of power.[11] Already Nietzsche had to resort to self-exemption from the verdict that truth is only a matter of perspective. Between the unstinting objectivism of scientism and the complete relativism of some constructivist approaches, a way forward has to be worked out which acknowledges that research is always contextual. Disciplines and the research results of the approaches within them are to be valued within their parameters. Nagl-Docekal concludes her analysis of the opposite extremes of positivism and of the subjection of all knowledge to a power matrix by taking stock of the results of the dispute: the realization that all knowledge production is situated; the need to specify the enquiry's guiding interests, being aware of its contexts of origin and of use without reducing research findings just to these contexts; offsetting possible biases and blind spots by casting the net wide when choosing perspectives and approaches for each project.[12] The truth claim of research is not overthrown when the awareness of the limits of reason, of its finitude and fallibility deepens. Yet research designs and their results are answerable to criteria of precision and inclusivity. This would require not excluding women, which should be obvious; but closer inspection reveals that research on women and their conditions of life, illnesses, participation in education and politics has been missing. What has happened often enough instead is that chronologies, data and conclusions from studies which de facto only included men have been wrongly generalized.[13] These failures show that research, however situated and fallible, is answerable to normative criteria.

---

[11] Nagl-Docekal, *Feminist Philosophy*, trans. Katharina Vester (Boulder, CO: Westview Press, 2004), 95: 'A strategy of blanket suspicion gets caught up in a performative self-contradiction: Those who try this extensive unmasking exempt themselves from it; they discuss the linkage of knowledge and power in a manner that they do not see as being itself guided by power interests.'

[12] Ibid., 102–10.

[13] Ibid., 89. Two of the examples she gives are the failure to research the effect of medical and pharmaceutical treatments separately, subsuming women to test results that apply to men; and the erroneous labelling of the granting of a 'general' right to vote when only men were given this right, and the starting date of the truly general right figuring as 'women's right to vote'.

Such critical awareness is important at a time when undesired research findings, such as the human-caused nature of climate change, are being contested. Those denying this link use the tools of an ideology critique which was once devised to uncover the interests involved in the economic, legal and intellectual structures set up by the dominating class. Dismissing that its causes are identifiable human uses of nature that could still be corrected is an ideological cover for continuing demonstrably ruinous practices. These conflicts show that vigilance regarding the goals and conduct of scientific enquiries is in the interest of a defensible concept of objectivity.

2. Sciences and technology as social practices and the role of ethics

A first conclusion from the observation of the situated nature of enquiries is that the individual sciences draw on cultural self-understandings, conceptual histories and perceptions of priorities. They can reflect on these conditions, but the ideal of 'value-free' research as proposed by Max Weber reveals itself to be mistaken. First, it ignores the embeddedness of the natural and the human sciences in a cultural value system and their task to examine and enable human competencies (a). Secondly, scientific enquiry is a part of human agency which to envisage as value-free would cut its tie to human reflection. Conceiving science and technology as part of social practices allows a different role for ethics assessments. With directions for future living implied in research projects, the different sciences need to take on board a hermeneutical reflection of contemporary trajectories and imperatives in their effects on lifeworlds (b).

(a) Assessing the parameters of a technological culture

The critical hermeneutical competence needed to understand contexts, directions and priorities of research will be spelt out in two aspects. The first examines how Habermas engages the individual sciences in the humanities in a programme researching the different levels of communicative practice (1); the second assesses the 'technological condition' of contemporary life in relation to agency (2).

(1) Habermas's concept of communicative reason offers a broader framework than the purposive rationality pursued in Max Weber's conception of modernity. It has critiqued the ideological aspects of a scientific culture and has sought to develop an ethics of recognition from the very foundations of language. In the analysis underpinning his programmatic reformulation of the status of philosophy in the early 1980s, the individual disciplines start 'primarily from the intuitive knowledge of competent subjects – competent in terms of judgement, action, and language – and secondarily from systematic knowledge handed down by culture (*überlieferte kulturelle Wissenssysteme*)', to 'explain the presumably universal bases of the rationality of experience and judgement, action and linguistic communication'.[14]

The task of the various disciplines is to investigate existing human life as it is found in communicative competences both in their genesis (such as language) and in the cultural expressions and institutionalizations they have taken; these could be systems of knowledge and of education, gender relations and forms of political governance. The task is not only descriptive, but also critical, in keeping with the origins of the Frankfurt School. Thus, it includes investigating the conditions for the actual use of these generic competencies, and identifying pathologies that hinder their realization. By investigating human capabilities one discovers internal criteria.

What should be added to this outline of an encompassing research programme in the 1980s on the basis of the critiques by Karl-Otto Apel, Dieter Henrich and others is the call to give equal attention to the reverse direction: does the empirical research format curtail possible aspects by reducing the starting points to what can in effect be researched in this way? By insisting on the independence of the philosophical method, Apel places research in a horizon where questions can go in both directions. The 'bases of rationality' should also be examined from the perspective of philosophical conceptions of self-reflection and freedom. In his dispute with Habermas regarding the understanding of 'metaphysics', Dieter Henrich put forward an objection regarding the origin of the consciousness of self which cannot merely be traced back to intersubjective relations.[15] Research designs have to be kept open to allow for an independent origin of self-reflection, distinct

---

[14] Habermas, *Moral Consciousness*, 15–16. I have amended the English translation which renders *Rationalität* as an adjective: 'the presumably universal bases of rational experience and judgment, as well as action and linguistic communication.'

[15] Dieter Henrich, 'What Is Metaphysics – What Modernity?', in *Habermas: A Critical Reader*, ed. Peter Dews (Oxford: Blackwell, 1999) [German original: 1987], 291–319.

from what is traceable to language and interaction. A further example of the need to specify the understanding of freedom, as already discussed in the previous chapter, can be found in Nagl-Docekal's critique of the neglect of 'inner freedom' in the 'post-metaphysical' paradigm of social and political ethics in the current Frankfurt School. She invokes the everyday consciousness of morality which is misrepresented, in her view, when it is accessed from the legal level of the external relations between citizens. In its orientation towards strict reciprocity, the law safeguards individual rights, but this means that it cannot account for a perspective that is not self-interested. Moral action which might generously renounce to legal equivalence cannot be reconstructed in this framework.[16] Thus, research designs and political theory are marked by tacit philosophical assumptions which need to be made explicit and opened up to debate. The need to avoid narrowing the understanding of what counts as 'knowledge' to data at our disposition has only increased in an age of digitization. How do these technologies affect the 'bases of rationality' and the scope of the competent subjects? What these and other scientific innovations promise is precisely a greater scope and power to act. How have the parameters posed by a technological culture been assessed by philosophers interested in individual agency?

(2) Comparing opposite claims regarding the role of technology, David Lewin draws on Ricoeur to conclude that it is a decisive 'context' for human freedom. Framing the debate in terms of alternatives overdraws each side: to cast it as being *either* a tool for free human agents, *or* a force of domination is caught in a 'stale dichotomy'. From a hermeneutics of culture across different eras, this does not do justice to the inevitable shaping of human agency by *all* cultural conditions: 'We are not victims of a technological fate, any more than we are masters of a technological destiny. This gives some indication of the problems with identifying human capability in the absolute terms that force us to take sides on the question of technological neutrality or determinism.'[17]

---

[16] Nagl-Docekal, *Innere Freiheit*, 21.

[17] David Lewin, 'Ricoeur and the Capability of Modern Technology', in *From Ricoeur to Action*, ed. David Lewin and Todd Mei (Continuum Studies in Continental Philosophy) (London: Bloomsbury, 2012), 64, with references to *The Conflict of Interpretations*, ed. Don Ihde (Evanston, IL: Northwestern University, 1974); 'Manifestation and Proclamation', in *Figuring the Sacred*, 48–67; and *Oneself as Another*. Regarding the question whether the power of human action can always contain the consequences, Lewin comments: 'With the catastrophes at Hiroshima and Nagasaki, the assumption that technology could simply be the servant of human will came to an end.' Ibid., 55.

Instead of assessing specific developments as either liberating, or as alienating and destructive, their potential to shape the self-understandings of those using them and exposed to them should be the focus of nuanced analysis. Based on Ricoeur, Lewin sees two dangers. One relates to the possible effect of instrumental reason on the ability to encounter a world that one can imagine, recognize in literary accounts, project oneself into, and transform. He refers to the imaginative resources found in narrative, myths of origin, conflict and utopias which could be depleted by an experience of a world that consists increasingly of user-friendly technological devices. The imaginaries of a culture which feed its productivity are threatened when rationality appears only in the form of purposive reason. The other risk is that of detracting from human initiative and receptivity – which are vital in relating to otherness – by being occupied with predictable technical effects. The gain through new functionalities could result in the loss of other ways of relating and could indirectly incapacitate individuals by reducing the ability to encounter a genuine 'other' who cannot be programmed. While the technological advances can also support humans in their creative and interactive agency, how do they affect its future shape? The ethical relevance of the fact that technology is a product of social practices but one that in turn submits human action to its effects is to be examined next.

(b) The concept of action and the position of ethics assessments in the course of technological innovation

As Habermas has pointed out, the individual sciences begin with something given, such as competencies found in humans which enable them to relate to their world and to others. Equally, the discussion on a proper understanding of 'objectivity' has questioned positivist views that endorse seeing scientific research as 'value-free'. This would deny a dimension that is given through the mere fact that science is a human practice; human action *is* subject to value- and principle-led analysis.[18] It is not a neutral domain for disinterested observers but a matter for critical evaluation. Humans need scope for action

---

[18] In *Reflections on the Just,* trans. David Pellauer (Chicago: University of Chicago Press, 2007), 152, Ricoeur formulates his objection as a point of internal criticism: 'How are we to hold together the *wertfrei* posture, claimed by Weber, with having to make recourse to the meanings experienced by social actors in the identification of the object of the social sciences?'

in order to work out their lives in accordance with their freedom; to insinuate that it is appropriate to recommend abstention from moral and ethical judgement contradicts especially the modern understanding of reason as practical.

A normative dimension is already introduced when one speaks of 'action', as distinct from a natural event or behaviour. It attributes a quality of intention to the act that can only be explicated by a fuller account of human freedom.[19] An analysis that remains at the descriptive external level fails to reconstruct the link to an individual's motivation and hoped-for outcome, which uncovers a dimension that is ethically relevant. Assessments are needed on how developments might affect the scope of individuals and societies for action, especially if it can be anticipated that they will be irreversible.

It is from the analysis that technology is 'not a given, but socially constructed', that Hille Haker demands turning around the burden of proof and to regard 'science and technologies as social practices that need to be justified in light of the normative framework'.[20] Technology is supported by societal systems, and should therefore be answerable to socially desired goals and rights already enshrined. In view of the speed of change, it becomes even more urgent to scrutinize the current practice of ethics assessments for its effectiveness. What is in question is the sequence: Does the reconstruction begin after the fact, when technological changes have already been introduced, as is the case with the ethical, legal, social assessment (ELSA) practice? *Or should one begin with the moral framework of a constitutional democracy oriented towards human dignity and committed to human rights, which protects ethical pluralism?* Technological advances would then be selected according to these criteria. Haker identifies both deontological and teleological dimensions in this reversed order. The Millennium Development Goals belong to the deontological obligations. But technological developments are also in need of assessment for their possible effect on teleological aims, that is, in relation to 'social imagination and social visions, but also norms of social interaction, practices of solidarity or group identities'.[21] By placing ethics assessments at the beginning, the specialists on contexts, internal motivations

---

[19] Nagl-Docekal, *Innere Freiheit*, 80: 'I can only call a specific occurrence "my action" if I am turning a decision into an act; in this case I have to be able to indicate why I have decided in this way ... If I can state why ... I am invoking – even if I am not explicitly making this clear to myself – a general principle ... One can only speak of a human action when a principle is involved.'
[20] Hille Haker, 'Synthetic Biology: An Emerging Debate in European Ethics', in *Ethics for Graduate Researchers*, 227.
[21] Ibid., 237–8.

and successful forms of learning how to live together in a pluralist world are heard first; they will be able to discuss their argumentations at a time when directions can still be changed. Instead of allowing terrains to be charted by an uncurbed new goldrush mentality, future-proofing would be put on the agenda by initiating public discourse at meetings and expert panels. By protecting spaces of deliberation in the informal public sphere, the early warning systems called for repeatedly in policy proposals would be enabled to avail of the knowledge generated at the level of everyday life. Questions of ownership or disappropriation, gain and loss of elementary skills can be accessed – informed, for example, by observations of educators from early childhood onwards: how does the advance of specific technologies change conditions for learning, not primarily at the level of didactics, but of anthropology, as a key characteristic of humans? And how can developments be steered towards goals agreed and promised, but not yet realized?

3. Integrating rationality operating in the disciplines with normative theories

Before considering the theoretical task of integrating the 'normatively human' with work in the disciplines, the embeddedness of policy formation in cultural and national parameters will be illustrated with a comparative analysis of three Western jurisdictions (a). This will highlight the practical relevance of determining more closely what is entailed in the task to integrate the two domains of reason – one, reflection on foundations as it appears in the schools of ethics; two, the diversification of rationality in the individual disciplines. Matters to be examined are how the encounter of issues in the disciplines with ethics takes place, which models exist and how convincing they are (b).

(a) Ethical deliberation as privatized or public in different national patterns of regulations

One decisive factor for the ways in which ethics is developed *within* the sciences and the humanities is what the technology analyst Sheila Jasanoff has treated under 'national strategies of normalization'. In her comparison of the United States, the United Kingdom and Germany as three different jurisdictions, she identifies factors that shape conditions for research: cultural memory, political institutions as based on a constitution or on other legal frameworks, the role of civic debate, and the degree of acceptance of leaving normative issues to market forces. She observes that '[p]ublic responses to biotechnology are embedded within robust and coherent political cultures and are not ad hoc expressions of concern that vary unpredictably from issue to issue'.[22] In the United States, she finds that regulation is by market; in the United Kingdom by expert committees and institutions regulating bioethical innovations, such as the Human Fertilisation and Embryology Authority; in Germany, the regulation is by law. It is significant for the role of public debate where the locus of accountability resides: it is 'judicial' in the United States, 'parliamentary and administrative' in the United Kingdom, and 'legislative' in Germany. Styles of deciding in cases of controversy differ accordingly, matching the allocation of accountability to different professional groups and levels of political governance or administration. Thus, settlements in Germany are 'reasoned (principled)',[23] they are 'consensual' in the United Kingdom, while both are based on centralized norms. In the United States, the 'decentralized norms' leave the decision to the courts where a 'Winner-take-all settlement of controversy' results.[24] She sums up the consequences of the differing weight of these factors for the role given to civic debate:

> Not surprisingly, opportunities for deliberating on the aims of innovation have been most conspicuously absent in the United States, the country most hospitable to the fact of innovation. Farmed out to public intellectuals and, lately, to presidential ethics commissions of uncertain legitimacy and purpose, the task of reflecting on the directions of biotechnological advancement has largely been excluded from the public sphere.[25]

The contrasting approaches to scientific innovation are given memorable tags: for the 'market-regulated' treatment of the United States, it is 'monsters encouraged', for the 'expert-regulated' innovation in the United Kingdom, it

---

[22] Sheila Jasanoff, 'In the Democracies of DNA: Ontological Uncertainty and Political Order in Three States', in *New Genetics and Society* 24 (2005): 139.141.

[23] This is to be expected, in keeping with the opening line of Article 1 of the Basic Law, 'Human dignity is inviolable' which 'to respect and protect … is the duty of all state authority.' It has been applied to the Embryo Protection Act of 1990 which Jasanoff mentions as relevant for one of her areas of comparison, human reproductive technologies.

[24] Jasanoff, 'In the Democracies of DNA', 151.

[25] Ibid., 153.

is 'monsters permitted', and in the 'law-regulated' scientific sphere in Germany, it is 'monsters forbidden', thus, limiting innovation: 'Only in Germany has the temptation to privatize ethical deliberation been successfully resisted and the normative and political questions surrounding biotechnology have been extensively debated in the public sphere. But the response has been to erect high, some would say unacceptably high, barriers against social and technological creativity.'[26]

Jasanoff's interest in the cultural factors behind the drive towards scientific innovation and risk-taking results in an insightful contextualization also of technological disasters like Fukushima.[27] Attitudes to scientific and technological research are shaped by national self-images and cultural memory, as of the criminal abuse committed by German doctors and scientists under National Socialism. The call for debate in the public sphere and in parliament is a result of this quest for transparent and principle-led procedures of decision-making.

(b) Dealing with plurality in two respects: regarding methods within the disciplines, and approaches to ethics

In his analysis of the academic and political framework conditions of applied ethics, the philosopher Marcus Düwell discusses the methodological requirements posed by interdisciplinary procedures (1), and identifies different models of understanding the contribution of 'ethics' as a scholarly discipline. These have a bearing on the actual task of giving normative assessments (2), and on the role left to the public sphere (3), especially in debates on new scientific and technological possibilities.

(1) Applied ethics provides 'mixed judgements',[28] relating research results sought for the issues under consideration from disciplines like biology, medicine, genetics, sociology, psychology and law to ethics in its different approaches. As in other cases of 'application', such as law, it is not simply a

---

[26] Ibid.

[27] S. M. Pfotenhauer, C. F. Jones, K. Saha and S. Jasanoff, 'Learning from Fukushima', in *Issues in Science & Technology* 28 (2012): 79–84.

[28] Marcus Düwell, 'Angewandte Ethik. Skizze eines wissenschaftlichen Profils', in *Interdisziplinäre Ethik. Grundlagen, Methoden, Bereiche. Festschrift Dietmar Mieth*, ed. Adrian Holderegger and Jean-Pierre Wils (Freiburg. i. Ue: Universitätsverlag/ Freiburg i. Br.: Herder, 2001), 175. In this case, I will include page numbers in the text.

matter of subsuming a particular case under a general rule, but of an interchange between foundational theories and cases. These show, for example, that key terms like 'personhood' or 'autonomy' need to be more precisely defined, thus challenging the underlying theory to engage in further development. The individual disciplines appear in two roles here: their findings are a necessary part of the moral judgement, and the aim is not to lose the 'level of differentiation' (173) achieved by them; yet they are also analysed by ethics for their premises and internally compared for their distinct standards of normativity (cf. 172). Düwell observes that there are 'descriptive' and 'prescriptive' senses of normativity, the first one analysing subject matters and disciplines for what is normative in them, the second one concluding with practical recommendations that are prescriptive (165, n. 2). Thus, several independent elements are constitutive of the process of evaluation: 'the factual information produced by the disciplines which in turn depends on their foundational assumptions'; and an assessment of the consequences of introducing a technology which comprises several factors: their 'relevance for social and cultural contexts', the 'realism of the goal envisaged, the goal-means relation, and the consideration of other alternatives for action' (173). All these argumentations from the individual disciplines have to be related to 'ethics', and if one point changes, or turns out to be unjustified, the whole assessment is affected and has to be revised (175).

Regarding the ethical part of the task, since ethicists differ in their views of the status and identity of their discipline, Düwell distinguishes different models. He questions them on their methodological standards and on the justification of their criteria of assessment that have consequences for the scope of application.

(2) Among the models of applied ethics, the first one discussed takes the task of ethics to be merely 'descriptive' by identifying 'options for action' and 'informing about presuppositions of moral judgements' (168). Düwell uses this understanding to show how the self-description of a model affects its scope. It does not reach into the practical sphere and cannot issue recommendations since this move to the prescriptive level would have to be justified by moral principles that are not just descriptive. All the other models seek to produce a practical outcome. Düwell identifies, second, a decisionist positing of normative premises that does without justification (177), and third, the attempt to reconstruct a network of coherent convictions; fourth, the use of international legal agreements (178); the fifth model is to account for a minimal or overlapping consensus (178); and the sixth, to argue out the different approaches to ethics: utilitarian, deontological, contract theory,

coherentism and an ethics of minimal consensus (178–9). Two points are decisive for declaring this model as the only way of being able to justify the normative foundations of one's assessment: the fact that there are existing convictions, as in the second and third, or a legal decision, as in the fourth, does not mean that they are morally justified. He points to the historical insight that values have turned out before to be in need of revision, and that this might also be true of our own era. The argument speaking against models two to five is that they cannot provide an integrative basis since each of them is itself a position, yet the theoretical justification is missing. This would require recognizing and engaging with the pluralism of theories so that a gain in knowledge, an exchange and a learning process become possible (177).

(3) As far as expectations from politics and the role of public debate are concerned, Düwell argues for a type of ethics advisory role that does not try to speak for civil society. Instead of summarizing the convictions of agents in the lifeworld from above, it should allow them to do so themselves. This avoids giving an 'aura of scholarly legitimacy' (181) to mere statements of minimal consensus. It also rejects 'internalizing political role expectations' (180) and a 'process of self-amalgamation in the understanding of ethics to a political assignment of functions' (179). The idea that ethicists will agree on one unitary answer, insinuating that just one solution is available, is dismissed. On the contrary, the need to legitimize its move to a prescriptive statement, such as that a technology should be pursued under specified conditions, means that the ethicist is no longer in a 'sovereign position of observing and reconstructing moral opinion formation' (182); she participates in the debate from the approach she argues for in the process of working out a solution that can be justified. Thus, after the individual sciences have contributed their information, the ethical adjudication does not happen at a general level. The conflict of interpretations cannot be avoided or replaced by retreating to an allegedly widely shared basis of convictions. This point is close to the warning expressed by Nagl-Docekal against socially existing values replacing argumentations on principles; since they merely express the conventions of a specific time and location, they can be exclusionary, biased and narrow. They are not to be accepted as a given but examined in shared discourse based on practical reason, taking citizens seriously as moral agents.[29]

---

[29] Nagl-Docekal, *Innere Freiheit*, 32. Cf. also 48, 53, 80.

Düwell admits that the integration becomes even more difficult if the whole range of moral theories has to be included into the process of searching for agreement. The expert cultures are needed to provide their insights but are equally learners from the other contexts involved. The role of philosophy is distinct from the individual sciences. It not only draws on the capacity for self-reflection, but also examines it with its dual standing as agent and as object of enquiry. Unlike the other disciplines which are marked by a specific formal perspective and a subject matter, the specialty of philosophy is general: it offers a critique of reason by reason, both as a faculty and in its differentiation into sciences, due to its capacity of pursuing overarching questions.

4. Integration as connecting to overarching questions of reason

Problems that may have been lost out of sight when following a discipline's internal debates can be retrieved by returning to an understanding of philosophy as a general enquiry into what it is to be human. This was one of the tasks proposed by Walter Schulz. In the specialization and fragmentation of knowledge, overarching questions including those of the limits of reason do not appear as part of research designs and need to be reintroduced also in their relevance for ethics. The fact that they fall outside the remit of the disciplines should not lead to them being marginalized. This would mean that the mode of generating knowledge that can be at one's disposition, such as data and conclusions from empirically researchable questions, would then become the only exercise of reason. It would not do justice either to the complex and more encompassing practical self-understandings of individuals in the lifeworld, nor to its own history of thinking. Cutting off the dimension of striving for the unconditioned, as *Vernunft* is defined in Kant, would interpret human conscious life in a reductive way (a). The failure to include a dimension which is closely linked with people's motivation, with aspects relevant in decision-making and with an overall understanding of the human person also affects the way of speaking about 'religion'. Used as the general category for the variety of historical faith traditions, it offers a specific way of dealing with questions of meaning. If these issues are no longer on the agenda of a philosophy which refuses to deal with problems for which it has no answers, religion could then only be approached as an empirical factor in past and contemporary cultures but without a link to reason (b).

(a) Reason in its quest for the unconditioned

Düwell's response to the question about criteria of evaluation which ethics needs to discuss if it wants to claim a scholarly status, was that the only way forward would be to engage in debate with the plurality of ethical schools which put forward different criteria. Instead of accepting a role of moderator in the political interest of consensus management, ethics has to engage with its own differences. Pluralism also in approaches to ethics requires an active effort of learning and mutual exchange, instead of merely stating differences descriptively. Some philosophical approaches to ethics keep the limit questions to philosophy of religion open, agreeing on that matter with Kant and with several existentialist, phenomenological and postmodern authors. In keeping with the emphasis on self-reflection, philosophy should continue to count as one of its strengths its ability to pursue questions which are so encompassing that they are not able to be definitely resolved. Leaving out this part of its previous agenda also in modernity, amounts to a prohibition to ask. Nagl-Docekal quotes a conclusion from Axel Honneth which does in fact cut off unresolved questions of human life and of philosophy. His view is that 'we all have become pure naturalists'.[30] If this is taken as the final word on the matter, the level of ongoing questions of meaning that a 'postmetaphysical reason' cannot answer is simply removed. Habermas, however, admits that these issues continue to stir humans and are relevant for exchanges between citizens on resources of meaning.

It should be acceptable also for philosophers who abstain from including existential questions of meaning to take on board Walter Schulz's diagnosis. The need to reconnect the isolated, specialized questions investigated successfully after abstracting them from everyday practices should be part of its brief.[31] With its ability to identify the concepts of self and world that are used, but not examined, in the various disciplines, and to relate them to a 'practical-ethical' orientation, philosophy should bring questions that the

---

[30] Ibid., 10, 66, with reference to Honneth, *Das Ich im Wir. Studien zur Anerkennungstheorie* (Frankfurt: Suhrkamp, 2010), 298.
[31] Schulz, *Grundprobleme der Ethik* (Pfullingen: Neske, 1989), 14, 17.

individual sciences do not pose back into circulation. These include the 'mutual conditioning of self-relation and world relation' which exposes the problem of the world's and of one's own facticity.[32] Realizing the groundlessness and sheer hazard of one's existence poses a foundational question that is silenced in an objectifying framework, but that remains a problem for agency.

(b) The theological integration of the four sources

Before portraying each approach to theological ethics with their treatments of the four sources in Part 2, one conclusion on the relationship to the sources from human reason can already be drawn. It is decisive for the external communicability of the Christian faith how it positions itself with regard to reason and to its diversified employment in the individual sciences. Will religions just be inhabited as an unquestionable empirical and historical fact, or is an internal link to reason recognized by theologians committed to different schools and confessions? What is at stake is the connection to the 'inner human being' that Kobusch elaborated as the key contribution of Christianity to Western thinking. Philosophers also have to be questioned on whether they expect anything from the historical religions, or whether universal human reason can do without all input from particular traditions. Questions that encompass the possibility of religious hope will persist and should not be wiped off the list of what can be discussed. Yet also the theological positions are called to decide whether it is correct to present religions as parallel worlds that do not communicate outside their own circles. Nagl-Docekal makes the case to thinkers like Rawls that the philosophical assumption of self-contained 'comprehensive doctrines' is inadequate. The histories of encounters between religions contain the evidence of exchange and transformation as well as polemics on key themes, such as attributes of God and human freedom. But Rawls's view also undersells the possibility of members of different faiths to communicate on the basis of the self-reflection that each one has access to as a human being. Instead of focusing on the potential for conflict between diverse traditions and 'representing them as systems of thought that are separated from each

---

[32] Schulz makes this connection between ethics and the awareness of one's facticity in *Grundprobleme*, 299.

other by unsurmountable differences', their ability to meet at the level of reason is to be taken into account.[33] They could, for example, relate to the concept of human dignity as the principle of ethics in modernity. For this process of reflective engagement, it is decisive in what capacity the members of religious traditions meet: not as 'citizens' who relate to each other on the legal basis of reciprocity guaranteed by constitutional principles, but as human beings in their morality. From a Christian faith perspective, an invitation to dialogue with each religion on their internal understanding of dignity should clearly be acceptable.

The four sources have shown themselves to be compatible in principle. The first source lays the foundation with the ethical monotheism developed through different periods in the Bible. Its view of the human creature as *imago Dei* can be translated into the modern intrinsic concept of human dignity. The second source, tradition, achieved the earliest task of translation by elaborating the 'inner person' discovered as a presupposition of hearing and responding to God's call. The perceptive insights into human interiority of the first two sources gave new prominence to concepts such as the will, remorse and forgiveness. Familiar both with the Bible and with philosophical sources, the patristic thinkers in their defence of freedom against Gnosticism changed the thought forms of their eras. Thus, the two sources from revelation and the two sources from reason are distinct, but not completely alien to each other.

Theological ethicists can contribute to connecting the two sets of sources more successfully by critiquing inadequate presuppositions and questionable alternatives which reduce both sides. Reserving 'public reason' for democratic officeholders is such a restriction which empties the public sphere of exchanges between traditions. While the plurality of religions and philosophical schools recognized by Rawls has to be welcomed, the terms in which this plurality is cast tie the diagnosis and the solution to a corporate level. Faith traditions, while coherent, are internally more diverse than this allows for, and they are able to communicate with other such life-shaping communities. Their long-debated, thought-through and renewed visions of the individual subject and the world, of history and the universe in relation to God, should be appreciated in their history of questioning and their engagement with the general consciousness of truth. Habermas's categorization of religions as 'opaque'[34] in distinction from other traditions

---

[33] Nagl-Docekal, *Innere Freiheit*, 13.
[34] Habermas, *Between Naturalism and Religion*, e.g., 142.

of reflection has been questioned by theologians. Instead of being cast as a counterpart to reason, they can be a partner in the ongoing struggle for inclusive living conditions and thoughtful self-conceptions. But they have to decide themselves in which language they want to offer their contributions to the public realm. This will be one of the differences between them which will be examined in the following two parts and in the Conclusion.

Part 2

Traditions of theological ethics

Part 2 will examine five distinct approaches to ethics as a theological discipline. It will analyse them in Chapters 5 to 9 on the backdrop of schools of ethics in the history of Western thinking. Each approach is presented in its theoretical framework and analysed according to criteria such as its use of the four sources, its internal debates, its theological consistency and its ability to contribute to the interdisciplinary task of theological ethics. Virtue ethics (Chapter 5) and its further specification as being founded on communal worship (Chapter 6) are two approaches that highlight the particularity of Christian living. Natural law (Chapter 7) and the autonomy school (Chapter 8) mark universalistic understandings of Christian ethics which relate it to a general consciousness of truth. However, there are different models within each of the two alternative directions that cross this division and develop their categories in such a way that combinations with the opposite type are possible; for example, an understanding of 'virtue' that is compatible with an autonomy approach (5.3), and a universalistic natural law framework which adds in virtue components (7.2). The feminist approaches treated in Chapter 9 work from the background theories they have chosen: revisionist natural law; care ethics which arose as a critique of the implications of a stage theory culminating in a 'postconventional' concept of justice; and an analysis of two understandings of 'autonomy'; they are illustrated within the field of new reproductive technologies where current cultural perspectives on women's bodies and self-understandings are put under review.

Varieties of virtue ethics

The rediscovery of virtue in philosophical ethics already in the 1950s, but with an even stronger impetus in reaction to contractual liberalism from the 1980s also took place in Christian ethics. This chapter will begin with virtue ethical reconstructions of biblical and Early Christian understandings of the lifestyle expected from followers of Jesus Christ (1). It will then examine ecclesial communitarianism, developed as an alternative to the liberal individualism it sees as the dominant contemporary political and intellectual framework (2). A proposal of virtues as 'images of attitude' (*Haltungsbilder*)[1] that have been wrongly neglected and complement, though not replace, principled ethics will complete the range of contemporary renewals of this tradition in Christian ethics (3).

---

[1] With this concept, Dietmar Mieth draws on Ernst Bloch, *The Principle of Hope*, trans. Neville Plaice, Stephen Plaice and Paul Knight (Oxford: Blackwell, 1986), vol. 3, 932.

1. Reading early Christian ethics as virtue ethics

The view that an ethics inspired by the New Testament can most adequately be grasped in terms of virtue ethics is shared by several exegetes and Christian ethicists. Arguments are the priority of judging goodness in a person rather than in actions; the emphasis on steady attitudes, not one-off acts; the setting of individual agents within a community; the model ethics put forward by St Paul, as well as the exhortations and lists of virtues and vices in New Testament Letters; an inclusive outreach of biblical and patristic authors in general in which the wisdom of other traditions is recognized and not dismissed. The claim that Christian ethics can most fruitfully be explained in a virtue ethical format will be examined in relation to three such reconstructions: the biblical scholar Wayne Meeks's portrayal of Early Christian ethics (a), the historical overview of its development in the first centuries by Jef van Gerwen (b), and the collaborative treatment of key themes from the Bible and moral theology by Daniel Harrington and Jim Keenan (c).

(a) Interpreting the ethical thinking of Pauline communities in virtue terms (Wayne Meeks)

Wayne Meeks concludes his discussion of the hermeneutical challenge of identifying what is specific to Christian ethics across the various ecclesial locations of the first and second centuries with three findings: 'Christian Ethics is an ethics of response', illustrated by the foundation of Christian practice on God's prior salvific action, as expressed in Eph. 4.32: 'Be kind to one another, tender-hearted, forgiving one another, as God in Christ forgave you.' Secondly, 'Christian Ethics is an interpretive enterprise', which can be understood as casting it primarily as a hermeneutics of the life of the Christian community. Thirdly, 'formation has priority over decision.'[2] As the language of the second and third conclusions suggests, the conceptual framework is Aristotelian. We can, as he explains at the start of his

---

[2] Wayne A. Meeks, 'The Christian Beginnings and Christian Ethics: The Hermeneutical Challenge', 181.

'ethnographic'[3] exploration of early Christian ethics in its different settings, learn from Aristotle

> one central insight into the genealogy of morals, which we moderns too often have forgotten: individuals do not become moral agents except in the relationships, the transactions, the habits and reinforcements, the special uses of language and gesture that together constitute life in community.[4]

While these terms and others, including 'character', 'dispositions' and 'attitudes' (rather than, for example, 'principles', 'decisions' and their 'justification') seem to indicate a specific perspective, the historical search itself is conducted also with the comparative methods of cultural studies and sociology. The focus is on exploring where the emerging Christian groups were similar to or distinct from Jewish Diaspora communities and the values of Graeco-Roman schools of ethics. The interest in historical accuracy, not in results that will dovetail with specific ecclesial self-understandings, is evident when he asks about pagan and Christian attitudes to the 'polis' as a place of belonging:

> But what did the polis mean for the Christians, those 'converts' who would come to accept their stigmatization as a 'third race', neither Greek nor Jew, who could sometimes say that their politeuma (a revealing term, often used of an organized body of immigrants, resident aliens, for example the Jews in a Greek city) was in heaven, not on earth (Phil. 3:20)? . . . Was the classical polis still their chief model for the language of morality? If not, what took its place?[5]

Meeks's answer to this question is the surprising finding that the framework chosen very often is '"the world," ho kosmos'.[6] He first notes a 'paradox' that is typical of small religious groupings and has been 'repeated in the history of religions: a cult that is, in the world's eyes, infinitesimal believes that the actions of its members take their meaning from a cosmic process. The One who called them into existence . . . is none other than the creator of the universe'.[7]

What is also remarkable, however, is that they had different understandings of 'world': 'The formative centuries of Christian morality are thus marked by

---

[3] Cf. Meeks, *The Origins of Christian Morality. The First Two Centuries* (New Haven and London: Yale University Press, 1993), ix, 8–11.
[4] Ibid., 8.
[5] Ibid., 13.
[6] Ibid.
[7] Ibid., 14.

oscillation between extreme visions: is it the Christian's moral task to do battle against the world, to flee from it, or to participate in its transformation?'[8]

A second enquiry into a key theme that can be seen as running counter to the typical virtue ethical emphasis on continuity and steady growth is about the role of 'conversion', which stands at the start of these communities. Meeks compares Thessaloniki and Corinth as they appear in St Paul's Letters; he highlights the questions arising in each location at their different stages of relating to the surrounding culture, and the psychological demands of reshaping their previous and existing relationships. The difference to other groups is not in the content of the virtues. It consists in the underlying consciousness that they belong to the Christian grouping held together by their faith in being saved by a founder who died the most shameful death the Roman Empire had for its enemies. With such a new and distinct motivation, it could be asked if the concept of 'virtue' used here is at all comparable to the Greek sense of organic development. A question to Meeks's insightful portrayal of Pauline communities is whether the virtue mode in which he states the ethical self-understanding of early Christians offers the most adequate framework. Or would it be more accurate not to select one school as the overarching allocation, but identify which of the traditions of antique moral philosophy appear in St Paul's categories, including, for example, Stoicism? Then questions about teleological frameworks, nature and freedom, continuity and conversion, polis-centredness and universalism could be examined across these schools.

(b) Identifying virtue ethics as the most adequate framework in the first centuries (Jef van Gerwen)

In the following overview of the origins of Christian ethics, the late Belgian moral theologian Jef Van Gerwen anchors the understanding of morality following from the person and practice of Jesus firmly in the tradition of virtue ethics. The contrasting terms give an important indication of what is seen as the alternative, showing the traces of the debate since the 1980s between liberalism and communitarianism: rules or principles, a universal scope, thus, a deontological instead of a teleological format.

---

[8] Ibid.

Early Christians all agreed that morality was a matter of training in the basic virtues, rather than just the application of a universal set of rules or rational principles. These approaches stress the particular features of moral education in a concrete sociohistorical community. Morality depends on the training of character, and seeing and imitating concrete examples, such as Jesus Christ, the saints, or the ordinary faithful.[9]

Key features are the 'training' effort, the contextual setting, and the role of models. The beginning of the article makes it clear that there is more continuity with antique understandings of ethics than with modern ones:

> (E)thics for early Christians was a matter of attitudes or habits, rather than just rules and commandments. Although the Jewish Law (especially the Ten Commandments) played a central role in it, Christian morality was primarily based on the practice of a number of virtues, such as love, hope, justice, forgiveness, and patience ... Consequently, it was committed to fight vices such as hate, envy, lust, sloth, and anger. Early Christian Ethics resembles more closely other antique schools of ethics, such as Aristotelianism or Stoicism, than our modern Kantian and utilitarian paradigms.[10]

Here, responses like 'hope' or 'forgiveness' that are equally significant in other systems of ethics as part of a person's moral self-understanding are subsumed under virtuous 'attitudes or habits'. Jesus' practice and proclamation are also seen as continuing the 'virtues' chosen by the prophets:

> The ethical teaching of Jesus of Nazareth fits perfectly into the tradition of prophetic and early rabbinical representatives of Jewish ethics. In the line of the prophets, Jesus stresses the importance of the virtues of justice and mercy over the ritualistic ethics of purity and cult offerings that had been developed in the Jewish Law (the books of Leviticus and Deuteronomy). In his interpretation of the Mosaic Law (Mt 5-7) he focuses on the purity of intention of the agent, rather than on the mere act of trespassing a rule of law.[11]

While it is helpful to see the lines of continuity drawn out, the question is whether the prophets fit into a framework of continuous growth in virtues, or whether their calls to self-critique and conversion are better captured in deontological terms. One of the moral concepts identified in the example

---

[9] Jef Van Gerwen, 'Origins of Christian Ethics', in *The Blackwell Companion to Religious Ethics*, ed. William Schweiker (Oxford: Blackwell, 2005), 213.
[10] Ibid., 204.
[11] Ibid., 205.

taken from the Sermon on the Mount also goes beyond the virtue tradition: 'the purity of intention of the agent.' It will be a matter of subsequent examination how this concern may link virtue and autonomous ethics against other, external approaches: judging goodness through outcomes, as in utilitarianism, and a citizens' ethics whose chief concern is to safeguard reciprocity in the external observance of the rights of the legal person, as in liberalism.

(c) Virtue ethics as a 'bridge' between biblical and moral theological perspectives on Jesus (Daniel Harrington and James Keenan)

After a historical overview of both their disciplines in the first chapter and an explanation regarding methodology, of how virtue ethics can serve as a 'bridge' between scripture and moral theology in the second, three questions are chosen for the following three chapters that deal with New Testament texts: 'Who ought we to become?' 'Who are we?' 'How are we to get there?'[12] Under the first question, the 'Kingdom of God' is treated as 'horizon and goal', under the second 'discipleship', and under the third the Sermon on the Mount. This first long speech of Jesus in Matthew's gospel serves as the path for present agents who define themselves as disciples towards the *telos* of God's coming reign. In keeping with a key Christological theme in Matthew, Jesus as wisdom, the New Testament scholar Daniel Harrington interprets the Sermon on the Mount in sapiential terms, as Jewish wisdom instruction. Using different genres, it elucidates elements of a way towards wisdom as a virtue in the Greek sense, as 'the personal characteristics' that are to be fostered. The discourse treats 'true happiness, the proper interpretation of the Law and the Prophets, genuine piety, wise attitudes and behaviour in everyday life, and the need to translate wisdom into action. As a Jewish wisdom instruction, it expresses the wisdom of Jesus.' However, Harrington points out that the virtues advocated are not conventional, recognized modes of behaviour: 'Jesus' list of values, character traits, and attitudes calls

---

[12] Daniel Harrington and James Keenan, *Jesus and Virtue Ethics* (Lanham, MD/Chicago: Sheed & Ward, 2002), 35, 49, 61. The same questions in the singular and beginning with 'Who am I?', taken from A. MacIntyre's *After Virtue*, are already used by James Keenan to structure his article, 'Virtue Ethics', in *Christian Ethics*, ed. Hoose, 84.

into question much conventional human wisdom about happiness and how to achieve it.'[13] Both Harrington and Keenan emphasize that these are achievable attitudes, not 'elitist or perfectionist', even if Keenan refers to 'grace' as a condition for living them.[14] In the face of conflicts between virtues, he also highlights Ricoeur's view that there can be a 'tension between two distinct and sometimes opposed claims'.[15] This does not put the model into question but calls for further elaboration. The role for directing the interaction between the revised four cardinal virtues, he proposes, falls to 'prudence' which 'determines what constitutes the just, faithful and self-caring way of life for an individual'.[16]

For each text and theme, the book draws on literature which it summarizes in its key points, providing a helpful overview of key participants in debates on the Bible and ethics. In his own detailed discussion of biblical scholars on ethics in the New Testament, Lucas Chan characterizes their purpose and their achievement:

> Harrington and Keenan set out a common framework built on certain ethical themes, and employ virtue ethics as their methodological approach. They acknowledge that their work is a heuristic effort 'at stimulating discovery and dialogue'... Despite the absence of an ideal, seamless integration ('interaction between the authors') ..., many praised them for modelling and inviting further collaborative and interdisciplinary work.[17]

The two authors put forward a programmatic claim, namely that virtue ethics is the most adequate framework, and elaborate it in their named contributions. The joint publication thus allows for distinct comments. One question to be put to Harrington as the biblical scholar is: does he regard the historical work on the Bible as having been completed and the truth on contested factual and textual points established? Does it now have to be taken to a different level? In his comparison of authors, Harrington contrasts, among other elements, a 'descriptive' treatment in biblical theology from a 'normative' one that 'yields standards or rules for Christian conduct'. Is an approach that expressly 'seeks to go beyond description', for example, by

---

[13] Harrington, ibid., 61–7, 61, 62.
[14] Ibid., 65, 71.
[15] Keenan, 'Virtue Ethics', in *Christian Ethics*, ed. Hoose, 92, with reference to Paul Ricoeur, 'Love and Justice', in *Radical Pluralism and Truth. David Tracy and the Hermeneutics of Religion*, ed. Werner G. Jeanrond and Jennifer L. Rike (New York: Crossroad, 1991), 196.
[16] Keenan, 'Virtue Ethics', in *Christian Ethics*, ed. Hoose, 94.
[17] Lucas Yiu Sing Chan, 'Biblical Ethics: 3D', 23.

proposing 'three focal images for synthesizing the moral vision of the New Testament: community, cross, and new creation,'[18] still subject to a scholarly evaluation of whether these organizing themes are accurate regarding its historical material? Can appropriations for personal and communal purposes in Christian contexts still be distinguished from research, and do biblical scholars continue to have an irreplaceable contribution to make that is separate from theological interpretation? Questions like these which already arose in Chapter 1, when analysing the Bible as the first source, return not only here but also in some subsequent approaches.

Ethics-related questions are: Among the objections to virtue ethics which James Keenan responds to is its 'introspective' appearance: 'While virtue ethics is at times introspective, the complaint that it needs to be more extroverted and practical has prompted a variety of writers to demonstrate that it can give specific advice.' Especially with regard to nursing ethics he points out that 'relationally-based concern for agents as persons is a more constructive ethics than any present rule- or code-based ethics.'[19] This comparison is useful, especially in the context of healthcare systems in which direct links between law and medicine risk leaving out the practitioner and the patient. But the question remains whether the role of prudence relates to any objective matter that requires analysis at different levels and by a variety of disciplines. How are natural and social 'reality' captured? How are institutions that include anonymous others brought into the horizon of ethical evaluation as factors that shape individual and communal life? And how does this assessment relate not only to the lifeworld, but to the systems that steer a society? The undoubted role that virtue ethics can have in the formation of professional identities has to take into account the structures in which they work: for example, selective school systems, health institutions serving different agendas, research and development departments that ask for individual 'integrity' but undermine it by conditions of competition, fragmentation and lack of transparency. So if one of the advantages of virtue ethics is its closeness to the 'terrain of the ordinary', instead of 'emergency rooms',[20] those conditions and their distorting effects for a virtuous or moral working life need categories of analysis that also include structures, not only 'character'.

---

[18] Harrington, in Harrington and Keenan, *Jesus and Virtue Ethics*, 21, with reference to Richard B. Hays.
[19] Keenan, 'Virtue Ethics' in *Christian Ethics*, ed. Hoose, 90.
[20] Keenan commends virtue ethics for 'moving ahead with less glamour and drama, but always seeing the agent, not as reactor, but as actor: knowing oneself, setting the agenda of personal ends and means in both the ordinary and the professional life'. Ibid., 90.

2. Ecclesial communitarianism as an alternative to Enlightenment individualism (Stanley Hauerwas)

The American Methodist Stanley Hauerwas builds his proposal of Christian ethics on the significance of a given ethos for shaping character and virtue through its rootedness in tradition and narration. It stands in contrast to the uncontextualized self-determination of an isolated individual which he identifies as typical for Enlightenment ethics. The starting point is the mutual endorsement of members of a community in particular traditions which are handed on through shared forms of life and storytelling. Prior to moral agency and decision-making is the socialization in a living ethos. Virtues as capacities for action are revitalized within the community. These points are shared with Meeks, van Gerwen and the joint approach of Harrington and Keenan. Yet while they accept virtues without hesitation as natural human expressions of an inherent capability for ethically reflected conduct as the basis also for Christian virtues, this connection is not valid for Hauerwas. The starting point for him is a concept of church that is defined by its distinction from the 'world'. To reconstruct his approach, it is necessary to begin by analysing this foundation (a). The roles of the Bible as narrative (b), and of the person and work of Jesus Christ (c), and a specific hermeneutics of tradition (d) will follow from this.

(a) The church as foundation

Decisive for Hauerwas's concept of church is that it constitutes a form of life which has been made possible by Jesus Christ and can only be learnt by participation. For the members, the emphasis is on evidence in action. Orthopraxis has priority as a criterium of truth. The 'fruits' by which Christians can be recognized are the virtues they develop. Regarding the method of ethics, however, it is descriptive and not prescriptive. The lived ethos is a matter for internal interpretation, it does not have to be justified. This approach can be seen as a social ethical parallel to the 'postliberal' concept of theology put forward by the 'Yale School'. Following George Lindbeck and Hans Frei, theology is about the internal grammar of the Christian faith which is to be explained primarily for its followers, and not in relation to other traditions or to the light of reason. For Hauerwas, only the Christian church fulfils the concept of a community united by shared convictions. Late liberal society is marked by isolation, diffusion and confusion of values. The lack of foundations to which the subjectivizing of epistemology and ethics in modernity has led can only be counteracted by turning to a basis safeguarded by God: 'The Church's One Foundation is Jesus Christ Her Lord; Or, In a World Without Foundations: All We Have is the Church.'[21] Correspondingly, the conception of church is dominated by biblical images which highlight its difference from the earthly polity, such as 'city on the mountain' and 'salt of the earth'. New Testament parables of the fishing net or of the chaff growing with the wheat are not given the same attention. A programmatic statement of the 'social', not the religious, task in *A Community of Character* makes it clear that the primary function of the Christian church does not consist in engaging in outside activity that could improve conditions in the world: 'My wish is that this book might help Christians rediscover that their most important social task is nothing less than being a community capable of hearing the story of God we find in the scripture and living in a manner that is faithful to that story.'[22] Therefore, its social function is to work out its internal understanding for the world to see and possibly imitate.

(b) The Bible as narrative

Based on the argument that the Canon is a creation of the church in the first centuries, the distinction discussed in Part 1 between the Bible as *norma normans non normata* and tradition as *norma normans normata* is not relevant for Hauerwas. Regarding the authority of Scripture, he makes it clear that it derives from the contemporary consensus of the church, and is not owed to a status of its own, such as being the 'Word of God'. In terms of genre, he stresses its nature as 'story' which gives it its identity-shaping power. Israel and the Christian church are both portrayed as examples of God creating a 'people'. In this respect, their stories are seen as belonging together. While this may be true for Christians, and while the necessary insistence on the ongoing covenant of Israel is to be appreciated,[23] the question is only treated from a Christian perspective. The narrative character is defended

---

[21] This is the title which Hauerwas has given to his contribution in a book he co-edited: Stanley Hauerwas, Nancey Murphy and Mark Nation (eds), *Theology Without Foundations: Religious Practice and the Future of Theological Truth* (Nashville, TN: Abingdon Press, 1994), 143–62.

[22] Hauerwas, *A Community of Character: Toward a Constructive Christian Social Ethic* (Notre Dame and London: University of Notre Dame Press, 1981), 1.

[23] For example, ibid., 244–5, n. 52.

especially against the concern that the literary genre could be left behind when moral principles are abstracted from the various modes of its original biblical expression. Hauerwas's linking of virtue and narrative is a countermeasure to such a replacement strategy that could only yield principles he would consider as rootless. It would make the stories lose their imaginative power which can evoke freely given responses. For him, the foundational role belongs to the narrative: 'Universal ethical principles become ethically significant only as we learn their meaning in stories.'[24] The danger of abstracting concepts from narratives is not only present with ethical principles, when, for example, the story of the Good Samaritan is reduced to an illumination of the demand to love one's neighbour.[25] Hauerwas is also wary of summative concepts like 'love' or 'covenant' in relation to God.[26] However, this reticence in relation to key biblical terms provokes a question regarding the use of the Bible: is there any legitimate way of specifying the 'character' of God? Are there criteria to decide which biblical narratives to prioritize? This is a problem that cannot be dismissed, in view of the controversies across eras between seminal authors and whole theological oeuvres about biblical narratives and their histories of reception.

One approach taken to the Bible is not only seen to represent one of the fruitless modern transformations within the Christian history of thinking, but even a transgression: historical-critical enquiries into the Bible, in his view, strip it of its standing as 'Scripture' and treat it just as 'text', comparable to other literature.[27]

Two questions can be signalled here that will need to be taken up in the following subsections. One, if the Bible is completely a function of the church, how can it fulfil the role of also being a counterpart to current Christian understandings? This is a function which Hauerwas clearly calls it to perform when he argues with biblical stories that upset mistaken and harmful values and theologies. And secondly, it may look ordinary and innocent to define the Bible as God's story with God's people. But does it risk narrowing the scope of God's salvific will to Israel and the church, instead of understanding the Bible as a reflection on God's action in history, recounted

---

[24] Hauerwas, *Vision and Virtue. Essays in Christian Ethical Reflection* (South Bend, IN: University of Notre Dame Press, 1981), 115–16.
[25] Ibid., 117–18.
[26] Hauerwas, *A Community of Character*, 56–9.
[27] Cf. Jeffrey S. Siker, 'Stanley Hauerwas: The Community Story of Israel and Jesus', in *Scripture and Ethics. Twentieth Century Portraits*, ed. Jeffrey S. Siker (New York and Oxford: OUP, 1997), 111, in his section on 'Hauerwas's view of the authority of Scripture'.

in a literary document in which God reveals God's love and care for all humanity and the planet entrusted to it?

(c) Truth claims on the work of Jesus Christ

From the long-standing debates on his approach, three issues shall be pursued: the nature of the truth claim proposed (1), the relationship between Christology and ecclesiology (2), and the standing of Christ resulting from a selective reading of the New Testament (3).

(1) On the one hand, as the Scottish theologian David Fergusson summarizes, the programmatic starting point is the particularity of God's action in history:

> The story of Jesus is not to be read as a particular instance of some universal truth . . . Jesus is of universal significance because of the constitutive power of his particular story . . . The narrative of Scripture is not simply a configuration of human stories constituting a social ethic. The narrative of Israel and Jesus is the story of God's self-revelation in history. It is, in a crucial sense, God's story before it is ours.[28]

Fergusson defends Hauerwas against the charge that truth is made dependent on the 'performance' or the actual delivery by contemporary Christians of virtuous action enabled by Jesus Christ. There is an 'ontological' basis of the Christian truth claim independent of its proclamation by the church. He reads it as a 'realist' conception of truth, as distinct from a 'regulative' one which stands or falls with the witness given by the currently existing disciples.[29] On the other hand, however, other propositions of Hauerwas's seem to put this into question by collapsing the very distinction between the biblical narrative (owned by the church), and the prior event to which it witnesses, 'God's self-revelation'. When Hauerwas refers to the 'essential nature of *narrative as the form of God's salvation*',[30] this difference is denied: there is no prior action in history, and the church which transports this narrative becomes self-referential. It is no longer about God's action but 'God's people' whose retelling of its own narrative engenders the ongoing

---

[28] David Fergusson, *Community, Liberalism and Christian Ethics* (Cambridge: CUP, 1998), 56.

[29] Fergusson is contrasting this statement which he interprets as 'realism' regarding the theory of truth, with the identification of truth with performance, that is, the orthopraxis of the believers, towards which followers of Lindbeck tend. In view of the close connection between the ethos and the virtue produced by it, as well as the following assertion by Hauerwas, the danger of the latter position is real.

[30] Hauerwas, *The Peaceable Kingdom* (South Bend, IN: University of Notre Dame Press, 1983), 23–4.

community of the faithful.[31] In philosophical terms, this is similar to a structuralist approach for which reference to a world and history outside the text is not deemed necessary.

(2) However this epistemological discrepancy is solved, a related theological concern of Fergusson's refers to the 'linear' relation between Christology and ecclesiology.[32] In Hauerwas's revelation-centred reconstruction, Jesus Christ's role is seamlessly passed on to the church, which is elevated to the position of being a 'linear continuation' of God's self-revelation. It is then no longer just made up of human recipients who remain a (more or less faithful) counterpart. For Fergusson, this sacrifices the 'once-and-for-all' character of salvation by Jesus Christ, and devolves it to the members of the Christian community as a task still to be accomplished:

> The church is not the extension of the incarnation, but exists to bear witness and to live faithfully in light of this unrepeatable and unsubstitutable event. Symptomatic for a failure to distinguish adequately the life of the church under the third article from the work of Christ in the second, is a somewhat reductionist treatment of doctrine of justification in Hauerwas.[33]

(3) This result is achieved through a selective reading of the New Testament which privileges the Synoptics, portrays Jesus as founder and as a model of ethical virtues, yet neglects decisive biblical statements relating to his person and work. As Fergusson notes, what is missing in this reduction of Jesus' significance to his ethical and institutional role are 'sufficient mention of Christ's overcoming of sin, evil and death; of our union with him by the bond of the Spirit; of the character of the community as the body of Christ; of the eschatological expectation that his Lordship will finally be exercised over all creation.'[34] One can conclude that it is a doctrinally weak Christology

---

[31] Siker, 'Hauerwas', 117, also refers to the quote of 'narrative' being the 'form of God's salvation' and interprets it under the title, 'A Communal Narrative Hermeneutic', summing up what is in effect a circular justification: 'The story of Israel and Jesus in Scripture reflects the life of God's people and in turn creates and sustains the community of believers.'

[32] Fergusson, *Community, Liberalism and Christian Ethics*, 70.

[33] Fergusson, 69. It is a 'domestication' of the Bible in the institutional church (71). Siker, 'Hauerwas', 123–5, equally directs his strongest criticism at Hauerwas's turn to a '*sola ecclesia*' foundation, having dismissed the Reformation principle of *Sola Scriptura* as a 'heresy because it displaces the community . . . there is the danger of Scripture's voice being muffled by the *sola ecclesia* position towards which Hauerwas leans' (123). Hauerwas's justification of the Canon on the basis of the need of the contemporary church is also seen as seriously deficient: His explanation in *A Community of Character*, 66, is that 'these texts have been accepted as scripture because they and they alone satisfy what Reynold Price has called our craving for a perfect story which we feel to be true'.

[34] Fergusson, *Community, Liberalism and Christian Ethics*, 70.

on which the massive edifice of his ecclesial ethic is built. Despite Hauerwas's justified concern about narratives being reduced to arid principles, his Christology can be seen as an instantiation of a diminished understanding of Jesus Christ: while the New Testament narratives include his status as Messiah, Son of God, Wisdom and Logos, what Jesus embodies for Hauerwas is the virtue of 'peacefulness'. The only difference from an Enlightenment view of him as moral exemplar is that this virtue is not natural, or not deemed possible for humans on their own. But this does not change the fact that the historical life of Jesus only illustrates a virtue humans could have known before his appearance, even if mainly through its absence; the self-revelation of God as love in Jesus' proclamation and practice recedes behind the feature of the peace-bringer.

(d) Which hermeneutics of tradition?

An analysis of the hermeneutical approach operative in this position has to include its understanding of narrative (1), of the methods of biblical studies (2), and of 'practice' (3).

(1) Hauerwas values the power of stories to create distance and insight, to suspend the impulse towards violence and to remind listeners of the aporetic constitution of human agency. Stories open up scope in four respects:

> power to release us from destructive alternatives; ways of seeing through current distortions; room to keep us from having to resort to violence; a sense of the tragic, i.e. an awareness of the moral conflict that besets even our best endeavours in a finite and imperfect world.[35]

How does Hauerwas link this general appraisal of narrative to its function within a specific ethos? What bridges are there between the basic openness, inherent pluralism and relativism of the narrative approach, and a Christian form of life?

In keeping with a story- and model-oriented type of ethics, the chance of revealing different aspects in the face of new opportunities and challenges is emphasized: 'We test our memory through Scripture as we are rightly forced time after time to seek out new implications of that memory by the very process of passing it on.'[36] Thus, it is not a static, repetitive

---

[35] Cf. Fergusson's summary, ibid., 55, with reference to Hauerwas and David Burrell, 'From System to Story: An Alternative Pattern for Rationality in Ethics', in *Why Narrative?*, ed. Hauerwas and Gregory Jones (Grand Rapids: Eerdmans, 1989), 185.

[36] Hauerwas, *The Peaceable Kingdom*, 69.

reading. But the statement also implies that no encounters with contemporary culture are envisaged. They could result in different understandings of the same stories and models in relation to new horizons. The 'new implications of that memory' are all produced by the internal life of the polity. Jürgen Werbick's comment on the effort to avoid transformation by engaging with current intellectual streams is that it renounces to the understanding shared both by the previous eras of Christian traditioning, and the Bible itself: if the process of tradition is only marked by 'self-stabilization', and not by an 'offer of conversation to the "others"', then it 'remains below the communicative level set by the biblical testimonies of revelation'.[37]

It is also not clarified which internal criteria are chosen for this continuous process of spinning forth the original message without dialogue with others outside the tradition; as a self-contained and circular development, it could appear as being closer to Spinozism than to an account of the historical self-communication of a creator God who is distinct from the world but engages with it.

(2) The impression that changing conceptions of world are not part of the hermeneutical task is confirmed when one looks at the evaluation of the historical-critical method as hostile and alien to the content of scripture. Hermeneutics, the discipline of understanding, is cast as being in competition with the church: 'Indeed, I suspect the project to develop general hermeneutical theories by some theologians is an attempt to substitute a theory of interpretation for the church.'[38] The 'living hermeneutic' of the church is deemed sufficient. The historical-critical method is viewed negatively as an 'adaptation of Enlightenment philosophy to interpret the Bible . . . as text, not Scripture, torn apart from the community of believers . . . that authorizes the Bible as Scripture.'[39]

So far, the church has assumed a heavy justificatory burden in two respects: for the Bible as its property, 'authorizing it as Scripture', and in effect

---

[37] Werbick, *Den Glauben verantworten*, 830. In that model, instead of appreciating 'revelation and tradition as a communicative nexus and not as one-way communication' (826), the 'new accentuations and new forms of faith (that) had to be formulated can only be accounted for as peripheral adaptations to a new era of a given that was in itself complete; they had to be marginalised' (822).
[38] Hauerwas, 'The Church as God's New Language', in *Christian Existence Today* (Durham: Labyrinth Press, 1988), 55, quoted in Siker, 'Hauerwas', 117.
[39] Siker, 'Hauerwas', 111.

by replacing all of humankind as its addressee.[40] How will the role of practical witness be spelt out?

(3) The 'performative' understanding of practice as the criterium of truth is specified also in relation to doctrine: 'A christology which is not a social ethic is deficient.'[41] But then this 'social ethic' is identified with the church: 'As such the church does not have a social ethic; the church is a social ethic.'[42] So the content of this 'social' ethic is not action in the 'outside' world; 'social' refers to what is actually an internal religious communal ethic. The equivocation that makes this transition possible lies in the term 'social'. It does not refer to 'society' as distinct from the church, as other praxis-oriented theologies would assume; its key content is the opposite to what is seen as Enlightenment individualism, an alternative for which the Christian community is taken to be the best representative. The meaning is that a Christology which is not an internal moral theology is deficient.

The specific hermeneutical approach taken is revealed in the claim that the church 'is' a social ethic. Instead of being a space cohabited by adherents who are both saints and sinners, and whose multiple intentions, actions and connections cannot be judged in the final instance by their contemporaries, the attribution of 'being' a social ethic transfers a near-salvific standing to a given community as an empirical instantiation of the 'Church'. The further development of this conception in the specification that the source of Christian ethics is 'worship' will be examined in Chapter 6.

What has become clear at this stage is that the strength of the narrative approach has not come to fruition since the plurality of meanings is cut off by a pre-established content. This unitary content itself risks being undermined by an inclination to think in dichotomies and to set up alternatives where it would often be more adequate to distinguish different compatible levels. An approach interested in integrating diverging

---

[40] This perceptive point is made by Christofer Frey, 'Konvergenz und Divergenz von Ethik und Praktischer Theologie', in *Reconsidering the Boundaries between Theological Disciplines*, ed. Michael Welker and Friedrich Schweitzer (Münster: LIT Verlag, 2005), 122: 'Due to this social dimension the church has to be one of the most important themes in Christian ethics. However, the church cannot replace human nature which still has to be presupposed', adding in a footnote: 'This has to be noted critically against Stanley Hauerwas, *Christian Existence Today: Essays on Church, World and Living in between* (Durham, NC, 1988).'

[41] Hauerwas, *A Community of Character*, 37. This claim can be defended in the way Fergusson interprets it in *Community, Liberalism and Christian Ethics*, 53: 'Christian confession is ethically situated in the form of life which Jesus makes possible.'

[42] Hauerwas, *The Peaceable Kingdom*, 99.

understandings would first have to acknowledge the fact of conflicting interpretations.

Siker's question at the conclusion of his sympathetic account is helpful in broadening the points of reference and reopening the closed circle between Bible and church: 'How is the authority of Scripture related to tradition, reason, and to experience, through all of which God speaks to the church?'[43]

3. Virtues as images of attitude (*Haltungsbilder*) in an ethics of ability (*Könnens-Ethik*) (Dietmar Mieth)

The third approach to be analysed for its use of virtue ethics begins with the element of 'experience' which, as Siker has just stated, belongs to the factors to be explored by a biblically based Christian ethics. Dietmar Mieth's rediscovery of virtue ethics is a consequence of his starting point, the ethical and moral experiences an individual makes in the course of her life. They are shaped by the following factors highlighted in an ethics of ability (*Könnens-Ethik*): the reflective ability to trace continuities and changes in one's convictions; the imaginative capacity to relate to the models depicted in literature and in the cultural and religious worlds that offer images of a flourishing life and of its conflicts; and knowledge of one's competences and frailties (a). From the concept of an 'experiential' ethics requiring a hermeneutical approach, virtues are accessed as 'images of attitude' (*Haltungsbilder*) which are to be analysed for the aspirations contained in them.[44] Christian virtues, while offering a motivating and critical perspective, are based on the general human ability to reflect on one's experience and becoming more proficient in those virtues that one makes one's own. A critical diagnosis of culture is directed towards finding 'attitudes' lived by

---

[43] Siker, 'Hauerwas', 125.
[44] Cf. Dietmar Mieth, *Die neuen Tugenden* (Düsseldorf: Patmos, 1984); *Moral und Erfahrung* (Freiburg i. Ue.: Universitätsverlag and Freiburg i. Br: Herder, 3rd edn 1982); *Moral und Erfahrung II. Entfaltung einer theologisch-ethischen Hermeneutik* (Freiburg i. Ue.: Universitätsverlag and Freiburg i. Br: Herder, 1998), 117–84; 'Zweiter Teil: Ethik, Moral und Religion', in Monika Bobbert and Dietmar Mieth, *Das Proprium der christlichen Ethik. Zur moralischen Perspektive der Religion* (Fribourg: Edition Exodus, 2015), 109–288.

social groups and individuals that can offer visible exemplifications of life forms and thus have relevance for structural, institutional ethics (b). Instead of limiting the enquiry to a set of alternative Christian virtues in order to provide a counter-model to the existing secular *polis*, Mieth insists on the link between human and Christian ethical experience. He also submits ecclesial endorsements of specific roles, attitudes and justifications to critiques from biblical, theological and moral sources (c). A more detailed treatment of the level of normative ethics will be provided in Chapter 8 on the autonomy approach of which Mieth represents the second generation; equally, the crucial elements which a Christian horizon adds to human morality will be explained more fully then.

(a) An ethics based on human experience

A key interest of Mieth's anthropological foundation of theological ethics is to elaborate human longings and abilities as a focus deserving as much attention as questions of justification. These are treated in an ethics of obligation which remains, however, largely silent on the continuity of lived self-understandings. The reflective, advisory role of ethics relating to hopes and images of human flourishing has a 'preventative'[45] rather than a 'reactive' function and engages in other types of access to the perception of reality: imagination and literary sensibility for a narrative, non-deductive logic. It does not imply less than morality: the standing of all human beings as ends in themselves has to be defended against instrumentalizing incursions by others or by the community; yet this 'ought' does not exhaust all aspects of human existence and practice that ethical reflection is called to explore. His corrective, but not dismissive approach to an ethics of duty implies several differences to modernity-critical versions of virtue ethics:

(1) Instead of anchoring virtues in a homogeneous *polis*, they are investigated within the ethos of the different eras and carriers to which they belong: from antique Athens to medieval knights and religious, to the nineteenth-century workers' ethos. They are expressed in a diversity of sources from philosophical treatises to the Bible, to literature like the medieval Tristan epos, to mysticism, and modern fiction.[46] They illustrate different 'model ethics'[47] to which the modern plurality of forms of flourishing life can relate.

---

[45] Mieth, *Die neuen Tugenden*, 56–9.
[46] Mieth, *Die neuen Tugenden*, 16–17.
[47] Ibid., 18, 58.

(2) Decoupling the concept of striving from the idea of a natural finality of human acts has the consequence that a more complex theory of subjectivity is needed than the term 'character' can express. Having discovered the Ricoeur of the *Time and Narrative* volumes as a philosophical counterpart to the 'narrative ethics' he had begun to develop from the middle of the 1970s, Mieth also discusses the concept of the self and the levels of ethics leading to the third, 'practical wisdom' stage outlined by Ricoeur in *Oneself as Another*. He sums up the result of the ninth study on 'practical wisdom' as uncovering the link between 'reason' and 'conviction': also discourses of moral justification draw on arguments that can be shown to be universally valid, yet as concrete instantiations, they include a personal assessment.[48]

(3) The contents of the general human desire of 'living well, with and for others, in just institutions'[49] – the formula with which Ricoeur describes the striving for *eudaimonia* as the entry stage of ethics – is coloured by the priorities of different eras. Thus, paradigmatic ethical attitudes or virtues change. For Christian ethics, this poses the task to analyse moral change in its effects on the decisions of moral subjects between old and new stocks of norms, virtues and values.[50] The fact of value pluralism is not to be taken as a sign of normative ties being corroded, to which only the prophetic counter-example of the Christian community could provide an antidote. Value change is to be expected, and the task is to identify the modern expressions of 'cardinal', that is, era-transcending and thus universally human virtues.[51] The interest in the substantive content of virtues which Mieth finds lacking in normative ethics, however, includes the modern link to self-reflection. It is responsible for their individual appropriation because they appear as convincing attitudes on the basis of one's life experience.

(b) Virtues as abilities and mentalities, not obligations

While the need for principled argumentation is recognized, for example on issues in applied ethics, it cannot eclipse the necessity of an ethics of the conduct of life in which long-term aims and hopes are anchored. From the

---

[48] Mieth, 'Ethik, Moral und Religion', in Bobbert and Mieth, *Proprium der christlichen Ethik*, 118.
[49] Ricoeur, *Oneself as Another*, 172. *Time and Narrative*, 3 vols., trans. Kathleen Blamey and David Pellauer (Chicago: University of Chicago Press, 1984–1988).
[50] Cf. Mieth, *Die neuen Tugenden*, 60–2.
[51] Ibid., 19–59.

perspective of a theory of freedom this turn is required. The principle of human dignity needs to be related to contexts where alternative paths can arise, calling for decisions on values conditioned by their contexts. Freedom at the concrete level includes principles and aims, inclinations and their conflicts. The advantage of the virtue approach for Mieth is that it signals an ethics of 'being able to', distinct from being obliged to.[52] Unconnected to duties, virtues offer images of attitude, narrative paths to biographical, moral and religious identity, a hermeneutics of life situations, contrast experiences and model ways of being human. This type of ethics does not work through argumentation but via exploration of how others, both living and literary models, experience life subjectively and perceive what is morally relevant.

By stressing ownership and appropriation over the imperative mode of deontology, Mieth elucidates how such an ethics of disposition, of the *habitus operativus bonus* is able to relate individual striving and a jointly lived ethos to each other. This is where the quasi-institutional status of virtue becomes evident, beyond the personal conduct of life.[53] There is a political dimension to 'character' virtues that give social movements their ethical grounding. As a long-standing tradition of thinking, supported by changing social bases in its different periods, virtues have the advantage of offering a visualization of alternative attitudes; they relate to institutions that need to be critiqued or defended in the face of cultural and economic forces. In an ethics of culture, the open models virtue offers can be analysed and compared.[54] By explaining the communal strength of virtues in this way, instead of in terms of either nature or identity, Mieth reaches a level that has been discovered as decisive, but also as ineluctable within a democracy. The German constitutional lawyer Ernst-Wolfgang Böckenförde stated already in the 1960s the paradox of the modern state: that it needs mentalities which it cannot procure itself; they are dependent on the free will of humans as social beings and the support of living traditions.[55] Mieth does not refer in this context to the debate about the need of democracies for such unenforceable attitudes; yet he does highlight the paradox it would pose if the free assent to a democratic

---

[52] Ibid., 48–51.
[53] Mieth, *Die neuen Tugenden*, 16–17.
[54] Mieth, 'Kulturethik', in *Angewandte Ethik und Religion*, ed. Thomas Laubach (Tübingen: A. Francke/ UTB, 2003), 293–308.
[55] Ernst-Wolfgang Böckenförde, 'Die Entstehung des Staates als Vorgang der Säkularisation' [1964], in Böckenförde, *Staat – Gesellschaft – Freiheit. Studien zur Staatstheorie und zum Verfassungsrecht* (Frankfurt: Suhrkamp, 1976), 42–64.

polity was not forthcoming: It could not be established through coercion without betraying its core.[56]

Thus, the social visibility and democratic relevance of free traditions of virtue are highlighted, resulting, for example, in a person opting for an attitude of trust versus an encompassing mood of scepticism or cynicism.[57] However, this role of 'virtue' is not the same as declaring an existing ethos as unsurpassable and as not requiring any further justification.

(c) Virtue as an appropriate entry point for Christian ethics

What Mieth finds lacking in normative ethics is attention to the constancy and resilience of basic attitudes which need to be reconstructed in a theory of striving and willing. He does not share the Neo-Aristotelian reason for minimizing the ought: that these norms are already immanent in the living community of faith which can be held up as a shining example to the outside world. For him, both the church and deontological ethics have neglected to spell out the connection to the hope for a flourishing life to which the gospel narratives speak. The decision for an ethics that does not begin with duties, neither autonomous nor ecclesial, is in keeping with the perspective of liberation or salvation by a God who affirms each individual and who reopens the future by forgiving.[58] The connection between *vita contemplativa* and *vita activa*, as investigated in the work of the mystical theologian Meister Eckhart, heralds an individualization of faith already in the Middle Ages. From this theological heritage, Mieth's differences to and immanent critiques of other Christian virtue approaches become clear.

(1) There is no apotheosis of the existing church and no assumption of a unitary understanding between members of the Christian tradition which would give them a closer alliance than those possible with other movements. The call is to forge allegiances with people of goodwill in the public realm on shared concerns. What can be learnt from the history of reception of the Gospel, is the creativity with which the early interpreters of the foundational Christian scriptures faced unprecedented challenges and set in motion historical changes in conceptions of self and world. In their joint chapter on 'virtue', Jean-Pierre Wils and Dietmar Mieth critique the receptive nature of

---

[56] Mieth, *Die neuen Tugenden*, 69.
[57] Mieth, 'Ethik, Moral und Religion', in Bobbert and Mieth, *Proprium der christlichen Ethik*, 179–83.
[58] Ibid., 257–60, on the 'vertical asymmetry of God's self-disclosure'.

Hauerwas's concept of virtue, in comparison with Alasdair MacIntyre's emphasis on the competence of judgement which credits the individuals with a capacity of their own. The self-enclosed, defensive periods of church and theology are judged as restrictive and unproductive hindrances to its message.

(2) The openness of virtues for an ethics in a narrative register needs to be expounded, not reduced. Wils and Mieth object to the promise of as yet undefined projects being narrowed down to a set of pre-established virtues, before the stories, biblical or literary, can be heard. The hope of greater context sensitivity, the interest in new projects of ethical-religious identity within the course of a life, and the maieutic roles of imagination and literary models are left unused; the virtues concluded from the Gospel narratives remain undiscussed and seem to be sacrificed to a dogmatic pre-conception of what constitutes adequate praxis for Christians. Thus, Wils und Mieth come to the conclusion that Hauerwas 'transports a fixed stock of virtues, as it were, in a narrative shell'.[59] The open, explorative process of ethical orientation which seemed to be announced through the category of narrative with the chance of giving access to the life of Jesus as a 'model' in its mystery and salvific nature, is closed off prematurely.

(3) Philosophical ethics is not superseded, but recognized in its ongoing role also within contributions of theological ethics to current debates. In matters of applied ethics, the argumentations offered by Christian ethicists are themselves philosophical. What has to be thematized, however, is their link to conceptions of the human person. Also approaches to philosophical ethics are not neutral, but put forward conclusions that can be analysed for their specific understandings, for example, of autonomy and dignity. This observation does not mean that each constitutes a 'comprehensive doctrine', just like religious traditions in John Rawls's view. But it indicates that every conception of the human has to be examined for its premises, and that 'not all of them are compatible with a Christian image' and its directives for action.[60]

In conclusion, analysing three current uses of the virtue tradition has revealed the following features: the first interpretation of biblical and early Christian ethics in terms of virtue relied on a contrast to a 'rule' and 'command' framework for their characterizations of prophetic, Pauline and

---

[59] Jean-Pierre Wils, and Dietmar Mieth, 'Tugend', in *Grundbegriffe der christlichen Ethik*, ed. Jean-Pierre Wils and Dietmar Mieth (Paderborn: Schöningh/UTB, 1992), 192.
[60] Mieth, 'Ethik, Moral und Religion', in Bobbert and Mieth, *Proprium der christlichen Ethik*, 118.

gospel pointers to an ethical life. The second model proposed a strong church-world contrast to develop its community-centred programmatic view of ethics for contemporary Christians. The third example emphasized 'attitudes' of individuals and social movements as the core of a virtue approach that is compatible with modern self-understandings and a necessary complement to principled ethics. The role of 'experience' and of 'models' in literary and other artistic expressions, but also within the history of Christian thought and practice was seen as the factor that normative ethics on its own does not capture.

The following chapter investigates the subsequent development of Hauerwas's ecclesial communitarianism into a more specific foundation on worship.

6

Christian worship as a foundation of Christian ethics

To include the ritual celebration of salvation as a source of renewal is in keeping with the esteem for the literary, narrative and symbolic genre of the Bible as the foundation of all theology, including Christian ethics. The consistency that a virtue or 'attitudes' entry point adds to a theory of Christian agency is also augmented by worship. In the *Blackwell Companion to Christian Ethics* this theme becomes the basis for a complete restructuring of the discipline. Edited by Stanley Hauerwas and Samuel Wells, the volume's authors develop areas of social, personal and applied ethics like justice and violence, friendship and silence, cloning and euthanasia under overarching titles given to the different parts of the Sunday service: 'Meeting God and One Another', 'Re-encountering the Story', 'Being Embodied', 'Re-enacting the Story', and 'Being Commissioned'.[1] The four chapters of the programmatic

[1] Cf. Table of Contents, in *The Blackwell Companion to Christian Ethics*, ed. Stanley Hauerwas and Samuel Wells (Oxford: Blackwells, 2004), vii–ix.

first part, co-authored by Hauerwas and Wells, entitled 'Studying Ethics through Worship', indicate delineations from other approaches through their headings. They classify Christian ethics as 'Informed Prayer' and elaborate an understanding of the ecclesial basis under the title, 'The Gift of the Church and the Gifts God Gives It'. A theory on the origins of the discipline is put forward as an explanation of 'Why Christian Ethics Was Invented', and 'How the Church Managed Before There Was Ethics'.[2] I will begin with this genealogy since it formulates the editors' understanding of the content and the methods of the discipline (1). Secondly, the core of the liturgical celebration from which this new conception of Christian ethics is being developed has to be identified, and how the eucharist is linked to an ecclesiology with a specific reading of the 'Body of Christ' (2). Finally, I will discuss the repercussions of the suggested re-ordering and reinterpretation on the tasks and the standing of Christian ethics and theology at the university (3).

1. Retracing the origins of Christian ethics

The edited volume presents as a new departure for Christian ethics by revoking its status as a discipline distinct from theology. This separation is attributed to the Enlightenment and judged to be a 'compromise' accepted by its Christian protagonists in order to be heard in a society that has departed from a previous political framework defined by faith convictions.[3]

The key objection is that practice is cut off from its source, and analysed in a comparison of different historical understandings as if it could be intelligible on its own, and without the meanings the faithful find in it. The Enlightenment is seen as casting ethics as something 'objective', to which a counter-position is claimed: 'This book . . . distrusts the notion of objectivity, if objectivity assumes there was ever such a thing as a disinterested observer.'[4] It is not surprising that in line with the original Aristotelian model of ethics as virtues existing in a *polis*, the distinction between the levels of what is and of what ought to be is minimized. Here, it takes the shape of insisting that

---

[2] Ibid., 3–12; 13–27; 28–38; 39–50.
[3] Ibid., 28. Cf. 35: 'attempts to distinguish ethics from theology in modernity have distorted the character of Christian convictions and practices.'
[4] Ibid., 5.

reflection should begin with the 'source' and not the practices themselves that flow from it. But it is not inherent in the antique virtue model to desist from spelling out a theory of governance, of law or of justice. There is an additional element in the new paradigm proposed which is not simply a consequence of a hermeneutical approach to ethics that sees its task as interpreting a given ethos. It is the turn to 'worship' as the enabling ground of Christian agency and theology, both of which are linked as functions to the church. How this counter-model to dividing theology into disciplines is established will be examined in three subsections: biblical foundations (a), theological conclusions (b), and a comparison of the style and intended audience to other types of theological analysis (c).

(a) Biblical foundations

What is found to be missing in 'conventional Christian Ethics' is 'the way God chooses to form his people',[5] making it 'capable of fulfilling all righteousness'.[6] It is this neglected resource that the book dedicates itself to elaborating, departing from the format they see as typical of the modern anthropological turn: it is 'not an attempt to ground an ethic on a reading of human nature and society in the style of Immanuel Kant.'[7] In order to uncover the unused potential given only in the church, they begin instead with an interpretation of the first words of Jesus in Matthew. It is in order to 'fulfil all righteousness' that he allows himself to be baptized by John. The explication of Mt. 3.13–17 as 'the foundation'[8] and 'the event of Christian Ethics' contains three steps 'that make possible the whole discipline'.[9] Unlike approaches to theological ethics that explain the anthropological premises of being able to be addressed and to respond to God's invitation, the single source that is specified has been 'revealed': Here, in the baptism of Jesus, 'is revealed the source of Christian ethics which lies in the interrelationship between the members of the Trinity: the Father who opens heaven and speaks, the incarnate Son who goes down, rises and fulfils all righteousness, the Holy Spirit who descends and rests upon.'[10] All three are interpreted

---

[5] Ibid., 13.
[6] Ibid., 16.
[7] Ibid, 14.
[8] Ibid.
[9] Ibid., 15.
[10] Ibid., 14.

consistently in a way that expands statements about Jesus Christ to his followers: (1) 'Heaven is open to those who stand where Christ stands'; (2) God's Spirit descending 'bears the promise that through him his people may become the Temple of the Holy Spirit, the place where God's glory dwells, the place of encounter'; (3) everything God 'gives to Jesus he gives through Jesus to his people. And, ultimately, the promise of this is that God's people mean everything to God.'[11] While constituting a systematically unified position, it restricts God's universal salvific will to the church.

Consequently, when two of the three offices of Christ are passed on to the church, the priestly office is explained as relating to the internal ordering of the community, while the prophetic office is directed at the world outside it.[12] Unlike biblical prophetism that reminds God's people of the covenant which it has broken, and takes a counter-position to the community, here God's people are in the position to call the world to order, but do not seem to need this office exercised by Jesus Christ as their counterpart. What first looked like Christomonism, concentrating on God's being in Christ in an attempt to correct a modern individualistic anthropocentrism, here slides into an ecclesiomonism. This also becomes evident in two verbs used interchangeably in the task assigned to Christian ethics: It 'names the ways in which the church inherits and embodies what God gives his people in Jesus.'[13] The 'inheriting' church is now also gifted with what theology attributes to the person of Jesus, to be the human 'embodiment' of God. The baptism account of God's confirmation of Jesus as God's Son turns out to have been really about the church. It is not humanity that means 'everything to God', but only 'God's people'. Scripture as well is not about God as creator of the universe and of the diversity of peoples on earth called to response and salvation; it 'is the story that identifies God's people.'[14] It is evident, then, that this understanding of theological ethics as already incorporated into the practices of God's people finds conventional versions of the discipline lacking. They fail to prioritize the unique 'resources' the church has to offer in its fulfilment of all righteousness.

---

[11] Ibid., 15–16.
[12] Ibid., 21–2.
[13] Ibid, 16.
[14] Ibid., 17.

(b) Theological conclusions about God, worship, the Church and the kingdom

By developing Christian ethics from the 'ordered series'[15] of the practices of liturgy, this approach clearly endorses it as a response to God's prior initiative. It focuses on a level before action, where motivation can be renewed, distance taken from a week of working, and God's goodness celebrated. With this move to another register, the enabled character of Christian responses is highlighted at the level of symbolic action. Coming together for the ritual of thanksgiving and commemorative narration allows for community ownership; more diverse possibilities of appropriation become available than in moral argumentations towards judgement. All these shifts can offer fruitful re-accentuations to ethics. So what conclusions are drawn about God and about the church's response from tracing the origin of Christian ethics to a church-centred reading of Jesus' baptism in Matthew's Gospel? 'Christians approach worship with an expectation that God will make himself known through liturgy, and Christians who approach ethics in ways informed by worship come with a similar expectation that God will make himself known in their deliberations, investigations and discernment.'[16] By giving the initiative to God who 'makes himself known', an open-ended parallel is stated between worship and ethical reflection. It is a matter of 'expectation' which cannot bind God but expresses a hope. The depiction of God and of the role of ethics that follows, however, is more definitive:

> God longs for his people to worship him in a friendship that is embodied in eating together ... it is in the Eucharist that the goals of God's creation and redemption come to fruition. The goals of Christian ethics are none other than these very same longings and realizations. This book is a study of how Christians ... may practice Christian ethics by fulfilling God's longing for them to worship him, be his friends, and eat with him.[17]

Here, it is not a matter of hoping that the ethical discernment carried out by believers does justice to God's intention for the world. The 'goals of God's creation and redemption' are said to 'come to fruition' in the celebration of the eucharist. If 'fruition' means complete realization, it would be a breathtaking restriction of 'God's intention for the world'. On the following

---

[15] Ibid., 7, 9–11.
[16] Ibid., 3.
[17] Ibid., 16.

page, it is conceded that the kingdom of God is more than the church: 'The kingdom is the fulfilment of the purposes of God, all creation in perfect service and harmonious relationship and joyful communion.'[18] Yet again, this definition of God's kingdom as reaching beyond the church to 'all creation' is qualified several pages later: 'When Christians gather they learn to value every person God has made, big, small, bright, slow, not because they are each individuals with rights (which inevitably conflict) but because each one has been given gifts by God that the Church needs to receive if it is to be faithful.'[19] This tendency towards binary qualification and pointed subordination takes away from the previous recognition of 'all creation' as being worthy of God's love just by itself, not because of its function for the church. The universality and the sovereignty of God's will of salvation are also diminished when the anthropomorphisms are extended to include that 'God longs for his people to worship him'. Similarly, roles are being exchanged when it is claimed that 'the Church is God bringing people out of slavery and exile through people coming together to identify with him and through him with one another'.[20] It is hard to decide whether this language is meant to be evocative by using poetic licence, or whether it is put forward in the concise theological sense of these concepts, 'church' and 'God', the first being identified with the latter. Then even God, after Jesus Christ and the Spirit, would be usurped by the 'Church'. Observations on the language used in this programmatic opening part on 'Studying Ethics through Worship', its theory decisions, and the relation struck to the history of Christian thinking will conclude this section.

(c) Style, theory decisions and positioning within the history of Christian thinking

The point that liturgy needs to be taken into account for an adequate understanding of the core of 'Christian' ethics is made as an overdue correction of other views, for example, merely activist ones. This critique can be taken on board by theorists of different models. Yet the style (1), the reduction of the sources to a unitary one (2), and the disruption of continuity with the history of theology and ethics (3) require some comments.

---

[18] Ibid., 17.
[19] Ibid., 25.
[20] Ibid., 23.

(1) The style chosen in the worship-based approach to theological ethics is not analytical and systematic, but paranetic. The model of theology that works at a distance from religious practice in order to elaborate argumentations on contested issues by analysing concepts and their premises, steps and conclusions, is left behind. The key addressees seem to be the members of the congregations centred around this approach who share its judgements on the world and on the type of church required.

(2) Regarding theory decisions, the first point that emerges in comparison to the models discussed so far in Parts 1 and 2, is a complete evacuation both of the 'normatively human' and of the 'individual sciences' as sources of Christian ethics. It is then no longer a *res mixta*, but derives totally from revelation, with no role for reason in theological, biblical and societal analyses, and on the premises of solutions proposed, especially for the realities that cause human beings to suffer. The authors' insight, stated as a critique of the modern turn to a critical epistemology, that claims to 'objectivity' have become suspicious, is not applied to their own reconstruction. If it is the case that enquiries for establishing knowledge are based on interests, the question of criteria arises. What insights does the turn to Jesus' baptism achieve, and what understandings are sacrificed if Christian ethics is reduced to this event as its only source?

A second theory decision lies in submitting biblical stories to immediate theological claims without utilizing the historical-critical knowledge available. They could have outlined the problem which Jesus' baptism by John posed for the evangelists, and drawn theological conclusions from how each of them dealt with it in their different accounts. It can be attributed to a selective reading of the tradition that the prophets' and Jesus' own critiques of the Temple, of ritual and exceptionless observances like the Sabbath are not considered as a criterium also for the Christian practice of the eucharist.

(3) The move to worship inherently reinforces the communitarian framework of virtue ethics by anchoring the narrative – which is accessible not only to in-groups – in the community's celebration of the liturgy. The complete focusing on an internal perspective is also stated explicitly, as already quoted: The new proposal is 'not an attempt to ground an ethic on a reading of human nature and society in the style of Immanuel Kant'.[21] What is ruled out by this clarification, however, is not just the approach that inaugurated modernity; rejected is a core position shared by the New

---

[21] Ibid., 14.

Testament and the two millennia of its history of effects. Proposed is a radical departure from the long-standing tradition of interpretation issuing from Paul's Letter to the Romans to recognize that also the gentiles have 'the requirements of the law ... written on their hearts, their consciences also bearing witness' (Rom. 2.15). Patristic theologians elaborated on the shared assumption that a Christian ethic is grounded on the general human capacity to discern between right and wrong. The Middle Ages followed them in this, with Thomas accepting the 'natural law' as a feature of creation, together with the cardinal virtues of antique ethics which are expanded and integrated, but not contradicted, by the 'infused' theological virtues. It has been a constant part of the Christian faith's contribution to the intellectual streams of different eras to propose a concept of human nature. Hauerwas's attempt to supersede this by positioning the church in this space has received a sceptical response. As mentioned in the previous chapter, Christofer Frey has pointed out the unsustainable role which the concept of church has to take over if the concept of human nature is eliminated.[22]

A final observation is that the virtue ethical rejection of the level of 'ought', which is identified with modernity and its individualism, as distinct from the contextualized ethics of communities, does not imply a lack of normative demands. These are still directed at the faithful whose only hope of being forgiven for their sins is the mediation of the church.

2. The event of the eucharist and dimensions of the Body of Christ

There is an obvious link between the ritual of the eucharist (a) and ecclesiology (b) in the history of Christian practice and thought. Yet, the verbal interpretations both of the ritual, and of metaphors for the church have given rise to such different theories that also the connections between them are marked by widely varying perspectives.

(a) Interpreting the eucharist

One of the ongoing controversies between different schools of theological thinking on the scope of God's salvific will becomes concrete in the

---

[22] Frey, 'Konvergenz', 122.

interpretation of the Last Supper. For whom was Jesus' dedication of his life as the new covenant, made on the evening before his death, intended? David Power sums up the New Testament foundations; beyond the Last Supper accounts of the 'breaking of the bread' in Paul and the Synoptics, they include the Letter to the Hebrews, chapters 6 and 13 to 17 in the gospel of John, as well as other texts, such as the feeding of the multitudes: 'These various features of the New Testament evidence facilitate a praxis-oriented understanding of the eucharist whereby it is seen in relation to the church's mission in the service of God's kingdom and to the church's aspirations to truth and justice for all peoples, in the memory and hope of Jesus Christ.'[23] Here, the 'moral implications of participation in the ritual'[24] point beyond the church to 'all peoples'.

Hauerwas and Wells propose an understanding in which the practice of ecumenism is visible in the inclusion of elements from the different denominations. Since the eucharist is identified as 'the most important thing we do in our lives',[25] the parts of its celebration acquire unsurpassable existential and corporate weight. Consequently, its conclusion carries an expectation well beyond the usual sending out of the participants into ordinary weekday life: the 'dismissal' concludes how what has happened in the service has 'informed, shaped, changed or transformed the Body'.[26] It is not about what is done after the service, but how the event itself has resulted in a change relevant for ethics. While the explanation of the dimensions of the 'Body of Christ' belongs to the concept of church to be examined in section b), it can already be noted here that the emphasis is on the present, not on the near or the more distant future. This accent on the immediate effect corresponds with two features. One (discussed already regarding his earlier work centred on virtue and character) is the tendency to take 'performance' as the criterion of salvation, with the risk of making salvation as the core of the Christian faith dependent on current enactments. The enactment is here narrowed to the eucharist. As David Fergusson pointed out even before the move to worship as foundational for Christian ethics, 'the Eucharistic prayer is traditionally one of praise and thanksgiving which

[23] In his chapter on the eucharist in *Systematic Theology: Roman Catholic Perspectives*, ed. Francis Schüssler Fiorenza and John P. Galvin (Minneapolis: Fortress Press, 1991), 270, n. 23, David Power refers to Raymond Johanny's statement that 'in the letters of Ignatius of Antioch, a reflection on the eucharist and on the celebration of the eucharist is the most basic form of early ecclesiology'.
[24] Ibid., 270.
[25] Hauerwas and Wells, *Companion*, 12.
[26] Ibid., 11.

declares what God has already done in creation and redemption'.[27] It does not have to be constituted by the faithful – it already exists as accomplished before their response.

The second aspect seems to reserve God's presence just for the members of the community, individually and collectively, by using the terms 'glory' and 'splendor' similarly to the *Shekinah* in rabbinic literature. There, it is the name for the presence of God that stands for God's own being: 'Worshiping God invites him to make the life of the disciple the theater of his glory. Worshiping God together invites him to make the body of believers the stage of his splendor'.[28]

Also Karl Rahner in his seminal chapter of 1956 that prefigured the Second Vatican Council's ecclesial and liturgical renewal identifies the eucharist as the 'event' of the church, which gives the local communities a foundational dignity that is not dependent on the universal church.[29] But this argument for the particular, local churches is not prone to a totalization of this celebration with a sole focus on God, as staged by the body of participants, with no memory of Jesus.

The strong statements on the eucharist's encompassing role require, but do not receive clarifications in relation to ongoing theological debates. The necessary verbal interpretations of the ritual diverge and can only be elaborated at a discursive level. Is the eucharist best expressed as 'sacrifice', and if so, in what sense, or as a meal of remembrance? Is it offered 'for the many', or 'for all'?[30] The issue of who is included in the community of salvation is a matter for debate also with Hauerwas and Wells. Apart from enquiring into the different premises of understanding the eucharist, what also matters are the structures of the church in which it is celebrated, including the question of access to ordination. David Power points out a tension in the theology and practice of the eucharist which counsel against isolating it from ongoing structural debates:

---

[27] Fergusson, *Community, Liberalism and Christian Ethics*, 69–70.

[28] Hauerwas and Wells, *Companion*, 25.

[29] Karl Rahner, 'Zur Theologie der Pfarre', in *Die Pfarre. Von der Theologie zur Praxis*, ed. Hugo Rahner (Freiburg: Herder, 1956), 27–39.

[30] The book predates the recent changes of the Roman Catholic missal towards a more literal wording – changing the meaning of the Greek in a way that could imply that Jesus' death was not for 'all', but only for 'the many'; or replacing the translation of *homoousios* in the Creed, 'of one being with the Father', with 'consubstantial', giving the medieval reception of Aristotelian categories priority over Nikaia. Cf. the theological assessments in, for example, *Gestorben für wen? Zur Diskussion um das 'pro multis'*, ed. Magnus Striet (Freiburg: Herder, 2007).

On the one hand, it is possible to speak of a legitimate plurality in unity, both practical and doctrinal. On the other hand, it is impossible to overlook a certain conflict of interpretations ... Some dialectic between apparently opposing positions is possible, as with the East-West positions ... It is also necessary to be attentive to the distortions that can creep into belief, theology and practice as a result of bias, naïve realism, or power structures that have inevitable effects on ritual and devotion.[31]

(b) The Body of Christ in its three instantiations

In the 'worship' approach to theological ethics, the Pauline metaphor for the church as the 'Body of Christ' is given priority to other biblical designations, such as the pilgrim people of God. Hauerwas and Wells distinguish three senses. The first denotes Jesus' body from his 'birth, suffering and death to his resurrection'.[32] The second is 'God's gift of the Church' that is 'always delivered and shaped by the incarnate, crucified and risen Jesus'.[33] The third is the eucharist with its 'regular rhythm of celebration' that 'comes to order the shapelessness of time'.[34]

Under the first aspect, the body of Jesus as a historical individual, and as resurrected, the gift of Scripture is included: 'a Story that shows the definitive workings of God, but invariably shows how those workings are laced around the strivings of his people.' Scripture which 'points back to the pattern of God's action expressed fully in Jesus' finds a counterpart in the actualizing work of the Holy Spirit who 'transforms the anticipated hope of the kingdom into action'. How is this seen to happen? 'Through the ministry of the Holy Spirit what would otherwise be words, stories, ideas become practices, habits, patterns of action'.[35] While it may not be intended that the word of the Bible is superseded, there is still a progression from mere 'words' to 'practices'. So already the body of Jesus himself finds its full definition in the virtuous life of the community. This transfer is justified with turning from the past, as narrated in the Bible, to the future of the kingdom. It is not clear whether the Spirit's work has to be related back to Jesus' earthly life and ministry. But by

---

[31] Power, 'Eucharist', 265.
[32] Hauerwas and Wells, *Companion*, 16.
[33] Ibid., 18.
[34] Ibid., 19.
[35] All three quotations ibid., 17.

finding its goal once again in the gathered church, already the first sense of the 'body of Christ' serves the continuation thesis, instead of according Jesus the position of remaining the ongoing counterpart to the church which is thus in a relationship of 'correspondence', not 'linear' continuation.[36] As noted before by Fergusson and Siker, the Bible is 'domesticated' by the church. One wonders how to account for those fresh readings in the history of Christianity that turned the Gospels' presentation of Jesus against the practices of the church of their time.

Under the second meaning, some of the institutional powers are covered. It belongs to the 'gifts' in the plural that the church offers intercessions in response to failures of its members, as well as 'admonition' and 'even punishment ... for the many times the Church's supposed witness and discipleship fail to imitate God and jeopardize his friendship'.[37] The following lines are the strongest indication that the impression gained from other sections that this ecclesiology borders on an immanent eschatology in which the kingdom is already realized, is, after all, misleading:

> God gives many gifts to the church to form, share and maintain its life ... practices, ... powers or charisms, faculties, that enable the Church to carry out the sometimes demanding practices God has given it ... in intercession, the Church comes before God with the anticipation of the kingdom and the burden of all in creation that falls short of the kingdom's fulfilment ... God gives the Church the practices through which he maintains and restores its character as the Body of Christ ... admonition, the speaking of truth for the sake of God and the sinner; ... penitence, the sinner's naming of his or her own sin and request for forgiveness ... They can require discipline, the use of persuasion, warning, constraint and even punishment in an effort to bring the offender to truthfulness, penitence and reconciliation.[38]

These disciplinary means belong to the third set of powers, after preaching, and 'deliberation of common goods and purposes' which is labelled 'politics'.[39] The term 'politics' is chosen, like 'social' before, for an internal activity, transposing it from its usual meaning to the inside world of the church. Worship 'is, or aspires to be, the manifestation of the best ordering of that body, ... the most significantly political – the most "ethical" – thing that

---

[36] Fergusson, Community, Liberalism and Christian Ethics, 70.

[37] Hauerwas and Wells, Companion, 19.

[38] Ibid., 18–19.

[39] Ibid., 18.

Christians do'.[40] This sounds close to the 'societas perfecta', the concept of an institution which has all the means it needs for its internal life at its own disposition, as found in the pre-Conciliar self-understanding of the Roman Catholic Church. A further clarification is added that in effect removes the possibility of dialogue or due process: In contrast to the liberal right of bodily integrity and privacy, the members of the Christian congregation are reminded that in baptism, they are 'called to give up any sense that they "own" their bodies ... the Body of Christ ... sees itself as being genuinely a body, rather than a mass of discrete individuals'.[41]

The weight falls completely on the side of the institution, and no protection is mentioned of the integrity of the individual Christian. Is it also deemed possible for the corporate Body of Christ to fail? Granting itself the power to be a stern disciplinarian on behalf of God has totalitarian overtones and offers no criteria for its decisions. The clearest contribution in the New Testament to the crucial question of how to deal with conflicts of interpretation and praxis among the followers and disciples of Jesus, is not considered: the parable of the wheat and the tares, in which both are let grow together until the harvest (Mt. 13.24-30), leaving the judgement to God.

3. Reconceiving Christian ethics from liturgy – repercussions on its tasks and its standing at the university

'What has the altar to do with the lecture theatre?'[42] It is clear by now that this question, asked on the second page of the co-authored first part, does not only enquire about the theory–praxis relationship of practical disciplines and professional courses like teaching, religious ministry or counselling. It announces a conflict in principle that will be resolved by abandoning the 'conventional' academic standards of enquiry of the discipline of theological ethics. Instead, a new format of worship-based reflection on the implications of that practice – which are indistinguishably at once theological and ethical

---

[40] Ibid., 6.
[41] Ibid.
[42] Hauerwas and Wells, *Companion*, 4.

– is inaugurated. In a certain way, the eucharistic turn of Christian ethics employs a similar procedure to the one developed by Friedrich Schleiermacher in his magnum opus *The Christian Faith*: only what is contained in the pious self-consciousness of redemption by Jesus Christ can be elaborated in the material dogmatics; other elements are shown to be accretions from metaphysics, speculation, or functionalizations from other sources outside of piety.[43] Being compared to the 'Father of cultural Protestantism' would not be acceptable to the authors, but a single-minded pursuit of a unitary source of validation, leading to a radical reconstruction of the field could be seen as being at work in both projects. Schleiermacher offered a systematically thought-through response to the new situation arising for theology after the anthropological turn and the critique of attempts to prove God from the existence of the world, as completed by Kant's philosophy. By contrast, the style of this proposal does not intend to convince through argumentations directed at a general consciousness of truth. It speaks to fellow participants in the type of church advocated, and proposes an alternative cast for theology including ethics.

A decade before the explicit turn to worship, in his chapter, 'The Church's One Foundation is Jesus Christ Her Lord', Hauerwas had anticipated the objections that could be levelled at him, as they had been at James McClendon's approach: 'Such a theology must surely be relativistic and fideistic since it lacks any "rational" basis ... it has no means to speak to the wider world, thus robbing Christians of any way to serve their non-Christian neighbor. Even worse, such a theology invites a triumphalistic attitude incompatible with Christian humility.'[44] At the end of the three sermons that make up the chapter he takes the perspective of an uninitiated reader: 'Many will find this essay confusing. Will this form or way of doing theology pass muster in the academy? It is so idiosyncratic. Assertions are piled on assertions, but no clear argument or method is apparent. How can one be expected to do theology in such a mode?' As an answer, one much-used, emblematic term is offered: 'through practice.'[45]

Before the price of this manner of doing theology is examined in conclusion (c), two elements of the intentional departure from accepted academic standards will be discussed: the turn away from theory-led

---

[43] Friedrich D. E. Schleiermacher, *The Christian Faith* (2nd edn, 1830/31), trans. and ed. by H. R. Mackintosh and J. S. Stewart (Edinburgh: T & T Clark, 1986).

[44] Hauerwas, 'One Foundation', 143.

[45] Ibid., 162.

enquiries conducted with some degree of distanciation, to an exploration of the community's experience (a); and a lack of criteria for justifying the strong claims put forward (b).

(a) Rejection of academic practices of enquiry

The new foundation of Christian ethics on worship critiques the academic practice of examining 'individual authors and their ideas', which implies for them 'that "ethics" is a subject that can be distinguished if not isolated from the liturgical life, daily habits, and elementary practices of the Church'.[46] This turn to the experience of the congregation gives rise to poetic, evocative descriptions,[47] but the use of concepts becomes equivocal. The firm foundation in one's own chosen ecclesial location is to counteract the misconception that 'Christian theology could be divorced from the ecclesial context necessary for theology to be intelligible'.[48] Yet it seems to make it impossible to reconstruct other existing positions on their own terms with their premises rather than in brief and vague summaries. An example is the series of oppositions by which the erroneous public perception of 'ethics' and 'worship' is characterized.[49] Ethics is classified as occupied with (1) 'the real', (2) 'the good', (3) 'the external', and (4) 'action', while worship is associated with (1) 'the unreal', (2) 'beauty', (3) 'the internal', and (4) 'words'. The adequacy of these ascriptions for 'worship' as well as its subordination to ethics are of course contested, yet ethics appears as simultaneously 'objective', containing 'obligation', being 'functional' and 'instrumental',[50] as if these were not contradictory terms. A closer examination of different approaches to ethics would have shown that a key contrast could have been turned around: instead of ethics being 'external' or 'public',[51] and worship 'internal' or 'private', an analysis of the moral subject would show that moral experience is

---

[46] Hauerwas and Wells, *Companion*, 34.

[47] The individual believer's role in the 'reconciling practice of God and the church' is spelt out as follows: 'the disciple enters into the rhythm of God's life, the pattern of the dance of the Trinity. The disciple who accepts the humility of repeating the same practices over and over again receives the wonder of discovering through them the God who is ever new ... Following the incarnate Christ means handing over to God the salient features of existence, and being surprised to receive back the humdrum as a wonderful gift.' Ibid., 24–5.

[48] Ibid., 34.

[49] Ibid., 4–7.

[50] Ibid., 5.

[51] Ibid., 6.

internal, based on the consciousness of inner freedom, while rituals are external symbolic practices which need interpretation to articulate their exact meaning. The danger of using concepts loosely or of trying to reapply them in an opposing sense (such as the term normally used to denote the secular sphere, 'political') is that they become empty. Hauerwas and Wells agree that contextualizing authors, schools, mentalities and research programmes is useful, but not to help understand their theories.[52] In addition, contextualization is only one element in academic enquiries, and is not sufficient to grasp the productivity and ongoing challenge of ideas and truth claims beyond their contexts of origin.

(b) Failure to justify criteria

A theological analysis of the self-understandings and practices of a local church would take account of the different forms and genres of participation. A crucial question would be how they are related, what their effect is on other practices, and how they contribute to the community's life. In the description that follows, this enquiry is replaced by an internal perspective finally attributed to the 'body':

> Worship is the time when God trains his people to imitate him in habit, instinct and reflex . . . Together, God's people . . . reflect on the patterns of life that build up the body. In discussing whether, how and when it is appropriate to speak in tongues or dance or prophesy or use contemporary music or pray extempore, the body discovers when it is appropriate to campaign, denounce, protest, or be silent. In discussing . . . the body discovers the gifts God gives the Church and the instincts of the community.[53]

It is partly the discussion of the members and partly the 'body' that are credited with being the centre of agency. It seems that authenticity, understood as being in relation with God, replaces criteria of justifying what are adequate responses.[54] The question of criteria also appears in relation to

---

[52] For example, after brief treatments of Troeltsch, Kant, Rauschenbusch, H. Richard Niebuhr and J. Gustafson (29–36), the reason given in contrast to Gustafson is: 'We think that such accounts . . . of the cultural, ecclesial, social and religious circumstances . . . are important in order to help us see how their worship shaped all that Christians do and did not do.' Ibid., 36.

[53] Ibid., 25.

[54] Monika Bobbert, 'Erster Teil: Zum Proprium der christlichen Moral; systematische Überlegungen angesichts neuerer Ansätze theologischer Ethik', in Bobbert and Mieth, *Das Proprium der christlichen Ethik*, 53: 'At times one gets the impression that the human person is to conclude what is morally right from her free relationship to God . . . and that moral theology consist of the genuine acts of interpretation of individual faithful Christians.'

statements on the 'politics of Church' which are to include 'partnerships in all corners of the world, especially the most benighted ones'.[55]

Against the rejection of the distinction between theology and ethics one can ask whether theological ethics may not also have an 'indirect function of critique for liturgy'.[56] But this critical standpoint cannot be actualized if both are established as secondary, derived activities, jointly originating from worship.

(c) Theology at the university

The combined effect of both traits is that it jeopardizes communication at the university, which is a key institution for the production of knowledge, and for monitoring research directions for the interests given with their context of origin and their context of use. Even more importantly, universities as well as broadly minded churches provide a venue for enabling shared reflection across disciplinary boundaries and worldviews, articulating problems, analysing intellectual frameworks, assessing projects both from their value for the 'good' and from their protection of the 'right' – a unique platform for the peaceful and respectful elucidation of controversial themes. If Christian theology and ethics withdraw from the opportunity of this exchange which they have access to in their institutions of higher education, a string of diverse committed religious communities will not be able to make up for it. What the authors may see as faithful countercultural witness, is equally likely to turn out as a gamble that affects the life chances of people without a voice as well as the intellectual formation of the next generation.

To maintain public discourse, all contributors have to relate to colleagues from other subjects at eye level, respectful of their expertise, and without the intent of missionizing or alienating them. Some claims are so hyperbolic that conversation partners will fail to detect any common ground in wishing to deal with global challenges such as climate change, migration, digitization and genetic technologies. Against a practical ethical orientation associated with Kant, the editors announce:

> More ambitiously, many of the authors of this volume would go further in terms of outnarrating Kant, and suggest that life is in fact a rehearsal for

---

[55] Hauerwas and Wells, *Companion*, 24.
[56] Christoph Hübenthal, *Grundlegung der christlichen Sozialethik. Versuch eines freiheitsanalytisch-handlungsreflexiven Ansatzes* (Münster: Aschendorff, 2006), 195.

worship – that, within an eschatological perspective, it is worship for which humanity and the creation were made, and it is worship that will make up the greater part of eternity, within which what is called 'life' and the 'real' will appear to be a tiny blip.[57]

Corresponding to this dismissal of current efforts to deal with 'the real', the new approach 'aspires to a politics that discerns the best use of the unlimited gifts of God, rather than the just distribution of resources'.[58] Chapter 2 ends with the judgement: 'It is these practices, not the crisis, that define ethics, for they are about being Christian all the time – not about acting Christianly, on occasion.'[59] Apart from the difficult question of how one can tell the difference, this evades the existing challenges and undermines collaborative attempts to use the God-given powers of intellect and of the ability for cooperation to analyse realities and structures as well as proposing participative solutions.

---

[57] Hauerwas and Wells, *Companion*, 5.
[58] Ibid., 6.
[59] Ibid., 26.

7

Natural law

Chapter Outline

In contrast to the communitarian approach which the Hauerwas School espoused and radicalized in replacing the concept of human nature by founding Christian ethics directly on the church, the natural law approach begins from human nature as a universally accessible given. The orientation towards God belongs to the natural inclinations of the human person. It is considered legitimate to start with the moral consciousness of the addressees of God's revelation, and the relationship between nature and grace is seen as one of correspondence, not of rupture. By assuming a 'natural law', the distinction from positive law is constitutive. Humans are beneficiaries of a law that is prior to and independent of the legislation of an empire, state or *polis*. Unlike the position of legal positivism, developed in the twentieth century, a link between law and ethics is assumed. In antiquity and the Middle Ages, its basis is a concept of the human person as part of a teleological system of nature. Before examining the inclusion, critique and reformulation of this tradition in Christian ethics (2), it is useful to take account of the philosophical framework and the key elements it combines. The classical understanding of natural law, however, has been affected by subsequent changes in the concepts of nature and of theoretical and practical reason (1). In view of the transformations required by modern theories of human subjectivity and agency, the debate on whether this anthropological basis should still be used by theological social ethicists needs to be assessed (3). How these questions appear in Catholic Social Thought, as one main concretization of the natural law approach, will be reviewed in the conclusion (4).

1. Key factors of natural law in changing philosophical frameworks

In his analysis of three core components of the natural law framework shared by Plato, Aristotle and the Stoa, the philosopher Ludwig Siep explains the understandings that were held in a productive tension in the antique era: (1) a teleological system; (2) a *polis* setting; and (3) the internal dimension of conscience.[1] The teleological order assumed all its participants to be directed towards inbuilt goals. The aspect corresponding to the *polis* setting was the understanding of the human being as a *zoon politikon*; it introduced a historical consciousness arising from dealing with the contingencies of praxis and of diverse agents, requiring a prudential use of reason. The internal dimension of reflection, specified further to the personal capability of conscience, could still operate within an encompassing natural order and the parameters of the community. Yet keeping the three factors in balance was already an achievement in view of the divergent dynamics of each. Modifications in one affected the connection with the others.

> In traditional natural law, natural teleology, political prudence with reference to a specific community and its experiences, and general reason accessible in inner reflection and scrutiny of conscience formed a unity which certainly had its tensions yet could be brought to the point of equilibrium. It came increasingly under pressure ... in the modern era, ... exerted mainly from three directions: First, the teleological explanation of nature yielded to the mechanic-technological theory of development, and finally to the theory of evolution as subject to chance. Second, the limits were partly removed from

---

[1] Cf. Ludwig Siep, 'Natural Law and Bioethics', trans. J. G. Cumming, in *Human Nature and Natural Law, Concilium* 46, ed. Lisa S. Cahill, Hille Haker and Eloi Messi Metogo (London: SCM, 2010), 50. Thus, 'from the start they contained a certain tension that became more acute in the modern era' (47).

processes of historical experience. Thirdly, the autonomy of the individual ran counter to every kind of predetermined natural or legal and rational order.[2]

With the system of natural teleology undermined, the understanding of practical reflection changes from working out conclusions for contingent circumstances from the governing natural framework of essential purposes. The leading role falls to a new understanding of practical reason as self-governance under the moral law. In his nuanced comparison of similarities and differences between antique and modern ideas of reason, Otfried Höffe singles out the concept of agency as the real game changer between Aristotle and Kant. Natural law is turned into the law of reason (*Vernunftrecht*) by basing the justification no longer on natural striving but on practical reason understood as will. Instead of pre-set goals which humans need to attain by rationally motivating themselves to actualize this potential of theirs, the idea of purposes of nature is abandoned and replaced by the one single entity that can be a 'purpose in itself': the human being in her capability for morality. Able to respect others and be respected as end in herself, she is the one to set the goals, rather than follow them. Höffe points out the reversal that takes place when the basis dissolves which had allowed a concept of nature or being (*esse*) to be established as predetermining action (*agere*). Human agency is no longer bound to a pre-set orientation. The direction changes from looking ahead to the *telos*, to scrutinizing the origin of an act. Distinct from striving or 'aspiration', willing

> is confronted with the question: 'Should I or should I not do x?' Whereas teleological aspiration is oriented towards a goal, and consequently is concerned with 'where to,' the strict concept of willing looks at 'wherefrom,' at the origin of the movement in what moves (i.e., at the will) ... When it comes to teleological aspiration, the highest, normative point of orientation, the superlative of unlimited happiness, consists in an absolutely highest 'where to' in the sense of ... eudaimonia. In the case of willing, on the contrary, the point of orientation is an originating 'wherefrom.' A superlative beginning replaces a superlative end, and this origin is established where the commencement of an action is not driven by something external but receives its impetus from the individual himself.[3]

---

[2] Ibid., 50. In German, the second factor is stated as: '*Zweitens* werden die historischen Erfahrungsprozesse gewissermaßen entgrenzt' (285). In other words, the insight into cultural contingency remains, but the limits of the *polis* are superseded.
[3] Otfried Höffe, *Can Virtue Make Us Happy? The Art of Living and Morality*, trans. Douglas R. McGaughey, trans. ed. Aaron Bunch (Evanston, IL: Northwestern University Press, 2010), 182–3.

The turn backwards, however, looking at the purity of the motives of an action, is in the interest of an inescapable moral imputability. Responsibility is no longer shared with a naturally given framework for action:

> The difference between the eudaimonic-oriented antiquity and the autonomy-oriented modernity is based not in the idea of an unsurpassable good, but in the concept of an action to which the idea of the good is applied. The decisive difference, then, doesn't occur on the normative side but from the side of the theory of action ... Interest in the intensification of responsibility speaks in favour of a shift from teleological aspiration to willing. In the case of happiness, the individual is only *for the most part responsible*, whereas in the case of autonomy the individual is potentially *totally responsible*.[4]

This point will be further explored in the next chapter on the autonomy approach to theological ethics. Yet the position of ethics between 'reason' and 'nature' in a teleological ontology is also the theme of an ongoing discussion on theological premises when a monotheistic creator God is assumed as the origin of the natural order.

2. Theological interpretations of natural law, classical and revisionist

The dual direction of natural law oriented either to reason, or to nature in the sense of a shared entelechy, also appears in the theological and ecclesial use of this thought form. I will first discuss the American moral theologian Richard Gula's insightful comparison of magisterial documents regarding the reason or nature point of departure for their interpretations of issues in social and in personal ethics (a). I will then treat the points of critique of Catholic ethicists revising, but not abandoning the paradigm (b).

(a) Order of nature and order of reason in magisterial documents

The analysis of documents of Catholic Social Teaching issued by the Roman Catholic magisterium reveals the presence of both readings of natural law, one relating to nature, the other to reason, as well as a consistent pattern of

---

[4] Ibid., 184–5.

their use for distinct areas: social ethical themes are elaborated as belonging to the order of reason, while matters of personal ethics, especially concerning sexual and medical ethics, are classified under 'nature'. This leads to what has been critiqued as a physicalist derivation of norms which more recently, however, has been supplemented by personalist categories. Gula concludes his comparison of the two interpretations of the teleological framework 'which have been operating in Catholic moral theology side by side' with the observation that in social questions, 'more modest, more cautious, and more nuanced' conclusions are drawn and that in 'social ethics, the church readily accepts the inevitability of conflict on the philosophical level as well as in social life'.[5] In contrast, on 'the basis of the order of nature criteria, Catholic sexual ethics and medical ethics pertaining to reproduction have achieved a degree of certainty, precision, and consistency of moral judgement which we do not find in documents on social ethics. The order of reason approach does not yield the clear unambiguous positions which the order of nature approach does.'[6]

For him, the way forward is to have a consistent approach that not only takes the changing historical contexts seriously but also implements the Second Vatican Council's move from 'nature' to 'personhood' for which 'Gaudium et Spes (1965) is a landmark document'.[7] Once it has been recognized that it is the moral subject who assesses physical structures as part of her moral experience, the appeal to a timeless finality of functions which set the frame for moral action loses credibility: 'The danger of physicalism is to derive moral imperatives from bodily structure and functions and to exclude the totality of the person and his or her relational context in making a moral assessment.'[8] Faith in God as creator does not entail an entirely receptive and obedient role for humans:

> To equate 'natural' with well-defined patterns in creation leads to a natural fundamentalism and yields a 'blueprint' of 'maker's instructions' theory of the natural moral law. Such an approach has no room for the distinctively human, creative aspects of moral knowledge and freedom. Moral knowledge would be simply the matter of discovering the given patterns in the world, and

[5] Richard Gula, 'Natural Law Today' (1989), repr. in Natural Law and Theology (Readings in Moral Theology No. 7), ed. Charles Curran, and Richard McCormick (Mahwah: Paulist Press, 1991), 377.
[6] Ibid.
[7] Ibid., 387.
[8] Ibid., 372.

freedom would be reduced to a matter of abiding by or violating what is given.[9]

In accord with other critics he quotes, such as Charles Curran and Louis Dupré, Gula rejects the isolation both of biological functions and of individual actions from the intersubjective context. In his exposition of the approach, the term 'natural' stands for a connection to 'reality': the 'force of the "natural"... is to ground morality in reality lest moral obligations become the product of self-interest groups or subjective whim.' At the same time, 'reality' is not seen as complete and closed but as filled with 'potential': '"Natural" is what is in reality providing the potential which would make it possible for each person to come to wholeness in community with others seeking wholeness.'[10]

In two books of 1985 and 1988 that chart and examine the English-speaking and the Continental debates between the different schools, such as natural law, autonomous ethics, and faith ethics, the Irish moral theologian Vincent MacNamara develops a position that equally rejects physicalism and argues for reason, but in the sense of moral autonomy.[11] If it 'is the design of God that the person is to be his own law-giver,'[12] this morality exists also outside of a theological framework and is explored by philosophical ethics. Non-religious self-understandings have to be recognized, as his reference to dialogue with secular humanists in his discussion of Joseph Fuchs and Franz Böckle shows. The assumption of the moral theological version of natural law that every human being is ontologically oriented towards God cannot be upheld as a shared philosophical truth. His questions to magisterial documents as well as to the philosophers of the 'New Natural Law approach', John Finnis and Germain Grisez, accord the key role to human freedom. Regarding the 'nature' version of natural law where 'biology reigns supreme', he asks: 'But why should one order one's life by submitting to the faculties-end structure?'[13] Equally instructive is his response to

---

[9] Ibid., 378–9.

[10] Ibid., 378.

[11] In *The Truth in Love: Reflections on Christian Morality* (Dublin: Gill & Macmillan, 1988), Vincent MacNamara clarifies: 'Morality, we have argued, is an autonomous human experience, in particular one that is independent of religion. It has to do with a perception about the needs of our interpersonal and social lives. Religion has to do with our ultimate concern about the meaning of ourselves and our lives – particularly our interpretation of the deity' (23–4).

[12] MacNamara, *Faith and Ethics: Recent Roman Catholicism* (Dublin: Gill & Macmillan/Washington, DC: Georgetown University Press, 1985), 55.

[13] MacNamara, *The Truth in Love*, 100.

Grisez's insistence that the goods identified as decisive – life, knowledge of truth, play, aesthetic experience, friendship, practical reasonableness, religion[14] are mentioned – 'cannot be weighed against each other' and that they 'are all equally fundamental'. MacNamara reminds readers that what makes them goods is that they 'serve the fulfilment of the human being: they do not have a life of their own'. It is therefore correct what the proportionalists argue, that it is 'not possible to pursue all goods independently', and that choices are required in which one may have to act 'against a good'.[15] His reason for maintaining that 'the physical structure will not of itself be allowed to be the determinant of what it means to act humanly', is theological: 'Culture ... is also a possibility from God – and not merely nature.'[16] These accentuations succeed in opening up a perspective that avoids pitting divine against human freedom: 'It is we who are the authors of natural law ... who make or discover the law. God is the author of it in the sense that he is our author.'[17]

MacNamara does not relate the 'natural' to 'reality', as an objective backdrop which limits 'subjective whim', but takes it as meaning a universal feature of human reflection: it 'is "natural" perhaps only in the sense that the experience of morality is a general human experience'.[18] This view leads to determining the relationship between community and individual differently from Gula, indicating that each human being has a standing that communal life is to serve: community is the 'context which ensures that in certain crucial respects the uniqueness, sacredness and needs of each are respected'.[19]

While there is agreement on key weaknesses in the ecclesial use of natural law – in Vincent MacNamara's view, the 'least creditable version had the greatest influence on Roman Catholic morality'[20] – the differences between the argumentations point to distinct counter-proposals. There is more than one type of moral realism, and there are other alternatives than 'natural' as 'objective' versus 'subjective whim', such as obligation as the free recognition

---

[14] Cf. ibid., 102.

[15] Ibid., 103–4. Feminist Christian ethicists make the same point, for example, Lisa Cahill *in Sex, Gender and Christian Ethics* (Cambridge: CUP, 1996), 103, quoted by C. Traina, *Feminist Ethics and Natural Law* (Washington, DC: Georgetown University Press, 1999), 46: 'Nussbaum and Cahill hold that even in an ideal situation, human goods would often be incoherent and that in fact we may need consciously to sacrifice one to another *in concrete circumstances*.'

[16] MacNamara, *The Truth in Love*, 104, 100.

[17] Ibid., 106.

[18] Ibid.

[19] Ibid.,107.

[20] Ibid.

of the moral law in oneself. But then one would have to distinguish morality from the flourishing life as separate understandings of the moral experience, a direction which will be examined in section c). The objections in the following section are internal ones, coming from moral theologians who want to make a case for this approach as being valid also under contemporary premises.

(b) Revisionist corrections of classical natural law

Revisionist natural law proponents maintain the ontological-teleological framework, but update its interpretation through historical consciousness. The good is not deduced from the given nature of the human being, but is determined in changing historical contexts by reflecting on how this nature is experienced. It is an inductive approach that aims at 'objectivity', as Richard Gula and Stephen Pope clarify: It 'affirms that moral standards are based on reality, and in this sense, "objective", rather than manufactured by human decisions'. Since the antique understanding of 'nature' as what is 'most excellent' differs from the modern natural scientific view, it is necessary to investigate 'how "nature" functions normatively within natural law ethics'. The pre-positive foundations it supplies, being 'morally prior to social convention and positive law'[21] are sketched from Plato to Cicero and Aquinas, and the challenges through subsequent shifts in worldview outlined by Pope. 'Both naturalism and historicism work with the underlying premiss that the world is valueless and purposeless, except when values and purposes are created by human choices.'[22] The counter-position of natural law ethicists is not that 'every event in the universe exists to produce a predetermined goal', but that human nature is 'naturally oriented both to specific goods, and more importantly, to the good as such', a fact to which '(m)oral systems around the world bear witness'.[23] Pope discusses key points and critiques of the 'new natural law theory' of Finnis and Grisez and of Pope John Paul II's personalist approach, as well as of different stages of Alasdair MacIntyre's thinking. He identifies under 'prospects' a combination of natural law and virtue ethics where 'true moral objectivity is achieved in concrete acts

---

[21] Stephen Pope, 'Reason and Natural Law', in *Human Nature and Natural Law, Concilium* 46, 149.
[22] Ibid., 154.
[23] Ibid., 160–1.

through the exercise of prudence'.[24] The social and communal feature of human nature supplies the transition to narratives and models shaping 'the affections, imagination, and practical rationality through which moral standards are interpreted'.[25] What other critics find absent in the universalist claim of natural law, namely a constitutive link to the Christian message, is thus made accessible. If the relevance of stories can be shown to be part of human specificity and as belonging to human flourishing, then it can offer a different quality of openings than 'simply time-worn platitudes and abstract, universal rules'.[26] In addition to the 'universal scope and claim to apply to all human beings' that makes this approach attractive, the insights from traditions in their particularity can play a role. The opening statement about the role of God can thus be seen as justified, although it goes beyond natural teleology and natural theology: 'Faith in this God leads one to affirm than an ordering wisdom lies behind both the inherent *logos* of the natural world and the explicit revelation communicated in Scripture and the Christian tradition'.[27]

The revisionist opening of the classical model includes modern biblical scholarship, a historical worldview and the finding that also the magisterium interprets natural law, as was evident in Gula's analysis of its documents. Yet also revisionists raise the question whether the Christian conviction of the self-revelation of God in the person of Jesus and core New Testament contents can be adequately conceptualized in this framework:

Is a 'natural law' ethics adequate as a Christian biblical ethics? Even if a 'reasonable' approach to 'common human experience' opens the door to interreligious and cross-cultural concerns and to public policy involvement, does it do justice to the example and teaching of Jesus, with its radical demands for love and self-sacrifice? How can a Catholic ethics in anything like the traditional 'natural law' form be fully a Christian ethics? In the Catholic tradition, moral conclusions have not usually been grounded explicitly in a faith perspective. What role, then, does faith play in the development of such conclusions?[28]

---

[24] Ibid., 163.
[25] Ibid., 164, with reference to William Spohn, *Go and Do Likewise: Jesus and Ethics* (New York: Continuum, 1999).
[26] Ibid.
[27] Ibid., 148.
[28] Lisa S. Cahill, 'On Richard McCormick', in *Christian Voices in Medical Ethics*, ed. Allen Verhey and Stephen E. Lammers (Grand Rapids, MI: Eerdmans, 1993), 83.

If it is possible to enlarge the approach by including the 'narrative' dimension of moral development and flourishing, the question whether this thought form can be hospitable to the particular content of the Christian faith could be answered affirmatively. The issue remains, however, this borrowing from a hermeneutical understanding of selfhood and of the role of cultural and religious traditions in relation to it does not in effect go beyond the paradigm by presupposing more than it can explain through its own categories. It is true that Siep and other philosophers point to the historical consciousness already present in Aristotle, and also, as the critics of the neo-Thomist approach show, in Thomas Aquinas. But for a full explanation of these human pursuits and of the possibility of uniting them in the moral capability of a speaking, acting, narrating and, decisively, imputable self, one would need to go to distinctively modern theories of selfhood. As Paul Ricoeur does with the duality of the continuity of the '*idem*', including 'character', and the '*ipse*' in its spontaneity, two levels need to be distinguished.[29] Beyond natural inclinations and a flourishing life, a more differentiated analysis of subjectivity is needed to provide an alternative to the 'classical' reading.

The position to be treated next includes the relevant modern proposals, such as those of Kant, Hegel and Kierkegaard, existentialism, and theories of justice, in their importance for Christian ethics; it is exemplary in its philosophical mediations. It argues for 'as much classical natural law as necessary, and as much modern law of reason as possible'.[30] The objections of two Continental theological ethicists to this part of Arno Anzenbacher's work will be examined, before returning to theory decisions in Catholic Social Thought in section 4.

3. Natural law as part of modern Christian social ethics (Arno Anzenbacher)

For the Austrian theological ethicist Arno Anzenbacher, the reasons for holding on to an element of natural law despite the anthropological turn

---

[29] Ricoeur, *Oneself as Another*, 116.
[30] Arno Anzenbacher, 'Sozialethik als Naturrechtsethik, in *Gesellschaft begreifen – Gesellschaft gestalten. Konzeptionen christlicher Sozialethik im Dialog*, ed. Karl Gabriel, *Jahrbuch für Christliche Sozialwissenschaften*, vol. 43 (Münster: Regensberg, 2002), 28.

which he endorses with Kant, are different from those identified by Gula and Pope. They preferred the 'objectivity' of natural law to two contemporary counter-positions they disagreed with: 'moral positivism' based on mere 'will' or 'decision' (linked either to individual agents, or to the state), and 'interest groups'. Pope describes a '"moral positivism", according to which binding moral claims are not discovered in human nature but rather are "posited" by the will of some authority. Outside such a will, positivism holds, there is no binding moral standard'.[31] Anzenbacher distinguishes between decisionism, for example in Max Weber, legal positivism, as in Kelsen, and the role of the will in Kant's justification of ethics.[32] The reason not to replace classical natural law completely with a modern law of reason is the role of a 'natural non-arbitrary' level (*das natural Unbeliebige*) expressed in the 'natural inclinations' which theories since Kant seem to overlook. I will compare the interpretations of his approach by Matthias Möhring-Hesse (a) and Christoph Hübenthal (b) as recent critical discussions of the tradition from a continental philosophical and theological background.

(a) Objections from a social ethics built on shared values (Matthias Möhring-Hesse)

Möhring-Hesse begins his contribution to the *Festschrift* for Anzenbacher by noting the extent of his agreement with a modern ethic of reason. In a pluralistic society, Christian ethics needs to accept that there is a variety of conceptions of the good. He quotes Anzenbacher's endorsement with its critique of versions of 'natural' that were 'aiming to foreclose or to limit the openness of the question about the human being – which is relevant for freedom – as much as possible through truth claims of material natural law ... Under conditions of freedom, a legitimate pluralism necessarily develops which cannot be brought down immediately to the denominator of truth and error'.[33]

---

[31] Pope, 'Reason and Natural Law', 150.

[32] Cf. Anzenbacher, *Einführung in die Ethik*, on Max Weber's misleading critique of 'Gesinnungsethik' (ethics of intention) as opposed to 'Verantwortungsethik' in which 'responsibility seems destined to take a Utilitarian form' (cf. 146–7), on Kant's starting point of the good will (72–3), and Kelsen whom he sees as continuing in the line of Hobbes, in *Christliche Sozialethik* (Paderborn: Schöningh/UTB, 1998), 66.

[33] Matthias Möhring-Hesse, 'Sozialethik als Naturrechtsethik – oder lieber nicht? Im Gespräch mit Arno Anzenbacher', in *Freiheit – Natur – Religion. Studien zur Sozialethik*, ed. C. Spieß, (Paderborn: Schöningh, 2010), 304, quoting Anzenbacher, 'Sozialethik als Naturrechtsethik', 31.

The modern distinction between the 'good' and the 'right' needs to be recognized in Christian social ethics; yet, as Anzenbacher holds, in order to counteract the privatization of questions of the good in modern society, both have to be 'integrated in a horizon of a *conception of the good* that encompasses both areas. While it can be differently accentuated – as common good, concrete freedom, or as the idea of a flourishing life – it ultimately points to a concept of the human person and her destiny (*Bestimmung*)'.[34] As the premises of proposals of the 'right', they belong to public debates on social and institutional issues, such as family, education or biotechnology. Möhring-Hesse questions Anzenbacher's stance to keep an overarching horizon of the 'good' on the agenda in its relevance for questions of the right. His own alternative to this position is to find 'shared or at least overlapping values'[35] that are already validated by society. They should not be endangered by pushing liberals towards some shared 'good', which might jeopardize coming to agreements on controversial issues.

There are a number of clues in Möhring-Hesse's reconstruction and critique that reveal his understanding of the task of ethics in a pluralist society. He makes no distinction between what is empirically 'valid' (*Geltung*) and what is 'justified' (*Gültigkeit*) when he describes the discipline's task as 'securing a sufficiently general acceptance'.[36] 'Autonomy' is mainly explained as 'self-determination', not self-legislation; the moral subjects appear as 'authors of their own lives in an unsubstitutable way',[37] thus veering towards authenticity; the 'ethics of the good' is spelt out as a 'hypothetical ought' depending on conditions applying only to specific people and therefore not a general ought, as in the categorical imperative.[38] The 'natural non-arbitrary' level which in Anzenbacher refers to natural inclinations as basic strivings of the human being is interpreted as the 'unconditioned'.[39] This seriously misrepresents the level at which it operates in Kant: the 'unconditioned' refers to morality, not to natural traits and directions which supply the material level towards which human beings can take a stance due to practical reason.

It can be questioned whether Anzenbacher's advocacy for an integrating horizon of the good amounts to a 'super-worldview',[40] as Möhring-Hesse

---

[34] Anzenbacher, 'Sozialethik als Naturrechtsethik', 28, quoted in Möhring-Hesse, 309.
[35] Möhring-Hesse, 'Naturrechtsethik – oder lieber nicht?', 320.
[36] Ibid., 321.
[37] Ibid., 312, 313.
[38] Ibid., 317–18.
[39] Ibid., 310–16.
[40] Ibid., 320.

fears who prefers to seek out a feasible consensus and overlap at the lower level of values. In a recent chapter, Anzenbacher pursues the parallels and differences between Thomas and Kant on decisive points. He points out the path that would have been possible in principle from Thomas's formal *lex naturalis* approach to a human rights ethics but which was not taken due to era-specific limits regarding equality.[41] However, as Christoph Hübenthal suggests in his analysis in the same *Festschrift* of 2010, the issue is whether debates are carried out at the ethical level of exchanges between particular worldviews, or whether decisions can be justified at the universal moral level by spelling out the principle of human dignity in concrete matters of justice.

(b) Critique from a theory of freedom (Christoph Hübenthal)

The divergences between Hübenthal and Anzenbacher appear on the backdrop of shared nuanced assessments of the distinctions between classical and modern natural law, of a medieval awareness of cultural diversity, and the deficits of current proceduralist interpretations of Kant (1). How the concept of God is introduced, matters both for the justification and the content of belief in God (2).

(1) In his analysis of teleological approaches, Hübenthal shows how onto-teleological thinking also included a 'practical moment that is commissioned and still to be realised'.[42] Also in Thomas, striving for the excellence that is possible for humans is not portrayed as following the natural inclinations automatically. They become a matter for ethics precisely because human beings can counteract them, for example, by lying. There is a role for self-determination in both the ethical frameworks of Thomas Aquinas and Kant. The teleological system in which individuals are embedded enables them by providing strivings that can be perfected only through their collaboration. Thus, freedom and the will are implicitly presupposed, but they are not elaborated as foundations, as they will be in the late Middle Ages by Duns Scotus.

While the plurality of the good was only able to expand in modernity since it presupposed the distinction of the 'good' from the 'right', and the

---

[41] Anzenbacher, 'Menschenrechtsbegründung zwischen klassischem und neuzeitlichem Naturrecht', in *Die Begründung der Menschenrechte. Kontroversen im Spannungsfeld von positivem Recht, Naturrecht und Vernunftrecht*, ed. Margit Wasmaier-Sailer, and Matthias Hoesch (Tübingen: Mohr Siebeck, 2017), 125–6.

[42] Cf. Hübenthal, 'Teleologische Ansätze', in *Handbuch Ethik*, 63.

authorization to engage in different visions and lifestyles, also for Thomas the good was not simply supratemporal. Its conclusions allowed for cultural differences.

In contrast to Möhring-Hesse, for Hübenthal the level of an overlapping consensus does not provide a sufficient, that is, more than minimal, basis to settle divergent moral judgements. Yet also Anzenbacher's combination of a modern law of reason with worldview components of classical natural law does not offer the argumentative stringency required. Both options are deemed unable to deal with profound disagreement. 'The hope that an overlapping consensus will emerge between different views of the good or of the destiny of the human person through institutions and procedures that pacify the pluralism of worldviews is in no way guaranteed'.[43] Against the impression conveyed by the term 'good', that it relates to contents that are all affirmative, not harmful, and shareable, his statement offers a sobering warning:

> As Anzenbacher concedes, also the conceptions of the good by which human rights or the democratic constitutional state can be legitimated, are anything but uncontested. But if none of them can any longer be justified rationally, then there is no argumentative provision available against those conceptions of the good which reject universal human rights or that present themselves as decisively antidemocratic.[44]

The universality of moral justification and the concreteness that are both required, in his view, can only be achieved by combining a transcendental concept of freedom with a theory of agency which allows for material and domain-specific elaborations.

(2) On the basis of a theory of human freedom, more adequate theological reflections can be put forward. In modern terms, it is no longer possible to assume the existence of God as part or anchor of a teleological system. As Anzenbacher points out, the concept of God used by Thomas in connection with the *lex naturalis* and the *lex aeterna* is philosophical, not mediated by revelation.[45] But this means that the concept of God is cognitively inevitable. The same applies to the purposes which the creator God has pre-set for the human person, resulting in a 'pronounced competition between divine and human freedom'.[46] From the conception of a natural order which assigns a

---

[43] Hübenthal, *Grundlegung*, 368.
[44] Ibid.
[45] Anzenbacher, 'Menschenrechtsbegründung', 123.
[46] Hübenthal, *Grundlegung*, 92.

specific position to the human being, it is necessary to move on to categories that can express a relationship of love both from God and from humans.[47] Their possibility is owed to God's self-revelation in history in the person of Jesus, an event that could not have been anticipated by or assigned to the insights of reason. Thus, the boundary between philosophical and theological thinking needs to be respected, and the free response of humans to commit to faith in God becomes visible as a consciously chosen practical option for their lives. The deepest discontinuity to the classical medieval definition of the human being is that this essence is 'profoundly practical'. It is captured in the practical initiating act (*Tathandlung*) in Fichte's theory of subjectivity as a further development of Kant's concept of practical reason.[48] The inauguration of this type of thinking can be followed back to the Franciscan tradition, with Duns Scotus as the key late medieval author. Hübenthal has interpreted his conception of the hypostatic union of humanity and divinity in Jesus Christ, in which human nature is already individualized and assumed in its *haecceitas*, as the theological foundation of a secular world in its own right.[49] It originates in the recognition, in keeping with Chalcedon, of Jesus' humanity in his free and loving response to God, a union in which the *Logos* does not replace the human self with its nature and will, as in the monophysitic and monotheletic heresies. Both in relation to theology and to social ethics, the modern starting point of human freedom offers solutions to previous impasses, created by the substantial-anthropological terms of their ontology. The relationship between nature and grace can be re-envisaged in terms of freedom, once the pre-modern ontological framework has been 'dispatched for good'.[50]

The two possible paths that arise from this analysis for Christian social ethics will be explored in the concluding section on the tradition of Catholic Social Thought.

4. Catholic Social Thought

The alternatives outlined are relevant for the future directions of Catholic Social Thought as one tradition within Christian Social Ethics. *Either* the

---

[47] Cf. ibid. 92–3.
[48] Ibid., 369.
[49] Hübenthal, 'Ethische Begründung aus dem theologischen Grund des Säkularen. Eine katholische Sicht', in *Ökumenische Ethik*, ed. Thomas Weißer (Fribourg: Academic Press/Würzburg: Echter, 2018), 55–6.
[50] Hübenthal, *Grundlegung*, 369.

whole discipline conceives of itself as operating at the level of worldviews and religious traditions. Their consideration in civil society and state institutions is then based on the empirical weight of the number of adherents, the historical impact on culture, and the protection of freedom of religion and worldviews granted as a human right in the Universal Declaration of Human Rights, the European Convention, and by national constitutions. Dialogical or polemic engagement takes place at the level of conceptions of the human person and of the good between traditions in their particularity. *Or*, as the alternative possibility to Anzenbacher's proposal, it begins from a philosophical foundation, here the unconditional nature of morality, and argues for this truth claim at the universal level of reason, as distinct from the particular.[51] This would anchor principles and their specification at a universal level of validity.[52]

I shall begin with a portrayal of Catholic Social Thought considered as a particular tradition that achieves resonance in public discourse through the biblical narratives and symbols it can draw on (a). The second model to be discussed argues from a 'non-negotiable deontological framework'[53] to which particular traditions are related and from which their maxims or principles can be reconstructed (b). The connection made by the American moral theologian David Hollenbach between the 'common good' and 'human dignity' will serve as an example of how the classical and the modern concepts can be brought together (c).

(a) Catholic social thought as a social and a narrative tradition (Johan Verstraeten)

The Flemish theological ethicist Johan Verstraeten examines Catholic Social Thought as a coherent tradition that has been able to undergo transformations in responding to new challenges, drawing from submerged and rediscovered elements within itself as well as from other social and intellectual movements. It is both an identifiable tradition of thought and praxis, and a participant in

---

[51] Ibid.

[52] It is a separate question of theological method concerning schools of thinking in theology, and not a matter of doctrine whether a theological anthropology is developed from the general human faculty of reason or freedom which is presupposed by revelation, or whether God's Word, or God's trinitarian nature is taken as the starting point from which the human creature is reached as the addressee of the Christian message of redemption. A universal and a particular starting point are equally possible in systematic theology and Christian ethics.

[53] Ibid., 365.

public debate and partner in social action: 'Catholic social tradition comprises a particular set of shared understandings about the human person, social goods and their distributive arrangements ... grounded in a living relation to the constitutive narratives provided by the Bible, integrated in a theoretical framework which makes it possible for the Catholic understanding to remain open to rational explanation and public debate.'[54] Because of its link to a specific historical community, it is in a 'process of continuous reinterpretation': 'when the Catholic community with its ethos changes, this has immediate implications for the tradition itself.'[55] Thus, the major transformations that culminated in the Second Vatican Council were reflected in the turn of Catholic Social Thought from natural law to the freedom of the person, and to a heuristic method of 'scrutinizing the signs of the times and interpreting them in the light of the Gospel (*Gaudium et spes* 4).'[56] In the rediscovery of the Bible as a source of the church's renewed understanding of its mission, a potential for internal and external transformation has been opened up. For Verstraeten, the ensuing new 'appreciation of its narrative and metaphorical forms'[57] unlocks 'new vistas of human possibilities' in the 'eccentric elements' of the parables that in the hermeneutical philosopher Ricoeur's analysis lead to a 'tension between everyday life and the extravagant world of the narrative' in the New Testament. With metaphors as 'vehicles of transcendence and freedom', Verstraeten explores the sea change in perceiving reality that they bring about. As Ricoeur observes, 'root-metaphors ... in the context of a tradition can persist through time ... because they can invoke a whole network of meanings and metaphors'.[58] They make a difference for how one conceives of society. Verstraeten contrasts an 'aggregate of individuals' who 'try to calculate their self-interest, whereby a (mechanistic) invisible hand leads to the realization of the greatest good for the greatest number', with a society 'based on solidarity and an invisible handshake', as the symbols of 'covenant' and 'mystical body' suggest.[59] The true effect of Catholic Social Thought lies in its ability to generate motivation. It 'brings in a radicalisation and

[54] Johan Verstraeten, 'Re-Thinking Catholic Social Thought as Tradition', in *Catholic Social Thought – Twilight or Renaissance?*, ed. J.S. Boswell, F.P. McHugh and J. Verstraeten (Leuven: Peeters, 2000), 64.
[55] Ibid., 65.
[56] Ibid., cf. 65, 71.
[57] Ibid., 71.
[58] Ibid., 71–3.
[59] Ibid., 74.

dynamism which go beyond every attempt to base solidarity on some form of enlightened self-interest'.[60] By enriching the conceptual mode of rational classification with the rhetorical and poetic resonance of the biblical source retrieved by the Council, Verstraeten achieves a change of register that engages the believer's self-understanding beyond the cognitive realm. It reveals the power of symbols, for example, of the cross which can lead 'to an understanding of social reality and historical achievements from the perspective of the victims of history' and 'opens our eyes to the tragedies of history'.[61] It does so with much greater effect than the objectifying tendency of its natural law framework that has been prevalent for so long. Combined with an instructive-theoretical understanding of revelation issued to humans as recipients of supernatural truths, it left out the dimensions of imagination, existential self-understanding and will.

(b) Reconstructing the ethics of religious traditions from a deontological framework

The opportunities of the narrative approach for thoughtful, productive and transformative exchange between adherents of different worldviews are obvious. The drawback is that it requires the dimension of the 'good' to deliver the solutions, sometimes accompanied by a minimalist interpretation of the 'right' as a legal concept protecting negative freedom. Yet despite their name, conceptions of the 'good' can be built on a Hobbesian fear of the other, on self-centred visions of power, self-interested 'rational choice' and other anthropologies that undermine a shared space of mutual recognition. It is precisely for this reason that Hübenthal makes the case for a foundation with a stronger claim. Using Alan Gewirth's 'principle of generic consistency', an explication of Kant's principle of human dignity that forbids instrumentalization of one human being for the purposes of others, he wants to go beyond the procedural level and put forward substantive proposals. It is not sufficient, as Habermas's discourse ethics assumes, to merely justify the 'discursive procedure of examining' policy proposals, and not also their

---

[60] Ibid., 75.
[61] Ibid., 76. Quoting Klaus Demmer on how the scandal of the cross can lead to a deeper understanding of life 'under the conditions of a kenotic existence', Verstraeten asks how it would affect thinking about 'human dignity, social action, ... justice and the redistribution of wealth ... it makes it possible to acknowledge that society bears the face of its victims', thus 'understanding the preferential option for the poor ... from this perspective.'

'substantive normative contents'.[62] This means for Christian social ethics that its contribution to civic debate should not consist in 'faith contents that have been translated into secular concepts, but in a philosophically justified substantial morality'.[63] If this looks ambitious, it is also due to a pervasive reduction of standards in what current philosophical ethics aims for. One of the contributions that a Christian motivation can make is to challenge this lowering of benchmarks. The points he mentions resonate with Herta Nagl-Docekal's observation that in contemporary social philosophy, the moral experience of obligation which a person makes in her internal freedom is being replaced by a merely legal understanding of a reciprocity of rights. Hübenthal sees

> the real danger in that ultimate meaning and encompassing justice are only spoken of in a diminutive way. Once the consciousness of the unconditioned has disappeared in the human being, it will become utterly impossible to continue to put forward the idea of a categorical ought, of universal justice or definitive meaning. The current tide of ethics proposals that break down the semantics of morality to mere utility, contractual validity, formal coherence, conventional plausibility or basic system functionality has its deeper reason in an anthropological reductionism which only perceives the human person in the mesh of his conditions. Once the unconditioned gets lost, the good, the just, and the meaningful can only be had in miniature format and can be realized with corresponding ease.[64]

Taking Anzenbacher's formula, 'as much modern natural law as possible, as much classical as necessary', as an 'open-ended work assignment', implies for Hübenthal that the 'effort of synthetizing always has to be accomplished anew'.[65] An example of this can be seen in David Hollenbach's sustained endeavour to relate Catholic Social Teaching with appreciation and critique to contemporary philosophical discourses on justice and to international human rights instruments.

---

[62] Hübenthal, *Grundlegung*, 363.
[63] Ibid., 364.
[64] Hübenthal, 'Groß vom Menschen denken. Sozialethik als theologische Disziplin', in *Freiheit – Natur – Religion. Studien zur Sozialethik, Festschrift Arno Anzenbacher*, 390–1.
[65] Ibid., 378.

(c) Connecting human rights and dignity to a communicative 'common good' (David Hollenbach)

The endorsement of human dignity by the Second Vatican Council as 'discernible in the transcendent power of the human mind, in the dignity of conscience, and in the excellence of liberty'[66] as a 'prime manifestation of the likeness of humans to God'[67] is the theological starting point of Hollenbach's connection of the 'common good' to a 'community of freedom'[68] based on human rights. By interpreting them in terms of '(i)nstitutionalizing solidarity', he directs them towards the goal of the 'dialogic universalism' which the Council stood for: 'Human rights are the moral claims of all persons to be treated, by virtue of their humanity as participants in the shared life of the community … The protection of human rights is part of the common good, not an individualistic alternative to the common good.'[69]

This key term of classical natural law is thus determined as the event and the outcome of free cooperation: the common good 'is the good that comes into existence in a community of solidarity among active, equal agents' and 'is not extrinsic to the relationships that prevail among the members and sub-communities of a society'.[70] Its communicative understanding makes sure that everyone's input is requested into elaborating what can count as 'common good', and grounds it in civic discourse across communities. In comparison with liberal theories of justice, especially that of John Rawls, it specifies the need for empowerment and an encompassing vision of the public sphere in which these understandings are worked out in 'intellectual solidarity' and curiosity about other traditions:

> The rights to religious freedom, free speech, and association are thus primarily positive social empowerments rather than negative civil immunities from

---

[66] David Hollenbach, *The Common Good and Christian Ethics* (Cambridge: CUP, 2002), 151.

[67] Cf. Hollenbach, 'Human Dignity in Catholic Thought', in *Cambridge Handbook of Human Dignity*, 253. In this chapter, the change in the Catholic church's view of human rights and especially of religious freedom is explained and discussed for its reasons, as well as related to new challenges.

[68] Hollenbach, *The Common Good*, 228 and elsewhere. 'Persons can live in dignity only when they live in a community of freedom … in which both personal initiative and social solidarity are valued and embodied.'

[69] Ibid., 159.

[70] Ibid.,189. 'Dialogue, therefore, is both a means and an end, both an instrumental procedure and a substantive good … Knowledge of what these universal goods are will be the outcome of enquiry and dialogue.' (158, 153).

coercion ... Religious freedom enables believers and non-believers alike to enter into a community of discourse that seeks to discover the truth of how they should live together. Commitment to intellectual solidarity leads to quite a different view of religious freedom from one that tolerates religion as long as it remains a private matter within the individual's conscience or inside the sacristy.[71]

Hollenbach attributes it to the notion of the 'common good' as expanding the idea of human rights beyond the private sphere that Rawls's problematic distinction between 'public', 'non-public' and 'private' no longer makes sense: 'When human rights are linked with the common good in this way, the division of human life into quite distinct public and private domains is implicitly being challenged.'[72] His apt critique of this division which allocates universities, professional associations and religious traditions to the 'non-public' dimension, regains the whole domain of culture and public debate for interventions by citizens. What is called 'non-public' by Rawls, and figures as the 'background culture', for Hollenbach 'plays a formative role in shaping what is politically reasonable'.[73]

By reinterpreting the 'common good' in terms of active dialogue on matters of justice, Hollenbach succeeds in bridging two eras and intellectual frameworks, as Dietmar Mieth recognizes: 'In social ethics the common good (*bonum commune*) as the social interpretation of the personhood principle offers the possibility to demarcate the distance from utilitarianism (the greatest welfare of the greatest possible number) ..., and from the individualism of the "libertarians" ... To understand the "*bonum commune*" as a "community of rights" is both a philosophical and a theological achievement.'[74]

Hollenbach's ideal of a 'community of freedom' is equally demanding as Hübenthal's call to 'think highly of the human person', and he would probably agree to the latter's concluding reflection that

> Christian social ethics as a theological discipline should tenaciously persist in advancing a conception in which the human being is not thought of as lesser

---

[71] Ibid., 161.

[72] Ibid., 166.

[73] Ibid., 168.

[74] Mieth, 'Ethik, Moral und Religion', in Bobbert and Mieth, *Proprium der christlichen Ethik*, 120, with reference to Alan Gewirth, *The Community of Rights* (Chicago: University of Chicago Press, 1996), and to Hollenbach, 'Human Dignity in Catholic Thought', in *Cambridge Handbook of Human Dignity*, 250–9.

than she actually is. Only if these efforts are successful and the unconditioned within the human person is taken seriously again at least as a possibility of thought, only then will the Christian vision of universal justice not be met with an incapacity to understand.[75]

---

[75] Hübenthal, 'Groß vom Menschen denken', 391.

8

Autonomous ethics within a Christian faith perspective

Like Natural Law, the autonomy approach begins with the capacity of all human beings for moral reflection. Distinguishing between good and evil is possible on the basis of one's humanity; its source, practical reason, exists independently of any religious tradition. The first section deals with the claim that morality belongs to a person's internal experience of herself, and how this self-legislation becomes practical (1). Section 2 will investigate how principled autonomy, as developed in Kant's deontological approach, is qualified in key components and in its status by decisive factors from the Christian faith in salvation (2). The chapter will end with a comparison of revisionist natural law and autonomous ethics as theological choices (3), before the feminist use of each of the two approaches as well as care ethics are treated in Chapter 9.

1. Principled autonomy as a framework for theological ethics

Chapter 3 on conceptions of the normatively human and Chapter 5 on virtue ethics have already indicated the point where a deontological ethics finds an ethics of striving unsatisfactory. While both may argue for similar conduct for much of the time, it is in cases of conflict that their different orientations become clear. The aim of a flourishing life turns out not to be sufficient, and a move is required to a different conception that takes self-interested and antagonistic ideas of the good life into account. In cases of doubt, priority is not automatically due to one's own interests; recognizing the 'obligation' to respect and recognize the others in their equal rights makes the potential conflict visible. Human agency finds itself in the dilemma that striving for one's own good can be at the cost of others; it has to face the need for taking a moral stance towards one's own wishes as a matter of principle. The 'ought' experienced by the self disrupts the naïve assumption that the agent's desires are inherently beneficial for other persons' agency, pointing to an unwelcome need to consider whose interests are justified. Happiness is therefore no longer a goal connected directly with action, but becomes an issue for moral reflection. The structure of praxis is marked by an antinomy, perceived at first when discrepancies arise between what one ought to do and what one is inclined to do.

The morality analysed in deontological ethics is thus a fraught experience; yet it is inescapable since the obligation is not located in an external system of rules but a truth that is discovered within the self. Analysing the sense of 'ought' as an internal expression of practical reason will help distinguish the principled understanding of 'autonomy' from another current use: based on what can be empirically established, such as evidence of consciousness or rationality, it is taken to express goals of life like independence and self-determination (a). How the interior self-obligation captured in Kant's categorical imperative becomes practical in everyday life needs elucidation. His concept of 'maxims' that provides this bridge will be compared with Dietmar Mieth's reconfiguration of virtues as 'images of attitude'. For theological ethics, both in view of its interaction with philosophical ethics within the New Testament as well as in its history of reception, and of its contemporary engagement with limit questions in ethics and philosophy of religion, it is important to find out where the real differences between Aristotle and Kant are to be located (b).

(a) Moral experience and discernment

Different aspects of this experience will be illuminated and defined in order to avoid misinterpreting and confusing them with alternative positions: such as taking normative ethics as a collection of rules; Hegel's critique of the role of personal decision as individual arbitrariness; and the sliding of the idea of self-legislation into self-realization. The Christian ethicist Margaret Farley identifies five aspects in the experience of finding oneself faced with an ought:

> (1) It is an experience of a *claim* made upon us, a demand made of us. But (2) the claim itself is experienced as *addressed to our freedom* … we experience this kind of claim as one to which we can respond or not. (3) As a moral claim, it is experienced as, perceived as, *unconditional* … simply (though with reasons), 'I ought to do X.' … (4) In addition, the claim must at least appear to be *justifiable*, and hence legitimate … (5) Finally, a moral claim is experienced both as an *obligating demand* and a *liberating appeal* … even when a response to it appears as extremely difficult, it is nonetheless experienced not as an alien imposition but a way of being 'true to myself' … Yet … it appears as 'larger' than myself or my own desires. It demands something of me. It is a form of command and even a call.[1]

It is hardly possible to mistake this internal experience for a body of external regulations, as which it appears in some efforts to contrast a 'being'-centred virtue approach with a 'rule'- or 'act'-centred deontology. Farley highlights that the analysis of the five factors 'provides a glimpse into what is at stake in the moral life – the springs of motivation and action, the determination of what one will be as well as do, the meaning of one's life'.[2] The Irish theological ethicist Vincent MacNamara appealed to a similar readiness for personal reflection in his interpretation of the moral agent: 'To be able to see what is the moral call in a situation requires self-transcendence, a going beyond the immediate interests, likes and fears … People change not only the scene around them but change themselves by their acts. Acts remain with us in a sense … We bring a unity, control or consistency into our desires and traits.'[3]

Insisting on the need to distinguish between being 'moral' as in Kant and being 'ethical' as in Aristotle therefore does not have to lead to 'quandary

---

[1] Margaret Farley, 'A Framework for Moral Discernment', in *Catholic Theological Ethics, Past, Present, and Future: The Trento Conference*, ed. James Keenan (Maryknoll, NY: Orbis, 2011), 140.
[2] Ibid.
[3] MacNamara, *The Truth in Love*, 117, 125.

ethics', or to the return to judging disparate 'acts' without their intention nor a longer-term perspective on responsibility, as in neo-scholastic moral theology. The sequence between moral 'experience' and 'discernment' can alternate, indicating that a deductive reasoning from the principle to the case can be exchanged in other instances with an inductive, growing awareness of an issue being morally relevant: 'Sometimes an experience of moral obligation precedes and prompts moral discernment ... sometimes the experience of moral obligation does not come first but last in a search to understand what ought to be done or left undone, or what kind of person we ought to try to be.'[4]

But another misinterpretation has to be dealt with at the opposite end of the spectrum, for which the problem is not the alleged impersonal rule orientation, but on the contrary an excessive subjectivism. The fact that for Kant only the individual agent in her interior freedom can be the arbiter in her own exercise of the test of universalization was read by Hegel as reducing ethics to an individual standpoint. Nagl-Docekal sees his '(mis)interpretation' as 'paradigmatic' for the history of reception of Kant:

> Hegel's objection is that the only thing that matters is the 'I want to' (das 'Ich will') so that the distinction between good and evil ultimately becomes obsolete. This reading disregards that practical reason is the measure ... and that it is not at all compatible with any optional kind of action ... It is not the case that I can assume (denken) each of my subjective principles to be a general law. Kant states: 'One has to be able to want that a maxim of our action becomes a general law.' A will that wanted to elevate a particularist interest into a general law would be 'self-contradictory'.[5]

From critiques in the tradition of Hegel which play down the requirement of 'self-legislation' under the moral law, it is not far to a self-serving reading of self-determination that aims for living out one's authenticity. By replacing the notion of principled autonomy with personal choices, the maxim followed is that of 'self-love'. Having clarified that Kant's conception 'does not endorse puritanism or self-sufficiency or detachment from others', and despite some 'much-quoted passages where Kant depicts preferences (desires or inclinations) as in themselves morally suspect', the philosopher Onora O'Neill concludes that moral failure only 'arises where duty is subordinated

---

[4] Farley, 'Framework for Moral Discernment', 139.
[5] Nagl-Docekal, Innere Freiheit, 85, with reference to Groundwork of the Metaphysic of Morals, trans. and analysed H. J. Paton, 91.

to self-love'.[6] This is why it remains important to speak of 'self-legislation' and to be vigilant when self-determination slides from a moral to a flourishing life perspective. Nagl-Docekal points out the consequent shift: '"morality" would thus lose part of its binding character and would become meaningless ... Distancing oneself not only terminologically from Kant's conception of "autonomy as self-legislation" runs the danger that the theme of "morality" is increasingly replaced by a theory which accords priority to self-interest.' The Austrian philosopher adds that this view would require refuting Kant's position by way of argument, and not to merely to 'push it off into history by labelling it as "traditional"'.[7] The maxim of '"active, practical benevolence" (§ 28) towards others, '"whether or not he finds them lovable"' (§ 27) is meant by Kant 'as the most plausible philosophical interpretation of the Christian commandment to love'.[8]

There is every reason for theological ethics to uphold the moral experience of an ought, of a moral law discovered by practical reason. Margaret Farley mentions 'Kant's description of "awe" before the law as well as the transformation of the will' which may result from the different formulations of the categorical imperative. It is 'categorical' because it does not depend on a further objective that provides the condition for following it: 'The key to a distinctive understanding of "moral" obligation lies primarily in the unconditionality of the claim.'[9] Moral self-reflection on one's guiding maxim in a specific situation for action and the readiness for an honest response that endorses and actualizes the will, or first has to transform it, already indicate that a foundational role falls to the good will. The next issue to be investigated is how 'maxims' relate to the substantive content to be adjudicated, constituting the bridge between real life and the principled level of justification. The question is whether maxims as subjective guidelines can be compared to virtues as 'images of attitude', in a similar way as the faculty of judgement in Kant takes up the function of 'prudence' in virtue ethics.

---

[6] Onora O'Neill, *Bounds of Justice*, 48. She mentions that 'there are also passages where he insists that they are good' (ibid), apart from the 'endlessly studied passages at the end of chapter I and beginning of chapter II of the *Groundwork of the Metaphysics of Morals*' (47, n. 33). Nagl-Docekal discusses the same question in *Innere Freiheit*, 94–5.

[7] Nagl-Docekal, *Innere Freiheit*, 96.

[8] Ibid., 98. For the two quotes from the second part of the *Metaphysik der Sitten* (MS), § 27 and § 28, cf. Kant, *The Doctrine of Virtue. Part II of the Metaphysic of Morals*, trans. Mary J. Gregor, 118–19.

[9] Farley, 'Framework for Moral Discernment', 138, 141.

(b) 'Maxims' as subjective principles and virtues as images of attitude

Farley, MacNamara, Nagl-Docekal and O'Neill noted the sense of ought as a reality of inner freedom and explored its implications. The result was a nuanced assessment: the human striving for happiness is not discounted but 'moral self-legislation has to be given priority before the maxims of our quest for happiness ... Am I primarily interested in my own well-being, or do I ask first whether the maxim of my action can be universalized?' To consider one's own well-being to be sufficient, is 'morally evil' for Kant.[10]

The material on which this judgement is made are the 'maxims'. They translate into action, or fail to do so, what is demanded in the categorical imperative. Thus, they concretize the respect for the inherent dignity of each human being, as manifested both in the prohibition to instrumentalize and in the (imperfect) duty to promote the other's happiness. If a similarity can be found between Kant's 'maxims' and the 'images of attitude' as which Mieth reconceives virtues, the assumed alternative between them would have to be dismantled. One could then try to identify where the real difference between antique and modern ethics should be located.

For the philosopher Otfried Höffe, it is misleading to pitch Kant's principled approach against virtues in Aristotle. There are normative dimensions also in the Greek account of ethics, and Kant prizes virtue and expands on it. What is different, however, is their theory of action:

> Supposedly, Kant is the primary representative of a non-virtue ethic. In point of fact, however, ... he makes a distinction that allows him to intensify the concept of virtue even in terms of its normative aspect ... The model of virtue ethics in Aristotle is, indeed, not satisfied with simple proficiency (*habitus*) through repetitive action ... because Aristotle insisted that virtues are combined with free will and with choice or decision-making ... As Kant explains, they do not occur simply 'by means of oft-repeated actions' ... there are elements necessary for the concept of virtue in an ethic of the will that are absent in Aristotle's ethic of teleological striving. Because Kant defines moral

---

[10] Nagl-Docekal, *Innere Freiheit*, 94, with reference to Kant's definition of 'evil' in *Religion within the Limits of Reason Alone*, trans. Theodore M. Greene and Hoyt H. Hudson (New York: Harper Torchbooks, 1960), 31: 'But by virtue of an equally innocent natural predisposition he depends upon the incentives of his sensuous nature and adopts them also (in accordance with the subjective principle of self-love) into his maxim. If he took the latter into his maxim as *in themselves wholly adequate* to the determination of the will, without troubling himself about the moral law (which, after all, he does have in him), he would be morally evil.'

virtue by means of this more demanding element, he represents in fact an intensified concept of virtue in the moral sense ... 'the firm resolve in following one's duty' that has become a proficiency (*Fertigkeit*).[11]

Since Höffe emphasizes that in Kant, the moral demand of virtue is not based on natural striving, but on the will, he can call it an 'intensification': virtue is duty appropriated by the will on a consistent basis. For others, however, aligning virtue with duty, or worse, absorbing virtue into it, is a rupture with virtue ethics, and specifically an abandonment of virtue as 'being able to' (*Können*) to an 'ought' (*Sollen*). It is worth discussing why this should be seen as a reduction, rather than as moving virtue unmistakeably from mere 'habits' to the basis of human freedom. The most basic 'ability' then is the human endowment with 'good will'. It is a strength to be able to judge one's maxims and one's past conduct by recognizing the dimension of 'ought' as relevant for one's self-conception. The reason that Dietmar Mieth sees 'duty' as diminishing the core of virtue is because the element of practiced 'ability' seems to be taken away. Yet Kant's position could equally be seen as being more ambitious and more critical of the human propensity to assume the best regarding its own motivation, not recognizing the elements of self-interest that are mixed into one's ordinary motivation. Both Höffe and Mieth emphasize virtues as the basic attitudes that help concretize the moral orientation. Höffe identifies 'maxims' as the place where the moral self-determination of the will is converted into different areas of life. Mieth highlights the sense of competence of practiced virtues, and the role these 'images of attitude' can play for a preventative ethics that not only reacts to the most recent social and technological developments. For both, there is a need to seek mediations, transitions and concretizations between the level of principles, encompassed in the respect for human dignity, and the diverse areas of actualizing and institutionalizing it. Both theorists appreciate that virtues and maxims provide a context sensitivity, flexibility, visibility and attraction of models which principles require in order to become relevant in ordinary conflicts. For Mieth, 'norms' are almost technical and at the level of pragmatic rules. As a theologian, he is interested in the link between anthropology and ethics that a Christian position spells out in its premises. The 'images of attitude' – such as hope against anxiety about the future, or generosity against insistence on private rights – fit what Ricoeur has called

---

[11] Höffe, *Can Virtue Make Us Happy?*, 262.

the 'enunciative' authority of a tradition.[12] It is an active response to offer alternative orientations to prevalent value trends and to do so at the level of basic orientations towards life, rather than at the 'casuistic' case-by-case level of applied ethics. Instead of being co-opted into an already fixed definition of a problem as seen from the angle of existing institutions, Mieth recommends beginning with the 'attitude' side. It can contribute creative ways of dealing with the discrepancy experienced between key needs and the delivery by established agencies. One key advantage of starting with the felt need, rather than allowing the relevant institutions to define the agenda, is that people's own capacities for detecting and solving problems are engaged. The 'heuristic' capacity nourished by stories and models of a flourishing life, as part of the cultural, religious and literary heritage, is a source of problem-spotting and of resistance against superficial solutions that in fact only prolong failing forms of life.

It is an insight that captures many of the points of dissatisfaction expressed against an ethics of principle, especially among Christian ethicists who fear that fields are being left unploughed that could bring a rich harvest of practiced, biblically inspired attitudes. With Höffe, however, it becomes clear that both are compatible and that Kant's inclusion of virtue into his will-based approach to ethics can be seen as an 'intensification'. The conflict in principle arises elsewhere, namely in the theory of action where Kant insists on an ethic of the will that leaves behind natural teleologies, reconstructing ethics in terms of freedom. What Vincent MacNamara observes can be accepted by both ethical systems: We 'do not really come afresh to each decision. We will see and judge as we are. It is not precisely the moment of choice that is the decisive one but all the moments that have gone into making it likely that this is how we would see and choose.'[13] There is no reason to see a principled approach as being at odds with the factor of time and the chance to reconsider judgements. Margaret Farley points out that evidences can change, that a conclusion, for example, on a war meeting the conditions of a just war, may no longer be 'able to be justified . . . and the experience of moral obligation evaporates'.[14] Nagl-Docekal outlines that the stock of one's maxims may turn out to be insufficient in concrete situations

---

[12] Ricoeur, 'The Paradox of Authority' (1996), in *Reflections on the Just*, trans. David Pellauer (Chicago: University of Chicago Press, 2007), 94, with reference to Gérard Leclerc, *Histoire de l'autorité. L'assignation des énoncés culturels et de la généalogie de la croyance* (Paris: Presses universitaires de France, 1986).

[13] MacNamara, *The Truth in Love*, 117.

[14] Farley, 'Framework for Moral Discernment', 140.

that pose new requirements; they may have to be revised or given up, if 'my existing conviction on them being generalizable now appears untenable to me'; Kantian morality is not a matter of one-off decisions but includes 'the obligation to be open to an ongoing moral sensitization'.[15]

A maxim a person could choose, as mentioned in Chapter 3, could be not to do anything that endangers her health, putting the needs of others unequivocally in the second position.[16] It is equally possible to aim for practising a different general orientation during one's lifetime, 'to make it one's purpose to contribute to the happiness of others'.[17] As Nagl-Docekal explains Kant's reflections on this point, this maxim requires 'a culture of listening' in order not to impose one's own conception on others.[18]

What Kant's 'intensification' provides for virtue is the will to aim beyond socially established boundaries and the limits imposed by finitude. Having spoken before of the 'liberating' appeal of moral obligation, Farley highlights this dimension:

> every choice is a choice of an action of our own. Our choices can affect our future actions, but they do so through actions in the present – such as commitment, resolution, promise making, planning, preparing. And we do sometimes choose actions that appear impossible for us, but we do so by choosing to 'try' to do them – if 'trying' seems possible even though we expect ultimately to fail.[19]

The human ability to aim for something impossible illustrates the 'unconditionality' of the moral intention despite the agent's finitude and the limitations of her scope of action. This orientation of the will beyond what is likely to be achievable could not have been conceived of in the thought form of a natural teleology where the aims and purposes of life are already given, instead of the agent being able to posit them. The autonomy approach in Christian ethics endorses the Kantian move to a distinct level of justification beyond the framework of anthropological givens, as will become evident in the five factors with which it qualifies Kant's ethics of ought.

---

[15] Nagl-Docekal, *Innere Freiheit*, 83–84, with reference to Kant, MS, 532. *The Doctrine of Virtue*, trans. M. Gregor, 60–1.
[16] Nagl-Docekal, *Innere Freiheit*, 81. It also signifies that 'I have relinquished control over the law of my action insofar as from then onwards, I am pre-assigned to doing whatever serves my health' (80).
[17] Ibid., 99, with reference to Kant, *The Doctrine of Virtue*, trans. M. Gregor, 117: 'The duty of love for one's neighbour can also be expressed as the duty of making others' *ends* my own (insofar as these ends are only not immoral)'.
[18] Nagl-Docekal, *Innere Freiheit*, 99.
[19] Farley, 'Framework for Moral Discernment', 142.

2. Factors from the Christian faith perspective qualifying the autonomy approach

Before specifying the modifications from a Christian faith perspective, it is worth outlining how 'autonomy' has been defined by the first and by the subsequent generations of this approach. Alfons Auer, its founder in German-speaking Catholic theological ethics, named as core contents of 'autonomy' the 'authenticity of the ethical (*sittlich*) sphere, the competence (*Zuständigkeit*) of reason for knowing it, and the unconditionality of its claim'.[20] In a 'Postscript' that deals with the objections raised in debates since the publication of the first edition in 1971, Auer explains three aspects: the 'ethical thesis' based on the 'conviction that a truth or reasonableness is inherent in reality . . . which can be known, stated and communicated at least to the extent as it is unrenounceable for human agency'.[21] Secondly, the 'theological thesis . . . sets the Christian message into a new horizon of meaning', a 'new determination by Jesus Christ'. Thirdly, the thesis relating to the magisterium gives it a role in the task of offering an 'integrating, criticising and stimulating effect . . . to the formation of ethical consciousness'.[22] The theological legitimacy of building on a general human capacity for morality is derived from Paul's reference to the 'law written on the hearts' of the Gentiles (Rom. 2.15), from patristic theologians and from Thomas Aquinas. While Auer refers primarily to the role of reason in interpreting the independent reality of the world, he regards the moral autonomy expounded by Kant as compatible with a theological position inspired by Thomas Aquinas. Quoting the philosopher Johannes Schwartländer, he excepts Kant's argumentation from the 'radical immanentistic claim of autonomy' of the later nineteenth century because of its 'openness to transcendence'.[23] Auer highlights the early reception of Kant by Catholic ethicists like Sebastian Mutschelle (1749–1800) and Franz Xaver Linsenmann (1835–1898), having written his doctoral thesis on his work which already at that time included secular sciences into the method of reaching judgements in

---

[20] Alfons Auer, *Autonome Moral und christlicher Glaube*, repr. of 2nd edn. 1984, with a Postscript of 1984 and an introductory essay by D. Mieth (Darmstadt: WBG, 2016), 211.
[21] Ibid., 212.
[22] Ibid., 213.
[23] Ibid., 220–1.

moral theology. Friedrich von Hügel is also mentioned as a precursor of the modern Christian autonomy tradition. But only the second and third generations of the School relate the term 'autonomy' to 'the ethical subject as the bearer of his actions', denoting 'self-obligation (*auto-nomos*) in freedom'.[24]

The independence of moral decision-making and its source in human freedom have a long history of recognition as theologically appropriate, offering a shared platform with philosophical ethics. Yet there are specific factors provided by the Christian faith context that shape and modify ethical understanding and practice. The first one highlighted is the ability of the Christian faith to provide integration (a). Its message offers a heuristics and critique (b), and supplies a horizon of meaning (c) which motivates praxis (d). Finally, it effects a relativization of morality through the message of salvation which also leads to a different view of moral failure (e).[25]

(a) Integration

For Auer, 'integration' is the most encompassing title for what a Christian specification adds to an autonomous morality that has its own justification in human reason and freedom. Having compared two other models, one by the Flemish theologian Edward Schillebeeckx, the other by the German moral theologian at the Gregorian University, Josef Fuchs, 'interpretation', and 'intention' respectively, he sees 'integration' as more encompassing.[26] There is a theological and a methodological reason for making 'integration' the first function exercised by the Christian horizon. Auer adds it to the two functions initially developed by the Dutch theologians Gerard Th. Rothuizen and Theo Beemer, 'critique' or 'correction', and 'stimulation' or 'motivation'. He clarifies that the perspective from which integration is undertaken is Christological: 'Christ is relevant as the salvation of the world and not only as the model of a new ethics of fellow-humanness (*Mitmenschlichkeit*)'.[27] The methodological need arises from the three-stage enquiry he proposes: analysing reality with the help of the human sciences, relating the results to a philosophical anthropology, and finding the appropriate ethical norms. Since disciplines with different methods are being drawn in, an overarching

---

[24] Mieth, *Moral und Erfahrung*, vol. II, 243. For an account and comparison of this school to other approaches, cf. V. MacNamara, *Faith and Ethics*, 37–55, and for its critique by 'faith ethics' (*Glaubensethik*), 55–66.
[25] Mieth, 'Ethik, Moral und Religion', in Bobbert and Mieth, *Proprium der christlichen Ethik*, 118.
[26] Auer, *Autonome Moral*, 173–81.
[27] Ibid., 189, n. 114.

perspective is needed in which the findings can be brought together. This theological framework, however, has to recognize the equal standing of the doctrine of creation and not absorb it into a 'Christomonism'.[28]

The consistently interdisciplinary layout of theological ethics promoted by Auer has led to a growing realization in dialogue with the individual sciences and philosophy that different normativities have to be brought together in a succinctly elaborated framework. For Auer, the individual sciences, social theory, philosophical anthropology and ethics can acquire coherence through interpretation in the light of the human hope for ultimate meaning. Here, the theological horizon of autonomous ethics is uniquely relevant in offering its interpretation of life to a question which is generally human.

What has accelerated in the decades since the first publication in 1971 is the dynamic with which different segments of life have changed together with the parameters of economic and political systems. The limits between workplace and private life have been under erosion by digitization; the protection of individuals by public institutions offering provision of healthcare, pension rights and benefits has been affected by globalization. The different roles individual agents have to service at the same time lead to new questions of self-interpretation. These transformations are being analysed by sciences like sociology, economics and psychology. But it is a problem that is equally faced by a philosophy which takes selfhood seriously. Dieter Henrich has pointed out that in view of the multiplicity of self-descriptions persons can give of themselves, individual answers to each of them 'at the first level, in relation to only one layer of self-description', miss the point. The 'explosive force of the question arises from the fact that it aims at a synthesis'.[29] It is the unity of the self without which there is no agency that is at stake here, and for which also the other four faith-related factors further specified since the original formulation of the approach are relevant.

(b) A critical heuristics

The second element revolves around the capacity for detection that narratives and symbols specific to religions and worldviews provide. The Christian trust in the goodness of creation, its openness to analysis by reason and to moral endeavour enables not only a critique of actions, elements and

---

[28] Ibid., e.g., 182, 184.
[29] Henrich, 'What is metaphysics – what modernity?', 296–7.

structures that counteract God's original intention for humanity; it also sensitizes and allows to spot issues for moral enquiry. The Christian faith provides a context of discovery also for what is not already apparent as a negative direction. Such 'motivating reasons from faith or from a Christian contrast experience' when encountering the suffering of people 'through which a moral issue is first of all perceived and formulated'[30] can arise, for example, from the stories and metaphors of the Bible. The ecological crisis can be understood as humans failing in their role of stewardship for the earth and of responsibility for each other. A current example emerging in the new context of discussion of the permissibility of genetic enhancement is the contrast between a religious appreciation of life and nature as gifts, and not as property or as results of human construction. This affects the sense of what should be legally permissible, for example whether the protection of patent law should be reserved for inventions, and not be extended to what remain discoveries, including natural sequences of genes. The monotheistic concept of a creator in its distinction from a neo-Platonic concept of emergence from God insists on the freedom of the creature which is not tied to the source of his or her being. Parents enhancing or editing their future children's genes would depart from the intended symmetry between the generations by installing their own preferences ineradicably into their somatic make-up.[31] The equal status of every human being as having been created by God and in the image of God has an obvious heuristic significance for the protection of the dignity and the rights of all humans.

(c) Horizon of meaning

The new horizon consists in the 'promised absolute future that stands behind all historical future' and in 'responding in the concrete ways of being in the world to the call of the creator heard in faith, . . . following Christ, moved by the Holy Spirit'.[32] By distinguishing the question of meaning from the question of why to be moral, and leaving it to practical reason to identify and justify what is right, Auer is in agreement with the separate roles of reason

---

[30] Mieth, 'Moralische Autonomie – Selbstbestimmung und Selbstverpflichtung nach Alfons Auer', in Auer, *Autonome Moral*, repr. 2016, vii.

[31] Habermas has commented on the ability of a faith perspective to see it as problematic when parents intrude and fail to respect what belongs to the child's free otherness. 'This creatural nature of the image expresses an intuition which in the present context may even speak to those who are tone-deaf to religious connotations.' Cf. *The Future of Human Nature*, trans. Hella Beister, Max Pensky, Walter Rehg (Cambridge: Polity Press, 2002), 114–15.

[32] Auer, *Autonome Moral*, 177.

and faith that Kant elaborated in the antinomies of practical reason. There are two points to be noted in this connection, even if Auer does not discuss them since his focus is on the autonomy of ethics in relation to reality, not to the moral agent: (1) The limits of human capability are not the limits of ethics. As Margaret Farley analysed in the experience of moral obligation, individuals 'try', even if they may reasonably expect to fail. It is decisive also for philosophical ethics not to understate the unconditional outreach of morality. The alternative would be a pragmatic calculation of probable success, an advance reduction to what is seen as feasible, thus curbing reason in its orientation towards the unconditioned. For theology, the trust that at the limits of human powers, God's promise still holds, defines its horizon of meaning.[33]

Worth noting is also that Kant's concept of happiness is not measured and rationally curtailed, but is 'unbounded and precisely not rationally limited' (*überschwänglich, gerade nicht rational gebändigt*).[34] It requires the postulate of God as the creator of a universe that is open to moral effort. Without such hope in meaning, in the face of unrequited and failing acts of kindness, the alternative would be a realm of desperation for which Kant already uses the term 'absurd'. The antinomies of moral praxis show that 'the concepts of "self-determination" and "happiness" point to the centre of a field of tension in which the question of meaning of human life becomes acute. (For Kant, this tension can only be resolved in the mode of religion. This is the conceptual focus of his account of practical reason)'.[35] The ground of justification of obligation to the other and to oneself is not God, it is the unconditional character of human freedom; yet the realization of this calling leads to the hope in a God who stands in where even the best human intentions fail.

(d) Motivation

It is because the fear of moral action ending in defeat and absurdity is overcome that Christians are motivated to engage also in apparently hopeless cases. Auer is critical of attempts to see the only difference between Christian and autonomous action in its motivation, leaving out what makes it possible, namely faith in God as the foundation of this hope. From that basis, however,

---

[33] Cf. Pröpper, 'Autonomie und Solidarität. Begründungsprobleme sozialethischer Verpflichtung', in *Evangelium und freie Vernunft* (Freiburg: Herder, 2001), 57–71.

[34] Nagl-Docekal, *Innere Freiheit*, 93.

[35] Ibid., 94.

he stresses the high ethical character of the New Testament demands with their immediate appeal to the followers of Jesus. This intensification stands in contrast to the fifth qualifying feature which completes the reflection of the Auer School on what is genuinely Christian in relation to an ethics of autonomy.

(e) Relativization

The concluding point consists in the theological assertion that the 'ought' explored so far by philosophical and theological authors is not the final truth about human agency. The human quest for salvation is distinct from and more encompassing than morality. What may look like a U-turn – from the previous insistence on exceptional demands like loving one's enemy, to putting restrictions on unconditionality – can more adequately be understood as a change of register. Believing that the ultimate designation of humans in their quest for meaning, healing and reconciliation is a God of salvation, allows for a hopeful distance from the capability for moral judgement. The Christian manner of dealing with morality is to accord it a penultimate rank. It sounds antithetical to what has been prized before, namely the foundation of human dignity on the capability for morality, for prioritizing the needs of the other over one's own entitlements. Yet this change of vantage point is taken for the sake of human agency:

> Faith in justification means that the human person knows herself to be liberated from the necessity of guaranteeing the ultimate justification of her existence (the *absolute* affirmation and the validity of her unconditional permission to be) by herself ... a dynamic that essentially overtaxes the human being and perverts also her moral action into a means of an intrepid, but ultimately unsuccessful attempt to certify herself (*Selbstvergewisserung*). By unburdening ethical agency from the problematics of meaning of our contingent existence, faith *limits* the claims of ethics. However, and this is decisive: it does so *for the benefit* of ethics.[36]

Mieth makes a similar point on the need to be attentive to the 'contingency of the claim to moral totality', 'since otherwise morality would become a religion, and that would overtax it completely. It remains a fact that the religious question about rescue and justification leads beyond moral

---

[36] Pröpper, *Evangelium und freie Vernunft*, 69.

questions.'[37] Thus, religion relieves morality of the risk of being made into a tool of securing identity. Morality cannot offer a solution to the question of meaning, of whether existence in its fragmentation can be made whole.

A final relativization of morality that changes the logic of action is that a person does not have to be 'worthy of happiness' to qualify for God's attention.[38] A faith position can assume this to be the case. Morality does not have to justify the self; instead, it is a response, by corresponding to God's love, to God's prior acceptance. This change of vantage point is something that 'ethics in its secular discourses could benefit from … not only preventively in view of human fallibility but also consecutively in view of failure and foundering.'[39] The claims of morality have to be limited, from the perspective of the Christian faith, so that agency can be liberated.

3. A comparison of revisionist natural law to autonomous ethics

How do the two approaches that are built on the general human capacity to distinguish between good and evil and promote a universalist claim to 'all people of good will' – autonomous ethics and revisionist natural law – compare in their philosophical foundations and in the space they give to Christian specificity? After mapping the elements they share (a), I will examine their differences (b).

(a) Shared positions between revisionist natural law and autonomous ethics

The points of dissatisfaction with classical natural law that called for revision were owed to changes of self-conception in the modern era. The need to reinterpret the universalist orientation to human nature in a historically conscious way, the reconfiguration of a Neo-Thomist concept of church into

---

[37] Mieth, *Moral und Erfahrung*, vol. II, 26.
[38] Pröpper, *Theologische Anthropologie*, vol. 2 (Freiburg: Herder, 2011), 678: 'The significance of grace is not primarily, much less, exclusively, to be explained in relation to the fact of sin, but by going back to the human basic constitution, by being attentive also to the neediness, the hopes and anxieties that are … founded on the antinomic constitution of human freedom in being both unconditioned and conditioned'.
[39] Mieth, 'Ethik, Moral und Religion', in Bobbert and Mieth, *Proprium der christlichen Ethik*, 118.

a role of service and collaboration of the national or local churches with other forces in civil society, and a new appreciation of the biblical sources after Vatican Two are corrections relevant for both approaches. It is remarkable what insights they share: an inductive route to establishing norms through the reflection of reason (both philosophical and in its social scientific applications) on experience; highlighting the role of freedom; understanding identity as a gift which becomes the basis of the capability of acting morally; spelling out the heuristic and motivational power of the Christian vision, as well as questioning the status and the way of dealing with morality.

Thus, the interpretive task of reason is underlined by natural law ethicist Richard Gula: 'The given physical and biological orders do not dictate moral obligations; rather, they provide the data and the possibilities for the human person to use in order to achieve human goals.'[40] Lisa Cahill understands Christian praxis as founded in the new identity that is freely bestowed by Jesus Christ and in the solidarity of the community. What the autonomy approach listed as the heuristic and the motivating power of the Christian context reappears in the functions distinguished by Richard McCormick in the Christian contribution to medical ethics: 'protective', 'dispositive' and 'directive' in forming ethical consciousness. Cahill spells them out in her analysis of his position: 'In a technologically advanced culture, … the Christian tradition can protect against a tendency to view persons functionally, by sensitizing the agent to human dignity not contingent on social worth or function.' 'Disposition' relates to love in following Christ which has a bearing on how the principles of beneficence, autonomy and justice are interpreted: 'Christian faith disposes the moral agent to exhibit charity or self-gift in action.'[41] Also the relativizing effect of Christ's antecedent love on the standing of value systems is articulated: 'The meaning of gospel commitment for the natural law system consists in "a profound relativizing of basic human values." They are to be pursued in interpersonal life as the meaning of neighbor-love but are always to be envisioned as subordinate to Christ's love for us.'[42]

At the same time, the framework of natural law is deemed revisable, governed by the philosophical concept of human flourishing from which the level of obligation is rarely distinguished.

---

[40] Gula, 'Natural Law today', 374.
[41] Cahill, 'On Richard McCormick', 88–9.
[42] Ibid., 89.

(b) Differences

(1) Philosophical foundations

Even if the significance of freedom is emphasized, for example by Charles Curran as the origin of values, and found in the call of conscience, also against ecclesial instructions, it is not the foundation of the system. A teleology of the goals and purposes of life still supplies the basis, for example, of many argumentations in applied ethics. In autonomous ethics, the principle of human dignity as the source of rights prohibits instrumentalizing anyone since each individual is an 'end in herself'. The question is whether natural law even in its revised form possesses the necessary categories to secure each individual as a limit against violations by others. The Catholic critique of negative rights as insufficient due to its insistence on the social and political nature of the human being becomes ambiguous in cases where only the unequivocal categories of undisposability (*Unverfügbarkeit*) and non-instrumentalizability of each individual offer the principled protection that is required. Vincent MacNamara warns against building consequentialist instead of deontological argumentations into a Christian ethic of love. Otherwise it would be less capable than secular ethics to protect persons adequately.[43]

Also for a revisionist, historically conscious ethics of the flourishing life, additional categories and approaches are needed. Without a theory of subjectivity, the level of philosophical ethics reached since Kierkegaard is not achieved. When the internal constitution of freedom in its duality of finitude and infinity is analysed, it becomes possible to see faith in the creator God as an answer to the question of facticity. A different understanding of sin, based on two distinct types of despair,[44] could inform ethics; the objectivizing concept of classical natural law of acts as 'intrinsically evil' could be replaced for good by a nuanced analysis of the human self in its dual capacity for good and evil, and 'flourishing' could finally be linked to the ability to become a self.

---

[43] Cf. MacNamara, *Faith and Ethics*, 159–60.
[44] For a discussion of their difference and of the question of their prevalence in male and female existences, cf. Valerie Saiving Goldstein, 'The Human Situation: A Feminine View', in *Journal of Religion* 40 (1960) 100–12, and William Cahoy, 'One Species or Two?' in *Modern Theology* 11 (1995), 429–54.

(2) Christian specificity

The revisionist opening of classical natural law to modernity includes a new turn to the Bible; yet there were doubts, as quoted in Chapter 7, whether this framework can accommodate essential contents from the New Testament. Lisa Cahill asked if natural law is 'adequate as a Christian biblical ethics . . . does it do justice to the example and teaching of Jesus, with its radical demands for love and self-sacrifice?'[45] The observation that moral conclusions are drawn on the basis of a philosophical argumentation is also true of the autonomous morality approach. McCormick's claim quoted by Lisa Cahill 'that "the Christian story" has a fundamental and formative function in shaping moral vision' is shared by both approaches. Yet the assumption already in the philosophical foundation of natural teleology that God exists, not only in the classical medieval version but also by revisionist authors, is an internal reason for the reduced relevance of the Bible. Autonomous ethics, in contrast, is acutely aware that the existence of a morally sensitive creator God would be the necessary condition for humans to be able to do the good without desperation. But practical reason can only postulate such a God. The reality of this anchor of a moral world order would need another source to support this belief as reasonable, namely a historical testimony to God and God's loving relationship to humanity. This gives the Bible and the person of Jesus a different standing that cannot be bypassed by assuming too much in the philosophical premises. How ethical self-understandings and moral visions are shaped also by biblical symbols and narratives, would then need to be elucidated with the resources of hermeneutical and literary theories. This route has been taken by Dietmar Mieth, Johan Verstraeten, Hille Haker and others in Europe and in the United States, often by drawing on Paul Ricoeur as a conversation partner for theological ethics.

---

[45] Cahill, 'On Richard McCormick', 83.

9

Feminist theological ethics

Having had to listen for so long, not only in classical natural law, to pronouncements on 'man', also in distinctly women-specific matters, the development of feminist Christian ethics has finally given women a chance to speak for themselves. This will become evident in the methods and the perspectives taken on both gender-related and general human questions. From the wide array of modern and postmodern approaches, three will be discussed: feminist elaborations of revisionist natural law (1); the care versus justice debate (2); and autonomy-based feminist moral philosophy and theology (3).

1. Feminist ethics from a revisionist natural law approach

In her study of feminism and natural law ethics, with the programmatic subtitle, 'The End of the Anathemas', Cristina Traina argues that judged by its own standards, natural law will remain one-sided and deficient as long as it excludes female experiences of being human from the material to be considered in its analyses of human nature.[1] The strengths of this approach,

---

[1] Traina, *Feminist Ethics and Natural Law*, for example, 1, 12.

taking embodiment seriously in linking justice to the human natural constitution, and using research to effect change, make it a counter-position to social constructivism and to the ideal of value-free science (a). It demands a differentiated treatment of gendered humanity in Christian ethics, requiring it to consider multiple perspectives. It thus stretches revisionist natural law with its awareness of different historical interpretations of 'nature' to check and expand its account, instead of taking male experiences as standard. At the same time, the theological questions already raised in Chapter 7 towards natural law in general will return, and will be specified regarding its elaboration in feminism (b).

(a) Positioning the approach against alternatives in feminism

While Cristina Traina admits that in view of the essentialist and denigrating statements of Aristotle and Thomas on women, natural law seems to be an 'unlikely ally' for feminism,[2] it offers an intellectual framework for spelling out the embodied constitution of humans. A theory of justice requires a link to human nature in order to justify which aspects of human life need to be protected and catered for by the community. The opposite view is taken by deconstructivist feminism. It critiques not only the effective social constructions of gender and role fixations but, more radically, holds that also the biological duality of sex is to be traced back to the forces that construct social reality. The consequence that 'sex goes the way of gender' has to be resisted, in Traina's view, while agreeing with Butler's finding that 'the body is a political construct' and that 'the category "woman"' is defined by 'people who fulfill not only biological criteria but ideological expectations'. Yet the critical need to 'ask continually what ideological assumptions "woman" binds up and whom it excludes'[3] does not turn the body into a complete site of construction; it still requires an analysis of the given elements of human existence, well aware of the fact that these cannot be had without interpretation: 'Sex differences will persist' and are 'always susceptible to an oppressive interpretation. Feminism must uproot oppression by

---

[2] Ibid., 11.
[3] Ibid., 4.

destroying oppressive interpretations of difference while leaving difference itself intact.'[4]

For the necessary 'political change' to occur, it is mandatory to be able to identify rights that can be justified. In view of the disproportionate suffering of women, the call is to create 'solidarity behind strong, positive, "universally shareable" rights claims'. In turn, 'to back up these claims we need an anthropology, a normative description of embodied human life.'[5] On the one hand, Traina is concerned that the position Judith Butler put forward in *Gender Trouble* (1990) and *Bodies That Matter* (1993) risked undermining the struggle for tangible improvements in the lives of women. On the other hand, objectivist statements about natural givens ignore the interpretive element which also cannot be dispatched in a monological way but must strive to take in the variety of lived and interpreted experiences. A complex task has to be delivered: 'the continuing existence of feminism depends on finding some third path that balances the need for universal claims against the need to attend to a genuine pluralism of experience and that takes the limits and possibility of a telic "nature" seriously but not deterministically.'[6]

To do justice to this variety, a 'procedure' is identified that takes the long road through widespread as well as marginal experiences: since 'without broad participation in moral discussion the parameters, methods and conclusions ... may be biased ..., the success of natural law *method* is best protected when there is a *procedure* for including the viewpoints of all, especially those normally underrepresented.'[7] She sees this path as the only

---

[4] Ibid., 311. Traina criticizes biological difference being dissolved and attributed to the power of discourse, but neither does she absolutize 'difference', as Luce Irigaray does. Saskia Wendel contrasts and critiques the positions of both Butler and Irigaray and concludes: 'While both subjectivity and sexual identity are always also conditioned discursively, they are in no way completely generated by discourse. That and how this is the case is not reflected in Butler's radical constructivism.' *Affektiv und inkarniert. Ansätze deutscher Mystik als subjekttheoretische Herausforderung* (Regensburg: Pustet, 2002), 88.

[5] Traina, *Feminist Ethics and Natural Law*, 6.

[6] Ibid., 7. The problem is that the 'universal claims' have taken the shape of essentialism in classical natural law. Susan Ross clarifies how this has been at the expense of women's agency: 'Women possess a unique human nature both distinct from and completing male human nature. Such thinking about gender differences is *essentialism*: that is, there is an essential quality to being male or female that is God-given and unchangeable ... When women are understood primarily as those who "listen" and who "wait", women's agency is lost. Women are, in effect, less than fully and normatively human when their capacity to define themselves is not affirmed and encouraged.' Susan Ross, 'Christian Anthropology and Gender Essentialism: Classicism and Historical-mindedness', in *A Time for Change? Open Questions, Concilium* 42, ed. Erik Borgman, Maureen Junker-Kenny, and Janet Martin Soskice (London: SCM, 2006), 45, 46–7.

[7] Traina, *Feminist Ethics and Natural Law*, 300.

viable alternative to three other theoretical 'alternatives to deconstructionism'. One extols nature as 'earth mother' in a 'biological determinism that identifies femininity with maternity'; another, 'liberal feminism', is credited with its political success: 'without its confidence in a common, transcendent human nature, feminist arguments for the equal dignity and common humanity of men and women might never have gained political currency. But it is only a short step from the liberal disjunction of fact and nature from culture and value to Butler's claims about the cultural construction of "nature".'[8] Against this separation, in Traina's analysis, a normative concept of nature is needed. Her critique of the third approach, 'inductive universalism', is especially perceptive. It explains why the search for an 'overlapping consensus' remains at the level of conventions and common sense which is below the level of a moral judgement presumed in political efforts of liberation. Two aspects can be distinguished in her critique of a 'consensus' consisting in an area of overlap of otherwise diverse segments. One is the lack of agreement on reasons in a procedure where elements of the ethos of different cultures – which can be partially oppressive – are averaged out or set at the minimal agreed level: 'A consensus is merely an uncritical intersection of myriad moralities ... oppressive patriarchal values infect cultures virtually universally ... Inductive universalism tells us only that the dominant classes in cultures worldwide concur, not why they do and whether their ethics are just.'[9] The second aspect is the 'two-dimensional' nature of a consensus observed from above, giving access to a surface view, as to a square measurement of its extension. In the opening pages she had already outlined a different aim for research: Instead of the image of a 'Venn diagram: two intersecting circles', the awareness of one's 'standpoint' needs to be included, in order to gain 'three dimensions rather than two. The slightest difference in experience produces a complete reorientation of perspective. Because we now see our "common" elements from entirely different angles each of us arrays and interprets them differently.'[10] Only by moving to the participants' perspective, can the real pluralism be made visible.

The task set for an inductive process of determining nature and flourishing is to engage in a wide-ranging collection of distinct experiences that preclude a premature, unvetted determination of female nature. Backed

---

[8] Ibid., 7.
[9] Ibid., 9. 10. The authors she names as endorsing this concept which was put forward by John Rawls in *Political Liberalism* are Robert M. Adams and John Reeder. Her critique of the lack of a shared basis is similar to Habermas's deontological critique of his fellow Neo-Kantian Rawls.
[10] Ibid., 3.

by a hermeneutics of lived experiences, it is also a counter-proposal to the concept of 'objectivity' espoused by scientism. No shortcut is available and it is not possible to define human nature single-handedly; after casting the net wide to capture relevant data, the community of researchers has to argue out the different positions with reasons.[11]

(b) Questions to theory decisions also in feminist natural law

It is remarkable how Traina succeeds in expanding the neo-Thomist reasoning of natural law that has left deep traces in the memory of the faithful on the standards they were held to, and why. Her feminist revision deepens and diversifies the concept of experience so that it can encompass the variety of gendered humanity in Christian anthropology and new, ideology-critical norms in ethics. Feminist ethics addressed the lack of 'awareness that theological anthropological reflection should itself systematically take into account minority and marginal accounts of the structure of being human, fulfilment, and reason'.[12] A hermeneutics of suspicion has been introduced, and in ethics, Christian charity has been connected to justice as an internal element.[13]

However, the philosophical and theological objections raised in Chapters 7 and 8 to the natural law approach as such acquire an added edge in the multi-faceted task of realizing equal freedom for women. The questions include the concept of self (1), the connection sought by some between the universalist thought form of natural law and the particularist one of virtue ethics (2), and the abiding concern of how natural law teleology relates to the Christian message of liberation (3). Are these premises in keeping with the justified and overdue, painstaking corrections theological feminists have made to a systematic edifice that predates the anthropological turn? The type of questioning spelt out under the following three subheadings is structurally similar to Traina's, Cahill's and other natural law feminists' critiques. They show how the current shape of the theory requires new openings and modifications to be able to deliver the tasks it has set for itself.

---

[11] This conclusion agrees with those of Chapter Four about the need for a more modest claim to the standard of 'objectivity' after the 'logic of science' debates, admitting the impact of context and of epistemological interests. Cf. Nagl-Docekal, *Feminist Philosophy*, 104–10.

[12] Traina, *Feminist Ethics and Natural Law*, 304.

[13] E.g., ibid., 265.

(1) Needed: A theory of self

Insisting on the link of individual flourishing to a community makes sense in a North American cultural context where a 'rational choice' anthropology of self-interested single agents has enjoyed some intellectual credence. Yet a subordination of the individual in her singularity to an unproven trust in a communitarian ethos towards which ethical 'formation' is geared sidelines, undermines, or even denies that moral agency is built on individual self-reflection. The consistent neglect of the first person singular in the natural law mode of ethics cannot be repaired by shifting the centre of responsibility from the self to either 'the' other, or to plural others. For example, one has to choose between Levinas and Ricoeur regarding the 'first philosophy' one wishes to commit to. Also the critique of deconstructivism cannot be completed without an alternative theory of identity which presupposes some analysis of self. The 'ends' towards which a 'telic' anthropology is oriented only become relevant if they are appropriated. Otherwise, they remain external, and women and men can ask, as Vincent MacNamara did in his critique of Finnis and Grisez: 'But why should one order one's life by submitting to the faculties-end structure?'[14]

Feminist ethics has demonstrated already in its distinction between sex and gender, natural difference and cultural roles, that it is reason which interprets nature. To account for the capability of taking a stance towards natural preconditions – for example, to become a mother or not – needs a theory of freedom that distinguishes between two levels: the formal, transcendental, and the concrete, historical.[15] The same is true for a theory of agency, in order to be able to understand 'acts' – as feminism does with its interest in narrativity – on the backdrop of the self-understanding and motivation of the agent. The meta-ethical question, what are the conditions of the possibility for taking one's distance from 'conventional' assumptions and specifying 'flourishing' differently, leads to a transcendental concept of freedom.

(2) Relating natural law to virtue ethics

While both are thought forms that share a teleology, their combination gives rise to conceptual questions. Answers to historical enquiries will affect

---

[14] MacNamara, *The Truth in Love*, 100.
[15] Pröpper, *Erlösungsglaube und Freiheitsgeschichte*, 182–94.

contemporary alternatives, as the following examples show. Lisa Cahill rightly points out that 'the most prolific and influential twentieth-century promoter of virtue theory in Christian ethics ... Hauerwas adopts a more radical Augustinian view of sin's effects than does Aquinas, and therefore focuses his ethics on Christian virtues rather than also on natural virtues.'[16] Does it make a difference in this context whether universalist natural law or particularist virtue ethics is the framework for Thomas? How does it change interpretations, if one or the other, or a specific interaction between them, is seen as the functioning, proper basis of his ethics? One of Jean Porter's precise analyses gives a differentiated account of three, not two, categories of virtue in Aquinas: besides the natural, cardinal virtues, and the infused theological ones of faith, hope and love, there are also 'infused cardinal virtues'. In her analysis, by including this third type against the ambiguity of virtue, Thomas is able, correcting Augustine, 'not only to preserve the gratuity of grace, but also to safeguard the integrity and intelligibility of nature, which operates through comprehensible principles in order to produce finite and attainable ends.'[17] Human finitude is recognized as a natural law insight into given structures of being human; yet these do not by themselves constitute a moral fault. It remains necessary to distinguish between real and pretended virtues:

> Falling short of divine goodness is transformed by Aquinas into a distinction between two principles of operation, nature informed by reason, and grace, aimed towards two distinct ends, naturally attainable happiness, and the supreme happiness of personal union with God. Aquinas makes explicit ... the real distinction between genuine virtues, whose proper goods can be oriented towards our final end through charity, and similitudes of virtue, which are vicious even humanly considered.[18]

But this insight into a self-serving use of virtue should not be connected to the difference between God and humans as such. For Augustine, who portrays its

> negative connotations ... humanly attainable virtue ... even at its best is never too far from outright sin ... Aquinas likewise insists on the infinite distance between divine and human perfection ... but does not imply that

---

[16] Cahill, *Global Justice, Christology, and Christian Ethics* (Cambridge: CUP, 2013), 272–3.
[17] Porter, Jean, 'Virtue', in *The Oxford Handbook of Theological Ethics*, ed. Gilbert Meilaender, and William Werpehowski (Oxford: OUP, 2005), 217, with reference to Aquinas, S.th. I-II 63.3.
[18] Ibid.

the latter is tainted or corrupt. The goodness proper to a creation does not cease to be goodness simply because it is not the goodness of the Creator ... the distance between the Creator and the creatures cannot ultimately be expressed within a scale of moral values. God exceeds every standard of comparison; yet his supreme transcendence has the effect of safeguarding, rather than undermining, the genuine integrity and value of created natures and their corresponding finite forms of goodness.[19]

The interpretation of the distinct theological ancestries also makes a difference for how church and society are conceived. Lisa Cahill concludes her observation regarding contemporary Christian virtue ethics with the comment that 'Aquinas retains a positive and constructive view of reasonable human morality, and of a social and political ethics oriented by the common good. The goods that constitute human flourishing can be generally known across communities; this is the source of an ethics of the natural moral law'.[20]

Thus, there is no reason to dismiss the capability of members of other communities for ethics. Yet there is a point of difference between medieval and modern moral philosophy, which is also relevant for feminist natural law with its links to secular liberation movements: its foundation.

(3) Morality founded in freedom, but hope founded in God

It is important both theologically and politically regarding shared initiatives with non-religious feminist movements to recognize that the overarching horizon of the Middle Ages, monotheism, is no longer shared. It is also not needed to found moral duty or human rights. It is possible to respect atheist humanism when it shares the same ground of moral obligation: human freedom. By distinguishing, as Kant did, the ground of obligation from the ground of meaning, God, secular self-understandings can be accepted as long as they are autonomous in the principled sense of respecting and promoting the other's and their own dignity. Unlike the synthesis of the Middle Ages, modern theology can relate to philosophy as a discipline in the search for truth that poses the question of meaning, since reason (*Vernunft*) drives it towards the unconditioned. But it has to be recognized that philosophy will keep the question open and will not answer it since it is

---

[19] Ibid., 218.
[20] Cahill, *Global Justice*, 273, with reference to S.th. I-II 94.

beyond the limits of reason. By contrast, theology as the reflection on the practical option of faith in God can draw on the testimonies about God's self-revelation, though not as necessary elements of cognitive knowing.

If it was possible for classical natural law to assume God as the highest common good, recognizable by all, this is no longer the case after the modern insight into the limits of pure reason. Yet for ethics as much as for theology, a more promising path has been opened up by the late medieval shift from human cognition to the good will, and from 'wisdom' as God's key attribute in Thomism to 'love' in Franciscan-inspired doctrines of God. Understanding salvation as liberation and as renewal of the sources of the good after failure should be much closer to feminist intentions than a theoretical or contemplative theo-philosophical approach to God.[21]

2. 'Care' as a challenge to 'justice'

One element that is common to natural law feminism and to the feminist critique of a concept of justice that neglects 'care' is their suspicion of an 'abstract' universalism. It is seen as bypassing difference, context and individualized attention to fellow humans in its principled and 'deductive' approach. Carol Gilligan's questioning of the justice orientation in Lawrence Kohlberg's stage theory of moral development has led to further conceptual enquiries of unexplored premises in moral philosophy. Practical debates in social ethics and social policy have shone a light on the invisible delivery of services without which market economies would not be able to function. Caring for the young, the old and the ill are ongoing tasks the scale of which has become more evident with globalization. It demands responses from Christian social ethics both in structural analyses and contributions to public debate (a). The challenge of the 'care' approach to moral theory uncovers fundamental disagreements about gender differences, alternative ways of moral reasoning, conflicting claims and goals, and the search for other models of ethics (b).

---

[21] For a study of Aquinas's concept of analogy in recognition of the inadequacy of human terms for God and a comparison with Ricoeur in relation to 'otherness' as a key theme of intercultural ethics, cf. Amy Daughton, *With and for Others: Developing Ricoeur's Ethics of Self Using Aquinas's Language of Analogy* (Studien zur theologischen Ethik vol. 146) (Fribourg i. Ue: Academic Press/Freiburg. i. Br.: Herder, 2016).

(a) Responding to the consistent human need for care: Between a gendered division of labour, personal responsibility and public policy

The extent of unpaid work provided by female carers in the home – looking after their children as well as sick family members and often the older generation, relieving others in the household from housework – has become more obvious with the increased participation of women in the paid labour force. As a consequence of this shift, as the Austrian Christian ethicist Christa Schnabl points out, the consistent need for care work has led to 'global care chains'; women from poorer economies, for example the Philippines and Eastern Europe, have taken over care tasks for the young and the older generation in the United States and Western Europe. Her structural analysis takes different factors into account, ranging from the 'precarious nature of different European retirement insurance systems' and health care, to inflexible working hours, and to the income hierarchy and unequal global status of countries.[22] Some of these could be organized differently and linked in a mutually supportive way, while changing others depends on concerted international efforts at quite another scale. Schnabl demands a 'just' organization of care for which one presupposition is the recognition that dependency is a given aspect of being human; this calls both for structural measures and for a decisive change in values from the ideal of independence and being in control, to a recognition of the constitutive vulnerability of all humans. At stake is the issue of 'how modern societies can integrate vulnerability, dependency, and care as partial aspects of individual human life and of living together in social contexts into societal, ethical and political self-conceptions'.[23] The task for theological ethics is to re-establish 'care' as a category of social ethics, not merely of an individual ethics directed mainly at women, and to combine the two elements, as the programmatic title, 'Caring justly', indicates, into a theory of justice.

The crisis in the availability of care in the modern labour market turns out to be a lynchpin issue which concretizes long-standing debates: on global

---

[22] Cf. Christa Schnabl, 'Vulnerability, Reciprocity, and Familial-Care Relations: A Socioethical Contribution', in *Catholic Theological Ethics: The Trento Conference*, ed. J. Keenan, 225.

[23] Schnabl, *Gerecht sorgen: Grundlagen einer sozialethischen Theorie der Fürsorge* (Studien zur theologischen Ethik) (Freiburg: Herder, 2005), 444, quoted in Susanne Dungs, Review, in *Theologische Literaturzeitung* 132 (2007): 995–7.

justice and on gender, on social contract foundations of the state, and conceptions of morality on what we owe each other. Its specific aim is to develop proposals for how unalterable conditions of being human can be catered for by creating appropriate support systems. 'Care' is to be regained as a task which is not gender-specific but part of the general expectation of justice that individuals commit to and that economic, political and social systems are required to support. For the German theological ethicist Marianne Heimbach-Steins this involves changes at the following three levels: the 'implicit duty' to seek a full-time working life in order to avoid a precarious post-retirement situation with uncertain and insufficient social benefits needs to be remedied by making the periods of care work relevant for social security and pensions.[24] It is a matter of justice that the mainly female family members who take over care should not incur the risk of poverty and uncertainty of their own needs being met when they have grown old. Secondly, when the care gap cannot be resolved by changing the inherited division of labour between male and female family members, and when professional care has to be 'bought in', this career option has to be made more attractive financially. Thirdly, fair conditions of work for migrant carers in private households have to be secured. There are two reasons why Heimbach-Steins advocates seeking country-internal solutions: 'strong traditions' as well as 'important legal and ethical reasons' speak for taking over the tasks of education and care in the family context, but equally the enormous human costs imposed on the children and parents of migrant women.[25] It exacerbates global inequalities when first world economies tear families apart by outsourcing the deficit in care work time to a global care supply chain of highly dependent female workers.

The discrepancy between predictable needs – augmented by the great success of increasing longevity and by the birth rates after the Second World War – and insufficient economic and political measures can no longer be ignored. An alternative solution to receiving attention from fellow humans is to develop a technological substitute: care and teaching robots. It would be equally possible technologically to provide worktime flexibility. However, the current endeavour of programming generic emotional responses into machines makes it visible that there is a strong current of cultural values

---

[24] Cf. Marianne Heimbach-Steins, 'Grund zur Sorge – Genderfragen im Feld der Care-Arbeit', in *Ethik in den Kulturen – Kulturen in der Ethik. Festschrift Regina Ammicht-Quinn*, ed. Cordula Brand et al. (Tübingen: Narr Francke Attempto Verlag, 2017), 237.
[25] Cf. Heimbach-Steins, 'Grund zur Sorge', 238.

which prefers anonymous technical, impersonal solutions. In order to resist developments in such a direction, equal recognition in terms of esteem and of financial security has to be given to those women and men who fulfil this part of the contract between the generations on which a society depends. Taking account of human fragility and of the need to be assisted at different times in a person's life could be the occasion for a wide-ranging process of consultation in the public sphere on how to engage in the rational life planning that is needed as a response to finitude.[26] It builds on a moral readiness to accept the other's expectation of human support, even asymmetrically, but not based on a one-sided, gendered division of labour. The insight into the specific relevance of interpersonal relations brought into the realm of moral theory by 'care ethics' now has to be examined for the questions it raises for conceptions of justice.

(b) 'Care' as an alternative to, or as part of 'justice'?

The 'facts of neediness and assistance, . . . as well as the conditions of freedom, autonomy, and justice'[27] highlighted by the care perspective constitute a decisive concretization for discourses on justice. Schnabl and Heimbach-Steins, the two female theological ethicists quoted in the first subsection, have already taken the stance that this is a dimension which has to be faced unrelated to gender, and that reserving 'care' functions for women is based on an essentializing perspective. In the course of her work, Carol Gilligan has clarified that her challenge to Lawrence Kohlberg's stage theory of moral development which culminates in 'justice' was meant to highlight two orientations: they are not reducible to each other, and they are open to both men and women. The initial impression that an essentially different female morality was being proposed was therefore corrected. What this productive controversy elucidated was a previously underestimated dimension in morality that needed to be spelt out and distinguished from the title of 'justice' with its implied standard of 'impartiality'. It was important to clarify against Kohlberg and Habermas that this dimension did not belong to the level of the flourishing life, that is, the ethics of the good, but quite distinctly to moral obligation, the ethics of ought. If the moral reasoning of women in

---

[26] At another level, rational life planning cannot avert or contain this finitude, and has to be addressed existentially, as is reflected in Kant's concept of 'happiness'. Cf. Nagl-Docekal, *Innere Freiheit*, 93.
[27] Schnabl, 'Vulnerability', 227.

these empirical studies never seemed to reach the principled level, but seemed to belong to a stage still assigned to be 'conventional', Gilligan was right to raise questions about the categories employed. However, greater precision in key terms was required, and some of the perceived polarities needed to be questioned, as will become clear in subsection 1. Secondly, I will treat a more recent link of the ethics of care to Paul Ricoeur's concept of 'solicitude'. It is seen to be anchored in an anthropology that accepts human fragility and the significance of the other for the self as basic (2).

(1) Clarifying misleading oppositions

The intention of the following discussion is not to resolve the variety of interpretations of Gilligan that is evident in the comments quoted, but the analysis of a crucial point in the feminist debate of an ethics of care: can the needs of the concrete other be encompassed in a principled understanding of morality, as part of 'respect' and 'imperfect duties'? Or is principled morality marked by 'deductive' reasoning and an 'abstract' concept of the moral subject, which are then identified with masculine thinking? Is a new moral theory needed? Seyla Benhabib defends a point of truth in both positions, the need to deal with concrete vulnerabilities, and the call to impartiality. Her objection is that 'Habermas and Kohlberg conflate the standpoint of a universalist morality with a narrow definition of the moral domain as being centred around "issues of justice".'[28] This is a perceptive critique which links Gilligan's emphasis on morality as needing to take account of the concrete other with a reminder of what a truly 'universalistic' justification consists in. Theories of justice, be they national or cosmopolitan, are exemplifications of the unconditional obligation not to instrumentalize the other, and to promote their intentions. Arguing from the original outline of a deontological ethics by Kant, Nagl-Docekal equally insists that no additional or alternative theory is needed to cover obligations of care towards individuals:

> It is not as if for Kant, the moral requirement (*Anforderung*) was exhausted by the obligation for justice; the categorical imperative has, as already elucidated, a more encompassing character. This has to be underlined against a currently prevalent assessment that Kant's conception corresponds to an "ethics of

---

[28] Seyla Benhabib, 'The Debate over Women and Moral Theory Revisited', in *Feminists Reading Habermas. Gendering the Subject of Discourse*, ed. and intro. Johanna Meehan (New York: Routledge, 1995), 183.

justice" which does not provide an appropriate place for considering human vulnerability and need for assistance – and for the appropriate caring attention.[29]

(2) Building a bridge between Ricoeur's concept of 'solicitude' and care ethics

If it is the case, as Jodi Dean suggests, that Gilligan herself has revised some previous polarities, then the discussion has moved on: it is possible to embed 'care' in an enlarged understanding of 'justice'.[30] The task then is to seek an approach in which the different dimensions of justice become visible and linked to a theory of subjectivity which distinguishes the transcendental from the empirical level, that is, the condition of the possibility of the use of practical reason, and concrete judgements. Because of the care or 'solicitude' that marks the first step of his tripartite ethics, 'striving to live well, with and for others, in just institutions',[31] Paul Ricoeur has been brought into the care ethical debate. By naming 'solicitude' as a fundamental orientation, he opts for a framework of recognition, not of power and fear for one's survival,[32] as Hobbes and Nietzsche and their contemporary followers do. The Dutch philosopher Inge van Nistelrooij and the theologian Petruschka Schaafsma try to make the case for the possibilities of Ricoeur's practice-oriented, but conceptual thinking, which sees a 'twofold movement' at work in 'the practical field': one of 'ascending complexification starting from basic actions . . ., and of descending specification starting from the vague and mobile horizon of ideals and projects in light of which a human life apprehends itself in its oneness'.[33] The horizon therefore is one of relating the

---

[29] Nagl-Docekal, *Innere Freiheit*, 90. For a more detailed discussion, cf. Nagl-Docekal, 'Feministische Ethik oder eine Theorie weiblicher Moral?', in *Weibliche Moral – ein Mythos?*, ed. Detlev Horster (Frankfurt: Suhrkamp, 1998), 42–72, and 'Ein Postscriptum zum Begriff Gerechtigkeitsethik', ibid., 142–53.

[30] Jodi Dean, 'Discourse in Different Voices', in *Feminists Reading Habermas*, 208–11.

[31] Ricoeur, *Oneself as Another*, 172.

[32] Ricoeur, *The Course of Recognition*, 162: 'the theme of *Anerkennung* has to be treated as a moral rejoinder to the challenge launched by the naturalistic interpretation of the sources of the political.'

[33] Ricoeur, *Oneself as Another*, 158, opening quote in 'Editorial. Ricoeur and the Ethics of Care', by Inge van Nistelrooij, Petruschka Schaafsma and Joan C. Tronto, in *Medical Health Care and Philosophy* 17 (2014) 491. The quote is from the sixth study, 'The self and narrative identity', which precedes his ethics, developed in Chapters 7–9. His ethics combines a teleological entry point (Ch. 7) with a necessary second, deontological step of the 'ought' not to instrumentalize others (Ch. 8), and with the third level of 'practical wisdom' (Ch. 9), a judgement that seeks to do justice to both prior levels, thus combining Aristotle and Kant.

actions and established practices of the self to the ideals relevant for its self-conception. Achieving such unity makes it possible to assume responsibility. In her response to this attempt at bridge-building across disciplines, the North American political scientist Joan Tronto judges his outline still to be located at the 'abstract' level. Yet the two Dutch co-editors insist that even if in the 'radically practice-oriented thinking of the ethics of care ... reflection ... must always emerge from the practices themselves', several traits of Ricoeur's approach make a dialogue promising: his highlighting of constitutive fragility, the critique of claims to sovereignty, and the role of 'solicitude' in narrative identity.[34] They point out that practitioners welcome 'non-professional outsiders' to help them engage in reflective practice for which 'conceptual tools' are needed.[35]

Perhaps the term 'practices' is charged with too many functions in Tronto's approach. Ricoeur provides not only a 'relational anthropology' but a theory of self that identifies the duality of *idem* and *ipse*. It can help clarify the relation and the distance between self, other and institutions. This allows to identify the different intentionalities and logics at work, as well as the differentiation of justice in accordance with its distinct spheres; for example, the upbringing and education of girls and boys, the research industry, and finance ethics. Ricoeur's outline of an ethics based on 'solicitude' for others offers an encompassing framework from which to judge aspects in tension, like 'care' and 'justice'. They have to be distinguished and analysed for their parts in the ascending and descending process in which the faculty of judgement (*Urteilskraft*) in its reflecting and its determining functions comes to decisions.

The final model of feminist ethics to be discussed includes consideration of these points into its framework, together with an analysis of culture as a backdrop to moral decision-making.

3. Principled autonomy as relational

The feminist specification of the autonomy school in theological ethics begins with an elaboration of the 'relational' meaning of this concept and its connection to an intrinsic, not an empirical notion of dignity (a). As part of their cultural diagnosis, they identify how the drive to perfecting empirical

---

[34] Nistelrooij, Schaafsma and Tronto, 'Editorial', 486–8.
[35] Ibid., 491.

features affects the constitutive condition of human embodiment; here, reproductive technologies assume a new role of intervention into the contingent physical basis of each human being's singularity, altering also the understanding of parenthood (b). Biblical images and guiding Christian motivations are elucidated in their relevance for biotechnological innovations which are carried out especially on women's bodies. They affect their self-understanding as responsible agents in a society marked by trends of perfection, control and exclusion (c).

(a) Relational autonomy, power analysis and hermeneutics of self

The theoretical strands combined by the theological ethicists in the autonomy approach are a Kantian concept of the intrinsic dignity of human beings in their fragility, the gendered power analyses of feminist philosophy since the 1970s, and the significance of the self-conception of the moral agent which requires the reflective approach of hermeneutics. In this framework, they reconstruct the different feminist positions as necessary angles of critique, overcoming the alternatives between care and justice, attention to the concrete and to the anonymous other, and the tension between difference and equality. By showing how some conceptual conflicts can be solved, they identify where the real alternatives lie, and do so from an encompassing view of Christian ethics as correlating with and helping to sustain a shared ethics of human dignity.

The liberal ideal of a rational agent choosing projects and contract partners, prioritizing negative rights with little regard for duties and the effect of decisions on third parties, is uncovered both as a myth that downplays the constitutive dependency of humans, and as an emptying of the moral concept of responsibility. Communitarians voice a similar critique; but they miss another decisive factor, namely a diagnosis of power relations expressed in the roles and expectations of communities and their sub-units, such as families. These have dominated women's lives far more than men's. The virtues and values they advocate belong to the external forces of social norms that structure practices also in oppressive, not just in benevolent ways.[36]

---

[36] Cf. Hille Haker, *Ethik der genetischen Frühdiagnostik. Sozialethische Reflexionen zur Verantwortung am Beginn des menschlichen Lebens* (Paderborn: Mentis, 2002), 24, n. 15, with reference to Marilyn Friedman, 'Jenseits von Fürsorglichkeit. Die Ent-Moralisierung der Geschlechter', in *Jenseits der Geschlechtermoral. Beiträge zur feministischen Ethik*, ed. H. Nagl-Docekal and Herlinde Pauer-Studer (Frankfurt: Fischer, 1993), 241–66.

Having situated itself between different intellectual traditions, feminist ethics has to clarify its status. Unlike virtue ethics or other schools, it is not yet another approach alongside these established ones: 'at times, feminist ethics is seen as a domain-specific ethics and is then pushed into the realm of "applications" of general ethics which levels its methodological claim.'[37] In some respects it is comparable to ethics in the sciences and the humanities by cutting across the different schools: 'Feminist bioethics is not an approach like preference utilitarianism, virtue ethics or "principlism" . . . It is part of feminist ethics which carries out an ethically founded criticism of acts, practices, systems, structures and ideologies that perpetuate the subordination of women.'[38]

This task raises the question of criteria in view of the divergence of feminist positions on what constitutes subordination, or empowerment, as exemplified by assessments of new reproductive technologies. Like ethics in the sciences, the remit of feminist ethics includes analysing cultures of knowledge with their key terms, premises, aims, values and means. It is a 'critical' enterprise that 'uncovers gaps in legitimation' and strives to 'change practices of knowledge' by developing 'normative statements that go beyond positive law and unquestioned, socially valid norms.'[39] Its comparison of feminist approaches shows that 'two distinct concepts of identity conflict with each other'. The liberal conception interprets autonomy as existing in relations of 'contract and exchange' with others and as being a citizen of a state that is aiming to achieve a 'fair balancing of interests'.[40] Parenthood veers towards being conceived on the 'model of defending property rights as the basis of human relationships'. The 'communitarian' alternative, the 'embedded self', considers the network of relationships with others as belonging to its self-conception. The idea of self issuing from a concept of identity oriented towards community gives priority to a common good co-defined and established by citizens over individual negative rights.[41] Against a concept of autonomy based on the single criterion that 'each woman must

---

[37] Haker, 'Feministische Bioethik', in *Bioethik. Eine Einführung*, ed. Marcus Düwell and Klaus Steigleder (Frankfurt: Suhrkamp, 2003), 169.
[38] Haker, 'Feministische Bioethik', 168.
[39] Cf. Haker, 'Geschlechter-Ethik der Reproduktionsmedizin. Ethik – Geschlecht – Wissenschaften', in *Ethik – Geschlecht – Wissenschaft. Der 'ethical turn' als Herausforderung für die interdisziplinären Geschlechterstudien*, ed. by Ursula Konnertz, Hille Haker, and Dietmar Mieth (Paderborn: Mentis, 2006), 258.
[40] Haker, *Ethik der genetischen Frühdiagnostik*, 186.
[41] Ibid., 187.

decide for herself', but also against accepting community-generated role expectations, these feminists argue for an autonomy that is 'in a position to integrate the rights of others into one's own free decision'.[42] The conflict between two positions marked by idealizations – 'autonomy' as autarchy, and 'community' as a tension-free haven of like-minded associates – is replaced by a proposal with different levels. Moral judgement draws from a self-conception that arises from the narrative formation of identity. This hermeneutics of self includes the symbols and shared self-understandings of a culture which structure perceptions and patterns of agency. This is why the contributing streams to a political culture are factors with resonance, and why also interventions from a Christian perspective can make a difference.

(b) New norms for the body

With the help of a diagnosis of contemporary culture, it is possible to discover factors of influence at the level of symbols: regarding human embodiment, for example, an unspoken rise of health to a status previously held by salvation; models expressed in films and novels, some of them dystopian; and changes in the priorities of values, such as economics intruding on the contents and aims of education, replacing its own criteria of meaning and successful interaction at the appropriate age levels. The heuristic task of ethics consists in identifying currents and possible counter-movements, in order to spot emerging issues that may turn out to be morally relevant. Two such features examined by these feminist theologians will serve as illustrations: the elevation of machines to model humans (1), and a new construction of 'normality' and 'deviance' based on the reduction of relevant factors to the genetic level (2).

(1) Machines as replacements for fallible and finite humans

In their analysis of cultural trends, Regina Ammicht-Quinn and Elsa Tamez note that 'the body gets established as a project' which 'aims at

---

[42] Regina Ammicht-Quinn, Monika Bobbert, Hille Haker, Marianne Heimbach-Steins, Ulrike Kostka, Dagmar Mensink, Mechthild Schmedders, Susanna Schmidt and Marlies Schneider, 'Women in the practice of reproductive medicine and in bioethical discourse – an intervention', in *The New Pontificate: A Time for Change?*, Concilium 42, 130.

perfection ... not only in the media and the beauty industry but also in the research and health industry ... the body is no longer a fate but a result of actions.'[43] At the same time, in films, literature, advertising and the discourse of transhumanism, a new direction can be observed: '"Never get a person when you can get a machine" – this seems to be the categorical imperative of this popular culture.'[44] In the construction of these artificial agents, Ammicht-Quinn sees a 'new normative picture of the human' emerging which has shed the factors of contingency, imperfection and mortality: 'The robotic revolution ... will leave behind ... the human inadequacies and fallibilities; human birth, human ageing and human death. The distinction between human being and machine ... is focussed on the negative aspects of humanity – perhaps also because spontaneity, fantasy and feelings are also on the programme of those developing artificial intelligence.'[45] It seems that embodiment as such has to be surpassed, instead of being valued as the medium of connection with a world and fellow human beings. What could just be seen as a revival of a Gnostic hostility to the body within one subculture in a pluralist society, in her analysis takes on a threatening character due to its inbuilt logic of exclusion: it exhibits a 'tendency to exclude the endangered, imperfect, contingent from the image of the human.'[46] Therefore, in order to protect the human being in her finitude and imperfection, resources are needed to value humans as 'more than a being which can be repaired and controlled ... There must be an ethical formulation of resistance to a picture of human beings which declares the liveliness and risk of human life first to be an illness and then an unbearable burden.' A 'new categorical imperative' is required in the face of aspirations to substitute the ordinary human condition with engineered perfection: 'pay attention to human vulnerability.'[47]

[43] Regina Ammicht-Quinn and Elsa Tamez, 'Introduction', in *The Body and Religion, Concilium* 38, ed. Regina Ammicht-Quinn and Elsa Tamez (London: SCM, 2002), 8.
[44] Ammicht-Quinn, 'Whose Dignity is Inviolable? Human Beings, Machines and the Discourse of Dignity', in *The Discourse of Human Dignity, Concilium* 39, ed. Regina Ammicht-Quinn, Elsa Tamez and Maureen Junker-Kenny (London: SCM, 2003), 35.
[45] Ibid., 38.
[46] Ibid., 42.
[47] Ibid., 44.

(2) Cultural imperatives and their counterparts: 'Perfect' bodies and 'inferior' ones

In an age in which the body has become a project, constituting an asset in the competitive course of everyone's life, and a threat, if it is not controllable, a 'non-instrumental relationship to one's body'[48] seems to be harder to achieve. The objectivism critiqued in physicalist natural law returns, but under the imperative to remodel the intrinsically deficient features of being human: limited by death, assaulted by illness, diminished by ageing, subject to suffering in body and psyche both by injuries and insults. The concern of the feminist autonomy ethicists, however, is not how auspicious or deluded these assessments and aims are considered to be, but the real effect they have in devaluing lives deemed to be inferior, and not to be capable of ever being a 'flourishing life'. Their 'intervention' into current bioethical debate and its tacit premises puts forward a counter-view. For them, 'what is required today is a new discussion as to how illness, suffering and the experience of imperfection can become part and parcel of life, and thus also of flourishing life'.[49] This requires rejecting the unnuanced view of the human constitution present in the understanding that in order to qualify as good, a life has to be 'as free from suffering as possible'. Their contrasting definition of what can count as 'flourishing life' is the 'creative engagement with one's own possibilities and limitations'.[50] By anchoring the task to be accomplished by every individual, regardless of their endowments and disabilities, in striving to do the best within their specific limits, they invalidate the 'judgements of inferiority' that are being drawn from genetic diagnoses. The feminist awareness of power differentials leads to a heightened attention and scrutiny of processes that construct 'normality and deviance under the sign of subordination'.[51]

The context of the articles, books and of the 'intervention' quoted includes the discussion of the permissibility of pre-implantation genetic diagnosis, as a planned selection procedure before initiating the pregnancy, that is, prior to emotional attachment. Their judgement from a relational concept of autonomy is that it undermines the normative concept of parenthood by suspending or revoking the unconditionality with which a child is accepted

---

[48] Haker, 'The Perfect Body: Biomedical Utopias', in *The Body and Religion*, 9–18.
[49] Cf. Ammicht-Quinn et al., 'Intervention', 119.
[50] Ibid., 132.
[51] Haker, 'Feminist bioethics', 178.

for its own sake. In such situations of difficult options, it becomes clear to them that support for 'reproductive autonomy' can be a society's declaration of indifference: 'This rhetoric of autonomy disguises the fact that women's "autonomous" decisions are shaped by asymmetries with regard to information and power, and depend on social assessments (e.g., with example to disability, parenthood of a disabled child, the social context). This rhetoric of autonomy perverts the principle of autonomy: autonomy is exploited.'[52]

A society that offers only rhetorical, but no tangible supports for families that have opted to give birth to their disabled child, falls short on its own highest principle: 'a society which upholds different understandings of human dignity with respect to genetically affected and unaffected human beings might misunderstand the concept of universal respect as well as the concept of tolerance.'[53] It is therefore apt if the 'Intervention' reminds potential parents and their societies that 'no human beings are responsible for the physical constitution in which they are born, and also parents are not responsible for the specific constitution of their children'.[54] Among the costs that a society shoulders – the cost of adequate provisions for periods of dependency as well as reliable, lasting support throughout a disabled person's life – is something it owes to itself, as a justified normative expectation of its citizens.

(c) Autonomous feminist ethics inspired by the Christian message

While this final section is dedicated to how the authors specify the contents of their own Christian motivation, it is important to note that secular society has to deliver the promise it has committed to by subscribing to the concept of human dignity which anchors human rights. The authors indicate in what ways the Christian faith as one of the formative traditions of Western societies offers decisive insights which may inspire other self-understandings, too. One addressee is the pluralistic society composed of many confessions and secular orientations (2); the other is theology and church which may augment or diminish the credibility not only of contributions to bioethical

---

[52] Ammicht-Quinn et al., 'Intervention', 129–30.
[53] Haker, 'Selection through prenatal diagnosis and preimplantation diagnosis', in *Genetics in Human Reproduction*, ed. Elisabeth Hildt, and Sigrid Graumann (Aldershot: Ashgate, 1999), 163.
[54] Ammicht-Quinn et al., 'Intervention', 120 (trans. amended).

and ecological debates but also the relevance of theological proposals as such (1).

(1) Critique of the ecclesial failure to support women's equal dignity and autonomy

For the feminists as for the autonomy approach in general, the ethical enquiries they engage in and their conclusions are aimed in two directions: On the one hand, the human dignity of women has to be defended against the role assignments inherent in the idea of a separate 'dignity of women' as put forward by the Catholic magisterium. On the other hand, biblical narratives and theological concepts that have shaped Western culture can be resources also for secular citizens in argumentations on choices that will shape lifeworlds in the future. The key concern of the authors of the 'Intervention' is that the ethical reflection offered by the Roman Catholic Church is restricted to deductive conclusions from a physicalist interpretation of natural law. This effectively disallows the experience of women to play any role in moral decision-making: '(W)hat is at stake is taking seriously the dimension of experience with regard to pregnancy and childlessness as *experiences* in their full extent and formative power'.[55] The problem identified before in relation to the 'objectivist' demeanour of the natural law approach, even in its revisionist form, is made visible by the feminist focus on the perspective of the moral agent in her context. Indispensable for moral reflection is the role of 'experience'; a person's self-conception is the pivot point between the moral issue that disrupts the continuity of her life and calls for a response, and her action.

(2) Christian narratives and symbols as horizons of meaning in secular society

Naming the biblical and theological roots of one's view of life is a service to a society made up of many traditions. It helps show that every view has its presuppositions which have to be laid open. There is no 'neutral', worldview-free position, as a hermeneutically conscious enquiry will accept. One of the effects of a faith position is the sensitivity it provides for spotting morally significant issues. It can help recognize secular conversions of previously

---

[55] Ammicht-Quinn et al., 'Intervention', 135.

ecclesial problems: it used to be the church that tied female humanity to the role of becoming a mother, if they were sexually active. Now, it has become a norm transported by secular images of what belongs to functioning male and female bodies. The new technologies have a more direct impact on the bodies of women than of men and 'seem to heighten the images of "female normality" – fertility, the role of pregnancy and motherhood'.[56] The 'new cult of the body' suggests that 'female bodies do not have to be chaste in order to be "good"'; rather they have to be beautiful and functional in order to be 'good', and this generally includes being fertile.[57]

Against this expectation imposed once more on women, the biblical narratives make it clear that life is a 'gift' from God. A child's life has the status of a completely un-owed and not meritable good turn of life, not a norm of functionality. The key point is that the 'Christian tradition sees each human being as un-interchangeable and dignified', and in no further need for justification, being a gift from God, made in God's image and likeness. 'Human existence is granted, not made, and open to a relationship with God',[58] is the foundational Christian conviction. It motivates the critique of instrumentalization for parental and societal interests and of the logic of exchange taking over human unconditional relationships: a thinking that makes partners, children, their fathers and mothers as well as the older generation substitutable and superfluous once a replacement with better features has been sourced. Making individuals dispensable also violates the general consciousness of what is moral. But lacking a more encompassing horizon of meaning, the human endowment with morality, as Kant saw, risks being undermined, exhausted by fruitless attempts of doing the good.

With their regard for the concrete other, as well as for institutional settings, the three schools of feminist thinking treated share a relational understanding of self-determination. Each analysed power structures and ideologies inscribed in conceptions of the body, in role definitions and contemporary expectations, such as full-time working biographies and cross-generational care. Judging by the criteria established before, the external communicability of the Christian faith, and the link to the 'inner human being' that gathers the relevant aspects and comes to decisions, the autonomy school has developed resources for both: in interdisciplinary settings deciding on permission, oversight and regulation of new

[56] Ibid., 125.
[57] Ibid., 126–27.
[58] Ibid., 134 (trans. amended).

technological possibilities, in teaching and research collaborations, in supporting initiatives within and outside their churches as well as by engaging philosophical ethicists in depth on the links between narrative, teleological ethics and principled autonomy.

The 'visions' to be compared in the Part 3 reveal the range of positions in theological ethics under a different perspective. The five traditions and their backgrounds in the history of European thinking presented in Part 2 can be recognized in the three alternative directions proposed. The focus will be on how they envisage and exemplify excellence in the discipline.

Part 3

Visions

---

10 Theological ethics as integralist, as praxis-oriented, or as discourse-focused
Conclusion

It became evident in Part 2 through the categories and traditions used that there is no unitary understanding of theological ethics. Just like theology itself, the discipline is engaged in ongoing debate with distinct perspectives on what constitutes the core of the Christian message. Each approach wants to relay its reconstruction to a contemporary world of possible listeners and practitioners. It is not surprising to find the discipline in this intense state of discussion which could be a sign of productive vibrancy. In the period of controversy between autonomous Christian ethics and faith ethics, moral theology benefited from having subjected itself to this thorough self-examination. Its social ethical counterpart in German-speaking universities did not engage in theory debates until later. It meant that Catholic Social Teaching in its neo-Thomist framework was then challenged with unexpected vigour and was replaced by a different view of church and society. The era of the 'Catholic milieu' through which the church had managed to survive the institutional challenges of secularization had ended, and a new mode of communication had to be sought. Having examined different models of theological ethics, this concluding third part will analyse the 'visions' of three authors for the goals by which they judge its success. Despite some overlaps, they set the discipline on distinctive paths.

The Conclusion will situate theological ethics in a debate that has been conducted over the past twenty-five years, between Rawls and Habermas and many other philosophers and theologians, on religion in the public sphere. The questions of what to contribute, how to engage and which language to use in speaking to non-religious fellow citizens will be illuminated from different angles.

10

Theological ethics as integralist, as praxis-oriented or as discourse-focused

Each of the concluding visions takes a specific position regarding the distinctions between church and world, faith and reason, theology and its practical effects. The first is ecclesiocentric to the furthest possible degree (1), the next praxis-oriented (2), and the third underlines the theoretical work to be done for three constituencies: university, society and church (3).

1. An ecclesiocentric vision (William Cavanaugh)

The most clearly church-centred vision alongside Hauerwas's community- and worship-based approach can be found in the introduction of the Radical

Orthodox conception of theology into Christian ethics by its American Catholic member William Cavanaugh. Unlike Hauerwas's two foundations, neither of which aim to supersede the state in their outline of a contrast community to liberalism, the radical orthodox vision is ultimately integralist. Of the four sources examined in Part 1, two are used: 'tradition', and some individual human sciences, such as history. Cavanaugh's key perspective of analysis is 'violence' and 'war'. A crucial thesis he sets out to dismantle first is the connection made by secular scholars between 'religion' and 'violence'. Beyond the goal of questioning this easy equation, he secondly seeks to uncover it as a 'myth' used for ideological purposes. The third step is to deny the validity of the distinction between 'religion' and 'politics', which is seen to have been 'invented' for a purpose, in order to divert allegiance from the church to the nation and its aggressive interests.

In view of the relationship of competition he establishes between the sovereign state and a religious ordering of community, I will begin with his critique of the distinction between religion and politics and of the 'nation-state' to which the 'common good' cannot be entrusted (a). Secondly, his counter-model of church together with corresponding interpretations of theological terms will be discussed (b). Thirdly, the method of this alternative model to other approaches to Christian ethics which accept the neutrality of the state will be assessed (c).

(a) Repealing the distinction between religion and politics

As a reader trying to identify the core thesis, one finds oneself balancing two sets of statements. On the one hand, assurances are made that 'the separation of church and state is generally a good thing ... important to uphold for several reasons, some of them theological'.[1] It is not a matter of 'nostalgia' for a medieval unity: 'To reject the myth by no means implies nostalgia for medieval forms of governance'.[2] At times, the key point seems to be that 'ideologies and institutions labeled secular can be just as absolutist, divisive and irrational as those labeled religious',[3] which for many is quite evident or at least less controversial than Cavanaugh tends to assume. The intention to 'help us to see that the foundational possibilities for social orders, in the

---

[1] William Cavanaugh, *The Myth of Religious Violence* (Oxford: OUP, 2009), 4, 179 and 192.
[2] Ibid., 179. Cf. 194.
[3] Ibid., 6.

Islamic world and the West, are not limited to a stark choice between theocracy and secularism'[4] is equally a project many would share. On the other hand, strong theses are put forward that make most sense if they are interpreted as part of an integralist vision: 'In my second chapter I show that the very separation of religion from politics is an invention of the modern West.'[5] The unspoken premise seems to be the illegitimacy of separating 'religion' and 'politics'. The exact meaning of the contrasted terms needs to be clarified. Is it possible to concretize 'religion' and 'politics' as 'church' and 'state', or does this fall under 'anachronistic' thinking, since 'state' is seen as a term typical for modernity? Is the point that a political order with separate foundations from the church is to be ruled out, and their original unity defended? Two observations can be made: One, the argument takes the shape of historical statements, for example: 'In the 16th century, the modern invention of the twins of religion and society was still in its infancy; where the Eucharist was the primary symbol of social order, there simply was no divide between religious and social or political causes.'[6] But was this the case, or is a normative view of the eucharist presented as a historical fact? It is not clear what the counterparts are, and at which level the critique of distinguishing religion and an autonomous worldly sphere is aimed. How does denying the validity of two orders relate to the medieval theological effort to recognize both faith and reason, each as a valid authority, but based on different sources? How is, for example, Anselm's argument for his satisfaction theory in *Cur Deus homo* that is made *remoto Christo* to be judged?

The second observation is that crucial concepts such as 'public' or 'secularism' lack precision. The referent of 'public' ranges from 'power' to 'square': 'Religion must therefore be tamed by restricting its access to public power',[7] is an example of the first use. 'In domestic politics, the myth serves both to legitimate devotion to the nation-state and to marginalize actors labeled religious from the public square',[8] of the second. If the latter were true, it would be the sign of a totalitarian state, insisting on allegiance only to itself. If the first use is relevant, then 'public' seems to be 'governmental' or 'state' power. If the first meaning applies, then portraying this view as a

---

[4] Ibid., 14.
[5] Ibid., 5.
[6] Ibid., 11.
[7] Ibid., 3.
[8] Ibid., 180.

secular, problematic reduction and wishing to reverse it amounts to abolishing the division of powers in constitutional democracies as well as the neutrality of the state regarding worldviews and religions. Such neutrality, however, is the condition and implication of the human right to freedom of religion. This right was recognized by the Second Vatican Council, which based it on every individual's human dignity and on the priority of the truth of the person to a previously objectivized understanding of truth. Clarity on the exact meanings would be needed to decide whether the vision proposed is indeed integralist. The intention to repeal the split between religion and politics then leads to a singular sacred foundation, as distinct from accepting the autonomous reality of the worldly order. To accept this independence was not seen as detracting from faith for theological authorities such as Thomas Aquinas. But Thomas also entrusts the state with guarding the 'common good' which Cavanaugh regards as a completely misplaced trust.[9]

(b) The church as 'the embodiment of God's politics'

The question mark arising about the basis of far-reaching judgements on allegedly shared positions in undivided medieval thought, such as being united in the eucharist before any other allegiance, continues in a chapter dedicated to the theme of 'church'. Doubts arise regarding claims, references and missing texts. Since genealogies are always contested, it is even more important to reconstruct an author's position, rather than merely state page references that might suit one's thesis. Before examining some pointers to Cavanaugh's ecclesiology (3), I will comment on two statements which to me seem to be not sufficiently specific and to ignore material available for inclusion: his references to the political theology of Metz (1) and to the medieval philosophy scholar Brian Tierney (2).

(1) Johann Baptist Metz's conception of political theology

The chapter on 'Church' opens with the statement that 'all political theologies at the end of the twentieth century can be read as so many attempts to come to grips with the death of Christendom without simply acquiescing in the

---

[9] Cavanaugh, 'Killing for the Telephone Company: Why the Nation-State is not the Keeper of the Common Good', in *Modern Theology* 20 (2004): 243.

privatization of the church.'[10] It is already a significant clarification that the concern is not about a liberal privatization of religion in the sense of individual believers, but of the 'church' as a body in the singular. He goes on: 'Nevertheless, Christian political theology has strangely neglected the topic of the church.'

While he discusses one of the founders of the New Political Theology from the late 1960s, Johann Baptist Metz, as an example of a 'politically indirect ecclesiology', he relies on a book that contains only the beginnings of political theology, namely Metz's *Theology of the World*.[11] Metz escapes the verdict of the 'pathology of atomism' which Jacques Maritain, John Courtney Murray and Reinhold Niebuhr are diagnosed with, because their 'emphasis is on the individual Christian citizen acting in the temporal realm'.[12] Metz, however, gives the church a role, namely, of being an 'institution of social criticism'. What could have also been mentioned is Metz's engagement with an actual church constituency by writing the document 'Our Hope' for the 'Synod' that took place from 1972 onwards. Its task was to translate the Second Vatican Council's renewals into the structures of the 'local' German church.[13] When Cavanaugh portrays Metz's view of the church's 'mission . . . as a service to the history of freedom unfolding since the Enlightenment',[14] important elements are missed: his subsequent narrative turn, the role of the dangerous memory of Jesus Christ's life, passion and resurrection as well as the critique of the Enlightenment from the perspective of the earlier Frankfurt School, and the contrasting of 'Jerusalem' and 'Athens', his ongoing commitment to the 'human subject' notwithstanding.[15] The key deficit even of Metz's less individualistic efforts for Cavanaugh is that it is not the church itself which is restituted to a direct political role. The model of 'Church as polity' or of a 'directly political ecclesiology' is outlined as Cavanaugh's concluding alternative. It is true that cautionary notes are sounded against a possible impression of triumphalism

---

[10] Cavanaugh, 'Church', in *The Blackwell Companion to Political Theology*, ed. Peter Scott and W. T. Cavanaugh (Oxford: Blackwell, 2007), 397.

[11] Ibid., 406, citing Metz, *Theology of the World* (New York: Seabury, 1969). This book includes articles and chapters from 1962 onwards, with two titles of 1967 mentioning 'political theology', stating: 'The deprivatizing of theology is the primary critical task of political theology.' (110).

[12] Cavanaugh, 'Church', 401.

[13] Metz's rediscovery of the potential of religious orders well before MacIntyre's *After Virtue* could also have been included: *Zeit der Orden? Zur Mystik und Politik der Nachfolge* (Freiburg: Herder, 1977). A collection in English, translated, edited and introduced by J. Matthew Ashley contains a chapter, 'A Passion for God: Religious Orders Today', in J. B. Metz, *A Passion for God. The Mystical-Political Dimension of Christianity* (Mahwah, NJ.: Paulist Press, 1998), 150–74.

[14] Cavanaugh, 'Church', 401.

[15] Johann Baptist Metz, *Faith in History and Society*, trans. David Smith (New York: Crossroad, 1980).

arising from identifying the church as 'the bearer of God's politics': 'The eschatological "not yet" means that the history of the drama so far needs to be told hopefully but penitentially, with room for marginal voices and conflicts. The story is not told in an epic manner, as if the church were made to rule. As the embodiment of God's politics, the church nevertheless muddles through.'[16] Would it not have been better to desist from applying the title of being the 'bearer' or even the 'embodiment of God's politics' to itself, if the second half of the sentence is true? The hyperbole of the first half cancels the admission of ordinariness in the second.

(2) Brian Tierney as a defender of the 'inherent inseparability of church and politics'?

The second example of neglecting to provide a detailed reconstruction of a relevant position for the context of his own enquiry is Brian Tierney's work on medieval philosophy. His 1964 book is used for a quote: 'Conflicts between civil and ecclesiastical authorities were due not to the confusion of essentially distinct responsibilities but, on the contrary, to the inherent inseparability of church and politics.'[17] Could a more comprehensive account of Tierney's studies have been provided,[18] or might that have put the claimed 'inherent inseparability' into question? Tierney, who has identified the origin of human rights in medieval Canon Law, has had more to say on the subject than the reference to 1964 contains. How does the thinking of, for example, Marsilius of Padua, whom Tierney has studied, relate to the 'inseparability' thesis? Can it be discussed in connection with Marsilius's breakthrough achievement of anchoring 'power over people and material goods . . . neither in laws of nature nor . . . divine command' but 'on the consensus of all those affected'?[19] This is clearly a distinct foundation, contrary to the overarching claims of radical orthodoxy. Whether these are accurate or ideological can only be decided by exposing them to the expertise of recognized international researchers. They are able to compare these authors and their reception by

---

[16] Ibid., 405.
[17] Ibid.,397, with reference to Tierney, *The Crisis of Church and State 1050–1300* (Englewood Cliff, NJ.: Prentice-Hall, 1964), 1–11.
[18] This includes Tierney's book, *The Idea of Natural Rights. Studies on Natural Rights, Natural Law and Church Law 1150–1625* (Atlanta: Scholars Press, 1997) and his earlier and subsequent publications on Marsilius.
[19] Mieth, 'Human Dignity in Late Medieval Conflicts', in *Cambridge Handbook of Human Dignity*, 77, with reference to Ruedi Imbach, *Laien in der Philosophie des Mittelalters* (Bochum: B. R. Grüner, 1989), 163, for the quote from Marsilius.

different intellectual traditions and to discuss how they have contributed to inaugurating paths towards the modern world.

(3) Tasks of ethics: Reflection on agency and on avenues of action?

As a final point of engagement, Cavanaugh's understanding of ethics and the role of ecclesiology in this theological discipline will be assessed. The consistency of the Radical Orthodox project becomes especially clear when it is transferred to ethics – which is after all a discipline interpreting human agency – as the interpretations given to 'peace', 'participation', 'eucharist' and 'church' will show.

Whether the alternative to this movement's proposal is stated as descending into 'nihilism', as by John Milbank, or into 'war', the dualistic conception of church versus a godless sphere of human action reveals an apocalyptic imagination. The disjunction is such that gradual work for change is effectively ruled out. It can be seen as a sign of a dualistic programme of categorization in itself when instead of distinguishing concepts and levels, the net of classification thrown over reality consists just of two counterpoles. It is also indicative when, as in Hauerwas, 'peace' is the catch-all term for the flourishing life to be enabled. Unlike justice, which is a complex goal to be specified according to criteria to be justified for different spheres, there is a stark alternative between 'peace', and 'war' or 'violence'. By attaching the task of ethics immediately to the worst case that exacerbates all other violations of dignity, the danger is that an apocalyptic framework is construed in which no remedial action is conceivable, such as steps of peace building, or creating institutions of shared sovereignty with agreed mechanisms of conflict resolution. When an all-or-nothing, calamity or salvation scenario is cast, there is no starting point for human action. It is not by chance that the pre-Vatican Two Roman Rite is revalidated as the most fitting expression of liturgy, against the Council's rediscovery of the whole 'people of God', and the ideal of *participatio actuosa* to guide its liturgy reform. The Radical Orthodox definition of 'participation', by contrast, relates to 'the Church' as well as the individual believer 'participating' in the life of the Trinity. One can hardly find a more effective way than this theological model to curtail the idea of the freedom of God's human counterparts.[20]

---

[20] Cf. Thomas Fliethmann, 'Radical Orthodoxy. Zu einer neuen Bewegung in der anglo-amerikanischen Theologie', in *Herder-Korrespondenz* 56 (2002) 407–11, esp. 411.

Cavanaugh concludes his 2004 article, 'Killing for the Telephone Company' by relativizing the distinction between church and world: 'God's activity is not, of course, confined to the Church, and the boundaries between the Church and the world are porous and fluid. Nevertheless, the Church needs to take seriously its task of promoting spaces where participation in the common good of God's life can flourish.'[21] This raises the question whether it can collaborate with other, including secular, traditions for causes like equality and justice, peace and ecology, or whether its work for Jesus' idea of the kingdom of God is restricted to fellow believers in the Trinity. But even more relevant for theological ethics is the description of its location at the start:

> the Church is not a merely particular association, but participates in the life of the triune God, who is the only good that can be common to all. Through the Eucharist especially, Christians belong to a body that is not only international, and constantly challenges the narrow particularity of national interests, but is also eternal, the Body of Christ, that anticipates the heavenly polity on earth.[22]

Does 'anticipating' mean it already actualizes it? From the timeless spheres of the eucharist and the city of God, Christopher Insole brings the biblical and theological motifs back to earth by returning to the real historical origin of the eucharist. It brings the criterium of Jesus' life to bear on the style of theology pursued, preventing a self-assured concept of 'church':

> It is worth remembering that the Eucharist is a re-enactment of a meal marked by real presence fully given within the reality – amongst the 'visible church' of the disciples – of fear, anxiety, uncertainty and imminent betrayal. As then, so today. The Eucharist is not the generating centre of political transformation, or the site of 'full participation' if by that we mean the elimination – from expectation and memory – of all confusion, frailty, complexity and fallenness. The Eucharist does not authorize or sanctify the actions or political vision of the communicants; for which of us knows who is Judas and who is Peter, and who can be certain that, for them, the cock will not crow a second time?[23]

---

[21] Cavanaugh, 'Killing for the Telephone Company', 269.
[22] Ibid.
[23] Christopher J. Insole, *The Politics of Human Frailty: A Theological Defense of Political Liberalism* (London: SCM Press, 2004), 153. See also Insole, 'Against Radical Orthodoxy: The Dangers of Overcoming Political Liberalism', in *Modern Theology* 20 (2004): 213–41.

(c) The genealogical method

The key tool in the 1998 book for contesting the adequacy of distinguishing politics and religion is to show that this is an 'invention' of modernity based on a new concept, taken to be transhistorical and transcultural, of an 'interior' religion versus a 'public' and independent social order. A genealogical method is used to reveal the distinction as relying on an 'essentialist' assumption which is projected back anachronistically into eras which were undivided. For example, medieval people are portrayed as having understood the eucharist not as something belonging to the religious sphere, but as the highest symbol of their social order. Thus, if the distinction is an ideological 'invention' in the era of the modern nation-state in order to draw allegiance from the previous integral understandings of politics over to itself, then the natural condition must be a united one. Contemporary accusations of Islamic countries for lacking this distinction only reveal a modern prejudice. How is this position argued for? The typical gesture of the genealogical method is to claim insight into the real origins or reasons behind current conditions of thinking and living. The goal is to unmask the intention behind the 'invented' thesis, that politics and religions are meaningful analytical categories to distinguish different spheres of human life and action, while accepting their confluence in people's self-understanding. As a heuristic thesis, the integrative view offers productive perspectives for further enquiries, also into nineteenth-century processes of organizing denominations as 'pillars', or into the distinction between milieus and lifeworlds. But the thesis is a normative one, namely that the unity they attach to the Middle Ages constitutes the true state of matters, which needs to be rescued from modern detractions and restored. Cavanaugh traces the division of what should have remained inseparably one back to 'power'.[24] This ominous answer invites the objection that has been put to Nietzsche's introduction of a genealogical method of ideology critique. Ricoeur's question about the self-application of Nietzsche's unveiling of language as a tool not of truth but of power can also be put to Cavanaugh's claim:

> As for Nietzsche's own philosophy, either it exempts itself from the universal reign of *Verstellung* (dissimulation), . . . or else it succumbs to it (but then how can one justify the tone of revelation with which the will to power, the overman and the eternal return of the same are proclaimed?) This dilemma, which does not seem to have kept Nietzsche from thinking and writing, has

---

[24] Cavanaugh, *Myth*, 4.

become that of his commentators, split into two camps: the faithful and the ironists.[25]

If for Cavanaugh the ultimate factor is power, then his own thesis also falls under it. The deduction of the constitutional state from an illegitimate split from an order integrated under God is just one more truth or power claim which would have to argue for its assumptions with a different method than genealogy. A 'nothing but' reduction to a different basis – be it nature, life, power, or the self-serving hands of the belligerent state – is always affected by the attitude of the revelatory genius explaining the world in incontestable terms. It is the end to dialogue with anyone outside the fold. Ricoeur's observation of just 'two camps: the faithful and the ironists'[26] seems also to be an accurate picture of radical orthodoxy and its reception.

The next 'vision' to be analysed differs from this one not only by its praxis orientation. One of many distinctions is its distance of a view of politics that is built on a Hobbesian framework of survival against hostile others, instead of a concept of practical reason as recognition. Cahill outlines her starting point:

> Political realism, not otherworldliness, liberal individualism, or secularism is the biggest contemporary threat to Christian Ethics and the preferential option for the poor. Political realism is the idea not only that the overriding motive of moral and political behaviour is self-interest, but that self-interest is politically normative. While self-interest is indeed a powerful (and often valid) motivator, human beings and societies are capable of altruism and solidarity. It is these capabilities that salvation regenerates and to which Christian ethics appeals.[27]

2. Theological ethics as originating in and returning to praxis (Lisa Cahill)

The second 'vision' to be treated reconstructs Christian ethics as a discipline that arises out of practical contexts and leads back to them by elaborating criteria and directions of change that can be justified on the basis of biblical interpretation and systematic theological argumentation. The use of the

---

[25] Ricoeur, *Oneself as Another*, 13.
[26] Ibid., 13, n. 20. Ricoeur sees the 'French commentators . . . generally in the second camp'.
[27] Cahill, *Global Justice, Christology and Christian Ethics*, 6.

individual sciences comes in not only at the level of the ethical issues, but equally for the exegesis of the Hebrew Bible, for writings of the Second Temple period like Josephus and Qumran, and the New Testament. As the source of the 'normatively human', pragmatism is chosen due to its practical concept of truth. Thus, in contrast to the first model, it is already apparent that it interacts with the cognate disciplines at the university, such as history and philosophy, and uses their results without theological barriers or a suspicion of their secular character. Three points will be discussed: first, how this vision analyses the practical constitution of Christian ethics, emphasizing the practical nature of theological truth claims (a). Secondly, it will become clear that theoretical enquiries occupy a central place, in that the justifiability of Christian activism is made dependent on the results of historical Jesus research. It offers a coherent interpretation of the historical figure of Jesus on the backdrop of a comprehensive consideration of current scholarship. The first source of theological ethics is thus treated much more stringently than merely by reference to key New Testament texts. Jesus' message of the kingdom of God is investigated in relation to alternative views of apocalyptic thinking, taking the result of this historical enquiry as the criterium for Christian action. It would delegitimize present political action by Christians if one had to assume that Jesus understood the kingdom of God to be entirely in the future. The debate demonstrates convincingly that Christian ethics must expose its claims to what can be historically researched about the person of Jesus (b). Following this exegetical enquiry, the third theme relevant for ethical agency is how the knowing subject is reconstructed. Besides William James, the other pragmatist author drawn on here is George Herbert Mead. His theory of the interactive constitution of subjectivity has an ongoing history of reception in social sciences and philosophy, including Habermas's discourse ethics. Yet it will have to be faced with an objection that is crucial for any concept of moral responsibility (c).

(a) Ethics and theology, practice and theory as a 'two-way street'[28]

Lisa Cahill locates her approach in 'the revised "natural law" tradition rooted in Aquinas';[29] being revisionist, it gives great weight to experience and its

---

[28] Ibid., 3.
[29] Ibid., 4.

interpretation, including from a gendered power analysis. In her review of Pope John Paul II's moral theological encyclical *Veritatis Splendor* she sees the key deficit in an objectivizing method that lists 'intrinsically evil' acts, based on physicalist premises, without considering the intentions of the agents and their effects:

> A key contribution of feminism is to highlight the social context of moral agency, and to be attentive to concrete human relationships … Perhaps the lesson to be learned is that we reject some decisions and practices as morally abhorrent not on the basis of properties they possess 'in themselves' and apart from the dispositions and circumstances of agents, but because of their concrete and practical degradation of the human persons involved. Moral evil will not be recognised as such simply because an 'intrinsic evil' flag is waved over it; substantive and reasonable arguments must be advanced about the specific nature of the acts in question.[30]

At the same time, the framework she chooses is Thomas's outline of general human inclinations, goods and different classes of virtues to organize what would otherwise be an endless sequence of singular events: 'Yet one problem that arises as a result of feminist theology's appeal to "experience" is the danger of replacing oppressive generalizations with bottomless particularity. If women's experience alone is exalted as the final moral standard, we run the danger of feminist relativism which is ultimately unable to give any real reasons for preferring equality rather than hierarchy.'[31]

Equality is the criterion that is lacking in Aquinas's concrete interpretations of natural law, as becomes evident from a modern perspective. Endorsing the thesis of the 'link of socio-political realities and theoretical knowledge', Cahill turns the practical intention into a mark of truth: 'Not only do biblical and theological claims about salvation in Jesus Christ require active commitment to social justice; the practices in which Christians are already engaged shape their theological vision, and the just or unjust practical consequences of Christian concepts and doctrines are indicators of the latter's truth and adequacy.'[32] She does not go as far as Hauerwas in making the Christian truth claim dependent on the performance of the faithful, for example, in the orthopraxis of peacefulness, but she links biblical and theological propositions to their history of effects. A problematic example in the gospels is identified in the way in which John 'terms all Jesus' adversaries

---

[30] Cahill, 'Accent on the masculine', in *Understanding Veritatis Splendor*, ed. John Wilkins, 58–9.
[31] Ibid., 54–5.
[32] Cahill, *Global Justice, Christology and Christian Ethics*, 3–4.

"the Jews"[33]. The scope of this criterium of practical effects is not just the Christian church but all of God's creatures: 'Theology must be tested by its effects in human life, judged not only in terms of spiritual conversion and the formation of religious community, but also in terms of the well-being of human and other creatures.'[34]

While this second type of 'vision' clearly contains key elements of the third, theory-oriented one, to be treated in the final section, it defines its own self-understanding as being praxis-oriented and directed towards Christian action groups in cooperation with other traditions. But as the above quote indicates, it avoids the objection that a vision of the discipline as uniquely church-oriented has to face: why should theological ethics limit itself to the matters that are being pursued by Christian communities? Why should it be kept from engaging with these burning issues directly, in their own right, because they are equally pressing for Christian and other human beings?[35] The choice of problems that are in urgent need of analysis and transformation is global, and the reason for putting them on the agenda is not that one's church is doing so but because these issues affect lives.

(b) Recognizing historical critical research on the Bible as a benchmark for theological and ethical proposals

Cahill's elaboration of an approach based on natural law gives much more space to the Bible than would be expected in a model that usually begins with universalist claims about human nature. She does not treat the Bible in an exhortative way as Scripture that unites its followers – as the first chapter of *Veritatis Splendor* does with Matthew's account of the rich young man who goes away sadly after Jesus' request to give his wealth to the poor (Mt. 19.16–22). Instead, she discusses the historical analyses needed to establish its meaning in the era of its writing. Examining it as a document in its own right before drawing conclusions for contemporary Christian living, her aim is to identify the best available evidence also in areas of ongoing debate. This approach can be traced back both to the natural law regard for

---

[33] Ibid., 116.

[34] Ibid., 3.

[35] This is the question Anzenbacher poses to a church-centred, liberation-oriented model in *Christliche Sozialethik*, 166, naming unemployment, the environment, and global inequality as 'actual social problems' that merit attention as such.

the light of reason, and to the feminist realization of the need to distinguish the message of salvation from the patriarchal understandings that are also contained in the biblical texts. The fact that this interdisciplinary project has practical import for present and future lives calls for hermeneutical watchfulness, in order to distinguish between biblical horizons and current interests: 'Historical understanding helps eliminate faulty readings that are unlikely to reflect how Jesus was received in his own era and helps make credible analogies from his time to ours.'[36] The search for 'integration' of the different 'sources' of theological ethics does not allow for premature conclusions. Cahill does not take it for granted that one can justify Christian action for justice with the practice of the historical Jesus. The decisive question for her is how to assess the status of the kingdom of God, as present or as future, in Jesus' proclamation:

> Given the now incontrovertible Jewish identity of Jesus, it must be agreed that his preaching of the kingdom of God is set in an apocalyptic framework. But to what extent did Jesus share or modify typical features of this worldview? What effect might this have had on his ethical and political outlook? And what difference does that make for Christian ethics today?[37]

Acknowledging with John Collins 'Jesus' purported apocalypticism as one of the most debated issues since the rise of the historical-critical approaches to the bible',[38] she makes it dependent on the research result whether Christians should be active in transforming the world: 'For Christian ethics and politics, the present dimension of the kingdom is essential to validate action and transformation.'[39] Or should they wait, in line with the apocalyptic literature, for 'God's decisive action'? Having so far presented much of the Second Temple and Historical Jesus research on their points of convergence, she selects Frank Matera's treatment of this question as a counter-view not to be ignored. Should the gospel of Mark with its open ending be judged as the document closest to Jesus himself, and the other synoptic authors as reflecting the early church's resurrection-coloured view? In this case, not Jesus himself, but only some of the gospel writers would have proclaimed the Kingdom of God to have already begun. Justifying all

---

[36] Cahill, *Global Justice, Christology and Christian Ethics*, 83.

[37] Ibid., 94.

[38] Ibid., quoting John Collins, *The Apocalyptic Imagination. An Introduction to Jewish Apocalyptic Literature* (Grand Rapids, MI: Eerdmans, 2nd edn 1998), and elsewhere to Historical Jesus scholars, such as Seán Freyne, *Jesus, a Jewish Galilean. A New Reading of the Jesus Story* (Edinburgh: T & T Clark, 2004).

[39] Cahill, *Global Justice, Christology and Christian Ethics*, 100.

efforts since then to contribute to its continued realization could then not be based on Jesus himself: 'If so, transformative Christian politics of the kingdom can trace its pedigree to the New Testament (and perhaps to the risen Jesus) but not to Jesus of Nazareth as a historical figure.'[40]

It is remarkable that Matera's position is not just dismissed as diverging from a mainstream view but that the question is argued out: 'If so, the Jesus of history does not licence an activist social stance, though the resurrection option in the later canonical materials does provide an alternative basis for a theology and politics of effective action for the church.'

Three reasons – historical, exegetical, and hermeneutical – are given to support the interpretation that for Jesus, through his actions of preaching and healing, the kingdom had already begun: the 'scandalous authority' he claimed, the exegetical rejection of Bultmann's disjunction of the kerygma from the figure of Jesus, and the point that a 'one-sided neo-apocalypticism ... is inadequate not only to the gospels, but to the complexity of Jewish expectations'.[41]

Paying attention to this controversy in biblical studies shows convincingly that details which could be seen as specialized and arcane have great significance for Christian ethics: 'the downside of a view of salvation that is almost entirely future-focused is that it leads to political disengagement or passivity, not likely to have been the stance of Jesus. And theologically and religiously, it amounts to a denial that salvation really arrived in the earthly Jesus.'[42]

(c) The pragmatist reconstruction of the self from intersubjectivity and the question of moral imputability

Respecting the independence of biblical studies from theology and ethics, Lisa Cahill has given an instructive account of what the natural law approach can deliver. The concepts in which moral agency is captured, however, confirm the previous critique of a weakness that can be traced back to its medieval origin: an objectivist format that lacks a convincing account of the subject as the centre of reflection, agency and responsibility which was established

---

[40] Ibid., 99.
[41] Ibid., 100.
[42] Ibid., 99–100.

through Kant's 'Copernican turn' as the critical epistemological starting point. There is no doubt that pragmatism can offer resources for theology and ethics. Yet the point that recommends it for Cahill as a modern philosophical partner for revisionist natural law is much-contested: the description that 'selves are socially constituted, their identities formed within particular worldviews and their attendant practices'[43] is only true at the level of the concrete, historical existence of individuals. But this cannot account for the capability of self-reflection. Cahill herself indicates the need for greater differentiation when she states: '(As a social ethicist whose watchword was "responsibility", [H. Richard] Niebuhr would certainly agree with Margaret Archer that the emergence of agency out of social structures need not be construed deterministically.)'[44] The quote that follows, however, Mead's position that selves derive 'from the social process in which they are implicated and in which they empirically interact with one another', only reinforces the view that intersubjectivity is the one and only origin of the 'self'. Dieter Henrich's critique of Jürgen Habermas on this point bears repeating: that this reduces a constitutive polarity to one pole, from which crucial capabilities cannot be explained. The opposite pole, self-reflection, needs to be accounted for; it relies, in Henrich's terms, on a 'prior familiarity with oneself' or an 'implied self-relation' that cannot be traced back to intersubjective relations.[45] The fact that distinctive approaches like communitarianism, natural law and discourse ethics continue to hold this view does not mean that the objection has been successfully refuted: in terms of Mead's theory, the unthematized element that makes it possible for the self to distinguish between the 'I' and the 'Me', and in terms of ethics, the lack of an accountable, imputable subject which cannot be established on the basis of the categories used. The factor that enables resistance to succumbing to the alleged genesis from intersubjective formation needs to be identified, especially in connection with a power analysis. The duality of the formal, transcendental level of freedom and its concrete realization, or the corresponding duality of *ipse* and *idem* in Ricoeur's theory of self are the basis on which one can distinguish between action and behaviour, morality and social adaptation, individuality and collectivity; without it, also the call of God to each human being as well as her response cannot be theoretically anchored.

---

[43] Ibid., 13.
[44] Ibid.
[45] Dieter Henrich, 'What Is Metaphysics – What Modernity?', 311. I have discussed his objections in *Habermas and Theology* (London: T & T Clark International, 2011), 48–56. 61–6.

Apart from this point, conceiving Christian ethics as grounded in praxis, as interpreted and directed further by bringing biblical and theological insights and criteria to fruition, and as seeking adequate institutional and legal structures to accompany local initiatives and protect subsidiarity is an encompassing and dialogical vision.

3. Theological ethics in interaction with three 'publics': University, society, church (David Tracy)

The third outline of a vision relevant for theological ethics follows David Tracy's mapping of the three 'publics' of Christian theology. While proposed by a systematic theologian, it extends to all the subdisciplines, and the work of several of the Christian ethicists used in this book exemplifies this model. The three publics are the 'academy' or university (a), contemporary culture (b), and the church (c). The modes of communication are conceived in accordance with the different interaction partners. Unlike the previous model, it sees its task as being centrally located at the level of theoretical enquiries. In what way contexts of 'praxis' play a role in them, is one of these examinations; it calls for a comparison of the philosophical backgrounds of devising the praxis–theory relationship, for example a hermeneutical or a naturalizing model. The theoretical work of reconstructing argumentations, of devising criteria for evaluation from what is discovered as morally relevant, and of mapping out different routes arising from them does not depend for its validity on being connected to movements and initiatives. While this is a desirable and motivating activity, it cannot make imprecise, incomprehensive or underdifferentiated analyses correct. Thus, while participation in ecclesial and political causes sharpens the awareness of priorities and offers access to the self-understandings of fellow activists, it cannot replace the task of in-depth treatment of the theoretical positions available in theology and philosophy, ethics and the individual sciences. Perseverance in continuing the dialogical work of theology and ethics when most of their peers kept within the limits of neo-scholasticism created the foundation for the current intellectual exchanges and cooperations that take place within a far more differentiated and complex society.

(a) The university as a 'public' shaping theology

Tracy defines the first level of publicness that theology engages in as a 'rational enquiry' with 'dialectical arguments'. 'Public' is understood as the effort to 'render one's claims shareable', to 'provide reasons for one's assertions'. For theological ethics, this means to relate its four sources to each other in transparent and argued steps. For Tracy, it is clear that even with striving for 'consistence and coherence' and giving 'the evidence, warrants and backings for those claims', all that can be achieved is 'relative adequacy ... for its complex and difficult claims'.[46]

For theology's dialogues within the university and with other religions, the model of theology as *scientia* or 'sure knowledge' is decisive.[47] By taking a step back from the scriptures and the practices developed from them in different cultural settings, and by using the capacity of philosophical analysis, the Anselmian brief for theology, 'faith seeking understanding', is pursued. As a second-order activity that reflects on first-order religious experience, theology is a conceptual discipline with typical forms like those developed in the nascent medieval universities, *disputatio* and *quaestio*. From the sociology of knowledge perspective he takes, Robert Schreiter has identified the two contexts in which this type functions best: 'the highly specialized and differentiated situations in urban economies, and wherever there is a plurality of competing worldviews'. In its skill of relating to different cultures of knowledge it possesses 'special capacities for cross-cultural communication'[48] which distinguishes it from the other three types.

The ability for dialogue across boundaries is a clear advantage arising from the distance it takes from its own religious practice, and from relating its truth claims to the general consciousness of truth, as it is constituted by philosophical reason in different eras. This interest had been signalled as a

---

[46] David Tracy, 'Three Kinds of Publicness in Public Theology', in *International Journal of Public Theology* 8 (2014): 331. Cf. 'Religion in the public realm: Three forms of publicness', in *At the Limits of the Secular: Reflections on Faith and Public Life*, ed. Willliam A. Barbieri (Grand Rapids, MI: Eerdmans, 2014), 31–50. Cf. Tracy, *Blessed Rage for Order: The New Pluralism in Theology* (New York: Seabury Press, 1975).

[47] For a comparison of four types of theology, each compared in relation to the knowledge cultures they respond to, cf. Robert Schreiter, *Constructing Local Theologies* (Maryknoll, NY: Orbis, 1985), 75–94. The other three are theology as variations on a sacred text, as wisdom, and as praxis.

[48] Schreiter, *Constructing Local Theologies*, 90.

crucial bridge by the natural law and the autonomous ethicists, including their feminist contributors. It is a capacity which Anzenbacher identifies as necessary once the living community settings of virtue ethics are no longer shared. The latter approach 'meets its limits where the praxis of social contexts is no longer normed unequivocally, but is marked by instances of dissent, as well as in places where the relevant traditions have become fragile and contested ... In these cases there is no alternative to using forms of argumentation.'[49]

Thus, especially for a normative discipline, it is indispensable to reflect on the level of theories, their origin and their intricacies; for example, the question whether a proposal is complete in itself, or whether it constitutes one pole of a polarity, requiring a higher level at which their opposition can be resolved. An example with great relevance for biblical and theological interpretation would be the balancing of claims between Gadamer's hermeneutics of belonging and Habermas's ideology critique, as accomplished by Ricoeur.[50]

Are political struggles for ecological justice, equality and participation left out of consideration when the need to continue the work of theorizing is defended? Or do practices of support and integration, for example of refugees, need backing also at the level of disputes between theories? In my view, the trust that the level of theory merits sustained, undivided attention is justified by the practical effect of such conceptions. Is, for instance, the humanitarian 'duty of assistance' stated by John Rawls in his *Law of Peoples* sufficient? Or is a more encompassing, global perspective needed from which existing regulatory frameworks, for example, for trade, may turn out to be unjust? As direct contributors to theories of justice, theological ethicists should join forces with other thinkers, also secular ones, who defend a universalist scope of ethics. In the Genesis account of creation, God in both stories gives the earth to humans as stewards. A political ethical equivalent can be seen in Kant's a priori conclusion from the idea of humankind and the earth's shape as a globe that every presently living member originally has a claim to owning an equal share of the surface of the earth as all the others. They also have a right to visit, even before treaties have been concluded

---

[49] Anzenbacher, *Einführung in die Ethik*, 149.
[50] Ricoeur, 'Hermeneutics and the Critique of Ideology', in *Hermeneutics and the Human Sciences*, ed. and trans. John B. Thompson (Cambridge: CUP, 1981), 63–100.

between states.[51] This thought, the consequence of a universalist perspective on morality and on justice between fellow humans offers a different starting point, for example, in the struggle for land rights than egalitarian liberalism does; it allows to challenge it and its libertarian and communitarian fellow theorists to reconsider tying justice to the borders of their own polity.

The second type of 'public' Tracy outlines with its appropriate mode of communication is not secluded from the academic exchange in its search for truth, and is in a position to take account of the major debates and alternatives put forward on current issues. But the task and the reasoning are distinct.

(b) The contribution of Christian 'classics' to renewing cultural self-understandings

The second 'public' to which theology contributes is society's process of developing an understanding of its cultural values and resources, their roots and future directions. Here, the method is 'dialogical' or 'hermeneutical', on contents that are also known to non-religious citizens as part of culture, 'the Christian classics', as Tracy calls them, using a term of Hans-Georg Gadamer. He notes that 'the public realm is a realm of civilized conversation before it is a realm of argument', a point he made against Habermas's sole focus on discourse already in 1989.[52] It is still a 'form of ... disciplined enquiry', dedicated to 'understanding the public dimensions of the ineluctable particularity of religion' as expressed in 'text, event, symbol, story, image, music, . . . persons, rituals'. Tracy points out their relevance for ethics, since it

---

[51] In *Perpetual Peace*, Kant argues that 'the law of world citizenship shall be limited to conditions of universal hospitality'. It is less than 'the right to be a permanent visitor' in someone's household, which needs an invitation. 'It is only a right to visit, to offer themselves as company, which all humans have. They have it by virtue of their common possession of the surface of the earth, where, as a globe, they cannot infinitely disperse and hence must finally tolerate the presence of each other. Originally, no one had more right than another to a particular part of the earth . . . In this way distant parts of the world can come into peaceable relations with each other, and these are finally publicly established by law. Thus the human race can gradually be brought closer and closer to a constitution enabling world citizenship.' In sharp contrast to this prospect is the behaviour of European colonialists: 'If we compare with this the *inhospitable* conduct of the civilised states of our continent, especially the commercial states, the injustice which they display in *visiting* foreign countries and peoples (which in their case is the same as *conquering* them) seems appallingly great.' Immanuel Kant, *On History*, ed. Lewis White Beck (Indianapolis/New York: The Library of Liberal Arts/Bobbs Merrill, 1963), 102–3 (L. W. Beck's translation slightly amended).

[52] Tracy, 'Theology, Critical Social Theory, and the Public Realm', in Don S. Browning and Francis Schüssler Fiorenza (eds), *Habermas, Modernity, and Public Theology* (New York: Crossroad, 1992), 19–42.

is 'especially the religious classics that provide visions of the good, including the good life of an individual and a society'.[53]

The level at which this significance is to be made available by theologians correlates with a 'model' ethics embodied by persons, and the narrative, literary traces of the search for meaning and hope, shaping attitudes also of emerging social movements. The strength of this proposal is that it includes questions of the good as well as of the right, and opens up a space of encounter for elucidating and listening to components of practical self-understandings: 'The paradox of the classic is that, however particular in origin and expression, it is public in effect; hence, classics are excellent candidates for discussion of ends and values for any enquirer in the public realm.'[54]

Such appeals to shared understandings can create a new cohesion which is important for debates on how ecology and migration, technology and biotechnology may change future lifeworlds. In ethics, the effort to outline a horizon under which segmented roles can be integrated into a reflective, self-determined life 'with and for others in just institutions',[55] can draw on 'biblical classics': 'religious thinkers should ... present their classical (especially biblical) resources as plausible candidates for public acceptance of their truth-value.'[56] Due to their literary and artistic history of effects, conversation is not about justifying what can count as correct interpretations, as in the first forum. Being classics, they have a 'permanence and excess of meaning that resists definitive, once-and-for-all interpretation'.[57] Rather than asking theologians and ethicists to 'translate' religious meanings into 'generally accessible' ones, as Habermas has put the task, in the dialogue with classics one can draw on a shared cultural heritage in which believers are naturally bilingual, knowing both the religious and the cultural side. Tracy sees the need to impart a new literacy as decisive for keeping the different uses of reason from withering:

> Without learning new skills to dialogue with all the classics of all the traditions (starting with our own Christian tradition): religion will be privatized with no claim to public truth; art will be marginalized with no claim to disclosing some truth about our condition; ... without new dialogical

---

[53] Tracy, 'Three Kinds of Publicness', 332.

[54] Ibid.

[55] Ricoeur, *Oneself as Another*, 172.

[56] Tracy, 'Three Kinds of Publicness', 333.

[57] Ibid.

skills, reason itself will become so technicized that it could join a privatized religion and a marginalized art. To avoid that fate, we need dialogical-hermeneutical public conversation with the Christian classics.[58]

One need only think of the recent changes to the public sphere through new media with their tendency to revert to closed circles which mutually confirm the positions of their 'friends' to realize the urgency of contributing to re-invigorating a public sphere in which exchanges across distinct worldviews can take place. For Tracy, each of the three publics as a community of enquiry and commitment has its proper criteria for publicness. It is easy to see the relevance of a hermeneutical perspective for self-conceptions. They are reminded of the heritage of the contingent encounters and transformations which have shaped the history of reception of the Bible in its interaction with Greek and subsequent philosophies, Roman law and institutions, and the cultures it later spread to. Tracy's encouragement of a 'dialogue with all the classics of all the traditions' by starting with one's own implies the hermeneutical insight that there is no pure, presuppposition-less entry point. Already being shaped by one language and culture enables persons to access other linguistic and religious traditions, aware of the role of key contents and turning points of interpretation in their own culture. An instructive example is the interest and effort of the monotheistic religions in antiquity and the Middle Ages to translate their own and other scriptures: the Hebrew Bible into the Septuagint, the New Testament into the languages around the Mediterranean and the Vulgate, and the transmission of Arabic science and Aristotelian philosophy through joint translations. It shows the potential for dialogue that the monotheistic religions had in them and how, despite their political and theological conflicts, they created new platforms for further intellectual developments.

(c) The church as a public uniting sapiential and prophetic-ethical orientations

The task assigned to the third public, the Christian church, is to connect the two main streams of the Bible, a meditative-sapiential thinking, and the 'prophetic-ethical-political primary character of biblical religion': 'The biblical monotheistic religions are prophetic-meditative religions, where the more universalizing, metaphysical and aesthetic wisdom traditions have an

---

[58] Ibid.

important role but are informed and transformed by the more ethical political prophetic traditions with their desire for the good as the dialectic of justice and love, especially for the marginalized and the poor.'[59] The challenge for theological ethics, then, is to elaborate how agency is affected by the 'wisdom' or 'mystic' dimensions of the biblical message. I will outline the concrete relevance of Tracy's point on the 'meditative' or 'mystical' for two current debates. One is by following his reference to Gregory of Nyssa, the other Ricoeur's use of the term 'mystic' in his debate with Hans Küng on the project of a 'global ethic' constituted by the world's religions, where Ricoeur insists on the relevance of the *'fonds mystique'* of each.

It is worth following Tracy's pointer to Gregory of Nyssa as one of the 'beyond-the-limit thinkers' who used the term 'mystical'.[60] He is portrayed by Kobusch as one of the key patristic thinkers of human freedom, including a dispute with Eunomius on the power of naming given by God to humans, according to Genesis, from which Gregory develops a philosophy of language.[61] Some of his counterparts were actual Gnostics, unlike what William Cavanaugh labels as being 'Gnostic' in contemporary society: those initiating sustained dialogue with other traditions are counted as 'Gnostics' since they seem to devalue or 'disembody' their own tradition by speaking to others.[62] If contemporary theologians see 'resourcement' from the patristic authors as a priority, Gregory of Nyssa seems like a highly relevant theologian to start with.

The 'mystical' level is also identified by Paul Ricoeur as the *'fonds'* of the truly particular. It does not cancel reason-led analysis but opens up a different space of encounter than the first, dialectical, platform of examining reasons. In his debate with Hans Küng on the project of a 'global ethic', Ricoeur makes the case for the relevance of particularity for ethics. Continuing a key thought from his 1961 article, 'Universal civilisation and national cultures',[63] he defends the unique and irreplaceable standing of the distinct cultures and religions which renew themselves from their *'fonds mystique'* in their historical encounters.

---

[59] Ibid., 331.
[60] Ibid., 333–4.
[61] Kobusch, *Christliche Philosophie*, 76–83.He also quotes Jérôme Gaïth's comment on Gregory's theory of freedom: 'the Sartre of Christian Antiquity', in *La conception de la liberté chez Grégoire de Nysse. Etudes de philosophie médievale* 43 (Paris: Librairie Philosophique J. Vrin, 1953), 106.
[62] Cavanaugh, *Church*, 403: 'There can be no question of a disembodied Christianity that serves only, in a Gnostic fashion, to inform the consciences of individual citizens occupying an autonomous political space.'
[63] Ricoeur, *History and Truth*, 271–84.

These original and abiding differences are of interest to philosophy. Küng, by contrast, wants to disregard 'dogmatic differences' in favour of 'practical agreements': 'how to live together does not depend on our conception of mystery'. One can see in this approach an analogy to the 'overlapping consensus' conceived by Rawls as a way of pacifying the pluralism of worldviews. For Ricoeur, what matters is to find out what in each religion 'leads to respecting life, the word, social justice'. He asks about the source, the '*fonds* of convictions which is more than ethical ... Religions can go back into the depth of their traditions, to the unsaid'.[64] Thus, Ricoeur, the philosopher, stands up for the particular, while Küng, the theologian, accompanies the different traditions at the World Parliament of Religions in working out the 'irrevocable principles and directives' which they can jointly endorse.

Tracy's argument for the 'meditative' or 'mystical' is equally not the opposite of the active, political and prophetic expression of a religious faith tradition, but a source of renewal within its changing cultural and political constellations. If ethics fails to explore this hermeneutical dimension, it will cut itself off from the ultimate ground of regeneration of each person's subjectivity in his or her evolving self-interpretations.

To conclude this final 'vision' for theological ethics: Tracy's distinction of three types of 'publicness' seems to me to identify succinctly at what levels the sustained intellectual work of this discipline is needed. It strengthens the philosophical and theological capacity for self-reflection against positivism, scientism, commercialization and 'self-instrumentalization'[65] that a technological culture will foster if it is left bereft of reason (*Vernunft*) as the search for the unconditioned, prioritizing instrumental reason (*Verstand*). The differentiated vision offered by Tracy identifies and relates three originary levels of reflection as well as the 'publics' relevant for the work of theological ethics in a productive and appreciative way. There is no need to play off the interior and the praxis-oriented, nor the intellectual and the ecclesial dimensions of religion. In view of the deep oppositions between conceptions of theological ethics this is a most helpful clarification and preparation of a space for renewing ethical reflection.

---

[64] 'Les religions, la violence et la paix', Entretien Hans Kung-Paul Ricoeur autour du 'Manifeste pour une ethique planetaire' (ed. du Cerf), ARTE April 5, 1996, Redaction: Laurent Andres, cf. www.fondsricoeur.fr, under ,texts on line', 2–9 (last accessed January 6, 2019). It is also published in *Sens. Revue de l'amitié judéo-chrétienne de France* 5 (1998): 211–30.
[65] Habermas, *The Future of Human Nature*, 66–73.

Conclusion

Reflecting on the overview of the field of theological ethics, I first want to highlight one insight from each part (1). Taking Christianity as one of the traditions that constitute the 'pre-political foundations' of a state, its ongoing vitality is relevant for civic and moral solidarity. With a critical understanding of the expectation to be a 'resource', Christianity can help shape future directions. The question is what mode of communication it should choose in its contributions to the public realm (2).

1. One conclusion from each part

The variety of approaches and of visions of this discipline could be a field of helpful complementarity, mutual critique and shared interest in contributing to working out solutions to contemporary challenges. Among these are climate change, the outsourcing of responsibility to digital decision makers and migration. At least for some of these questions Christian theology is well equipped to propose thought-through and practicable ways of engaging, due to its biblical foundations and its tradition of encounter and reasoning. It can help create conditions for peaceful and fruitful coexistence by welcoming strangers and negotiating a framework of terms of mutual recognition for individuals, groups, cultures and religions.

The reality of the discipline of theological ethics shows that these opportunities are not being used sufficiently in a constructive way. Internal struggles for legitimation to converse with philosophy, law and the human sciences continue, as the ongoing debate about autonomous ethics reveals since its beginnings almost half a century ago. Christian ethics should not leave the public sphere devoid of its competence to compare premises and parameters. In this task, it can join forces with other theorists to mark out tendentious interpretations, lacunae and failures to teach the next generation of practitioners and communities about shared basics and current controversies. If the culture wars in liberal as well as traditional societies are being replicated, and not overcome, Christian theologians are contributing to the polarization within societies; they should be concerned whether they are misusing the Bible and failing to question an inward-looking defence of identity.

(a) Sources

From the four *sources* of the discipline, the authoritative foundation is to be found in the Bible. The survey of approaches has shown how problematic it is not to use the capacity of historical reason for its interpretation, thus doing justice to its authority as the counterpart to the churches of all ages. Contemporary congregations and their theologians are not in a relationship of linear continuation but in one of response to the founder Jesus Christ and his message of salvation. The antidote to using the New Testament as a projection screen for present interests is to research it with the methods of historical and archaeological, philological and hermeneutical, literary and other enquiries.[1] While the integration of their findings is a further task that goes beyond biblical studies, using these secular disciplines rules out taking a shortcut to the desired results.[2] A striking example of such an

---

[1] In 'The Virtue of Hospitality According to the Bible and the Challenge of Migration', in *The Bible and Catholic Theological Ethics*, 35–36, Alain Thomasset discusses methods of interpretation: 'Christians have used the Bible as a quarry from which to extract neat proof texts in order to support a demonstration based primarily on philosophical arguments. This method is obviously inadequate, because it separates the text from its literary and historical contexts, and reduces the Bible to a tool within another type of thinking altogether. The historical-critical methods, which seek to understand the text on the basis of its original setting, are much more adequate. For their part, synchronic methods of analysis illuminate the interpretation of the text by unveiling the literary structures and the forms or styles of writing.' He concludes with a further task: 'But neither of these more enlightened approaches can tell us what impact the revealed text should have on our lives.'

[2] An example for building a bridge to theology from the historical research of biblical studies, and with a hermeneutical consciousness of its history of reception, is Seán Freyne's article, 'The Galilean Jesus and a Contemporary Christology', in *Theological Studies* 70 (2009): 281–97.

instrumentalization of the New Testament is the way in which the Hauerwas school in its more recent specification towards worship has based a whole approach to Christian ethics on one verse, taken from Jesus' explanation of his baptism in the gospel of Matthew, 'to fulfil all righteousness' (Mt. 3.13–17). It is interpreted as 'the foundation' and 'the event of Christian Ethics', making 'possible the whole discipline'.[3] This is done without comparing Matthew's account of Jesus' baptism by John to the other gospels and their emphases, for example, on Jesus' praying in Luke's version, with the trajectory of each gospel. It is significant that Matthew ends with the call to 'go and make disciples of all nations, baptizing them in the name of the Father and of the Son and of the Holy Spirit' (Mt. 28.19). This conclusion of Matthew's is the opposite to the inward orientation of the worship approach and a highly relevant question for theological reflection: How do Jesus' first words in Matthew relate to this post-Easter interpretation of his intention?

(b) Approaches

A key distinguishing factor between the five *approaches* was the choice of philosophical schools that spell out the third source of the 'normatively human'. The need for precision became evident in the characterization of counter-positions: for example, not to identify a late twentieth-century liberal concept, such as 'rational agent', with 'the Enlightenment'. This period, together with Romanticism, constitutes an 'axial age' for the modern concepts of the subject, of freedom, and public reason, as well as for understanding 'the other', and for devising institutions that are in keeping with the dignity of each human being. There were several distinct and mutually critical approaches that were put forward, starting with Rousseau in the 1760s, to Kant, Fichte, Hegel, Schelling and the Romantic philosophers of subjectivity. Instead of assuming a non-existent homogeneity between the different 'Enlightenment' authors, it is necessary to ask further whose specific work is being critiqued from today's perspective. Theological ethics cannot proceed without taking account of the history and of the present stage of philosophical interpretations. As became clear in Chapter 8, also theological authors agree that the experience of moral obligation cannot be captured as an external rule. Instead of branding 'autonomy' as 'monological subjectivism',[4] two concepts need to be distinguished: one is principled, the other choice-based.

---

[3] Hauerwas and Wells, *Blackwell Companion to Christian Ethics*, 14–15.
[4] Cf. Pröpper, critically, in *Evangelium und freie Vernunft*, 62.

It turns out that it is the second, authenticity-oriented version, which is prone to downplaying the discrepancy between self-interest and recognizing the other as an end in herself. It is foremost the agency of every fellow human that is owed support, requiring both the legal protection of scope for action, and personal initiatives to help. Without 'free space (*Freiraum*) individuals are not able to realize their competence to act. This free space requires legal protection which can only be conceived in a stringent way by using the paradigm of contract; only under this premise can the same freedom be secured for all citizens.'[5] But this level is not sufficient, and the relation of self-legislation to the happiness of others has to be actively pursued both in what it prohibits and in what it calls for: 'It is of the greatest importance that the connection of "self-legislation" to happiness is not about one's own happiness but that of others', expressed in the 'narrow' and the 'wide' duties contained in the categorical imperative. Its demand to 'always respect human beings as persons implies, on the one hand, the prohibition to instrumentalize them against their will, and, on the other, to offer support and promote their well-being.' Instrumentalization for one's own purposes means 'robbing them of their innermost competence – to shape their own lives'. The 'wide' sense of making available 'means that enable their self-determination' corresponds to 'what social and development political conceptions call "empowerment".'[6]

Thus, 'autonomy' in the moral sense of supporting the self-determination of others remains distinct from the 'authenticity' people strive for as a key to a flourishing life. Monika Bobbert has noted the additional danger that 'authenticity' can become a replacement for the task to work out the best moral and institutional responses under the given circumstances.[7] This would include using all the information that is available from the four sources. While promoting the virtue approach, James Keenan has cited the critique that virtue can be 'introspective'.[8] Its agents may be found to perceive existing problems – that would need interdisciplinary analysis and justified proposals for action – mainly in terms of their own virtuous integrity.

[5] HND, *Innere Freiheit*, 89.
[6] Ibid., 97.
[7] Bobbert, 'Zum Proprium der christlichen Moral', in Bobbert and Mieth, *Proprium der christlichen Ethik*, 53. Instead of assuming that a person's experience of God will lead to the right moral answers, she clarifies that it would be necessary to indicate the points of transition, first, between anthropology and an ethics of striving for a flourishing life, and secondly between the dimension of personal identity and of coming to a judgement at the normative level (ibid., 54).
[8] Keenan, 'Virtue Ethics' in Hoose (ed.), *Christian Ethics*, 90.

Reducing principled autonomy to different versions of the 'good' that leave out the 'sieve of the norm'[9] or the element of critical self-scrutiny may have similar effects as the ideal of the 'unencumbered self' that is being critiqued.

(c) Visions

The theological premise of the deontological critique of approaches and concepts that do not reflect on the human propensity for rationalizing one's motivations is the universal salvific will of God. It is the criterium by which also the *'visions'* of theological ethics have been judged. Here, a thought of Magnus Striet in the context of questioning the requested change in Roman Catholic liturgical texts from remembering Jesus' death 'for all', to, 'for the many', is incisive. Striet concludes his critical reflections with the call to the participants in the liturgy to pray themselves that it will be possible for God to extend God's mercy to all, including the perpetrators of the most horrific crimes. This would presuppose their remorse, which one can only pray for.[10] This need arises if, as he assumes with Thomas Pröpper, God's forgiveness cannot happen over the heads of the victims.[11] Emphasizing God's universal will of salvation is thus not left at the level of a theological position in the debate on the outcome of the Last Judgement; it is made accessible to modes of agency open to the faithful. Their prayer enacts a hope that realizes what reason could not accomplish on its own: its striving for the 'unconditioned'. This outreach beyond its own powers is not discredited by the fact that humans in their finitude cannot make it happen retroactively for each victim in history. But it shows a possibility that is unique to people with a faith commitment, to remember their suffering with the hope that the victory of evil and death will be overcome by the even greater power of God's love.

---

[9] This is how Ricoeur entitles the deontological step in his tripartite ethics, *Oneself as Another*, 170.

[10] Striet, 'Nur für viele oder doch für alle? Das Problem der Allerlösung und die Hoffnung der betenden Kirche', in *Gestorben für wen? Zur Diskussion um das 'pro multis'*, ed. Magnus Striet, 90.

[11] In a text originally published in 1993 in a *Festschrift* for J. B. Metz, Pröpper asks: 'However, not only God would (*dürfte*) forgive, also the victims themselves would have to want to do so and thus be respected in the dignity of their violated freedom . . . Do we not have to trust that God's love may also enable persons for such reconciliation?' *Evangelium und freie Vernunft*, 274.

2. Particular traditions as 'pre-political foundations' as resources for civic solidarity and as contributors to the public sphere

Regarding reflection on moral action and proposals for policy directions, theological ethics is the steward of a tradition that has shaped the symbolic foundations of Western society which it helped create.[12] After taking account of the 'paradox' on which the secular state is founded (a), and of examples from the conceptual development of philosophy which Habermas traces to the biblical heritage (b), I will examine in conclusion the question of the mode of interaction of Christian and other religious traditions with the public sphere (c).

(a) The neutrality of the state as a principle and as a risk

Under the title, 'Pre-political Foundations of the Constitutional State?', Jürgen Habermas and the then Cardinal Ratzinger discussed the question whether the 'pacified, secular state is reliant on normative presuppositions that it cannot itself guarantee'.[13] This question from 2004 sums up a thesis of the constitutional lawyer and later Supreme Court judge Ernst-Wolfgang Böckenförde of the mid-1960s which has had a long history of debate.[14] On the one hand, the neutrality of the state was realized for reasons of principle, to protect the freedom of religion and worldview; on the other, this act of

---

[12] In *Woher kommen wir? Ursprünge der Moderne im Mittelalter* (Darmstadt: WBG, 2008), Ludger Honnefelder traces the origins of modernity to the Middle Ages. He points out that 'our historical origin (*Herkunft*) determines to a high degree the horizons in which we live and understand ourselves ... which lasting traces has it left in our own cultural identity? What are the convictions and assessments that were born in the dramatic developments of this era that shape our cultural self-understanding up to today ... without which what we call *European-Western modernity* cannot even be thought?' (9–10)

[13] Habermas, *Between Religion and Naturalism*, 111.

[14] Cf. Detlev Horster, *Jürgen Habermas und der Papst. Glauben und Vernunft, Gerechtigkeit und Nächstenliebe im säkularen Staat* (Bielefeld: Transcript, 2006), 42, quoting the theologian Friedrich W. Graf that there is hardly any recent German-speaking contribution 'on the relationship between the democratic constitutional state, civic virtue and religion which does not cite Ernst-Wolfgang Böckenförde's dictum'.

respect for individual freedom is also its risk because it has made itself dependent on the vitality of the moral sources that feed self-understandings in civil society. These 'pre-political foundations' have to deliver imaginative, conceptual and motivational resources that support the ability to live together, to accept the rule of law, and other attitudes, like not treating strangers in a hostile way. Law cannot operate sustainably without ethical foundations, but to keep these alive is not in its gift. This puts high demands on each human person to mobilize inner resources for dispositions that go beyond respecting only the negative rights of other citizens. It is the space where communities of conviction can draw on their narratives and conceptual traditions to revive motivations and to present contemporary culture with contents that others might also find meaningful. This thought is similar to what David Tracy has described as the appeal of the 'classic', and why he urges to develop literacy also in the symbolic worlds of other origins.

While Habermas points to the resources of secular humanism, he also sees the need for 'all cultural sources that nurture citizens' solidarity and their normative awareness'[15] to be engaged. He regards the 'democratic bond' as being under threat of 'corrosion' by markets 'assuming regulatory functions in domains of life that used to be held together by norms – in other words, by political means or through pre-political forms of communication'.[16] It is in this context that Habermas speaks of the danger that an

> uncontrolled [*entgleisende*] modernization of society ... could ... undermine the form of solidarity on which the democratic state depends even if it cannot enforce it. Then the constellation that Böckenförde has in mind would transpire, namely the transformation of the citizens of prosperous and peaceful liberal societies into isolated, self-interested monads who use their individual liberties exclusively against one another like weapons.[17]

The contributions of religious traditions to re-energizing the social bond and a normative consciousness lie in the heuristic and motivating capacities that their world-disclosing language makes available: 'Pure practical reason can no longer be so confident in its ability to counteract a modernization spinning out of control armed solely with the insights of a theory of justice. The latter lacks the creativity of linguistic world-disclosure that a normative consciousness afflicted with accelerating decline requires in order to

---

[15] Habermas, *Between Religion and Naturalism*, 111.
[16] Ibid., 107.
[17] Ibid.

regenerate itself.'[18] Thus, to reinvigorate the democratic project with its high moral expectations, Habermas regards it as vital that mutual translations are undertaken between citizens with religious and with secular self-understandings.

(b) The legacies of 'Athens' and 'Jerusalem'

For the Frankfurt School theorist, it is philosophically evident that central concepts of modernity would have been unthinkable without the biblical understanding of God. Unlike the different conceptions of the divine in Greek metaphysics, this God in 'calling into life communicates within a morally sensitive universe'.[19] He identifies the impact of biblical monotheism by indicating the key components of modern self-understanding that have been shaped by it:

> Without this subversion of Greek metaphysics by notions of authentically Jewish and Christian origin, we could not have developed that network of specifically modern notions which come together in the thought of a reason that is both communicative and historically situated. I am referring to the concept of subjective freedom and the demand for equal respect for all – and specifically for the stranger in her distinctiveness and otherness. I am referring to the concept of autonomy, of a self-binding of the will based on moral insight, which depends on relations of mutual recognition. I am referring to the concept of socialized subjects, who are individuated by their life histories, and are simultaneously irreplaceable individuals and members of a community; such subjects can only lead a life that is genuinely their own through sharing in a common life with others. I am referring to the concept of liberation – both as an emancipation from degrading conditions and as the utopian project of a harmonious form of life. Finally, the irruption of historical thought into philosophy has fostered insight into the limited span of human life … This awareness includes a sense of the fallibility of the human mind, and of the contingent conditions under which even our unconditional claims are raised.[20]

The recognition of the imprint which religious faith has left on key concepts emerging from the encounter of Jerusalem and Athens gives a

---

[18] Ibid., 211.

[19] Habermas, *The Future of Human Nature*, 115.

[20] Habermas, 'Israel or Athens: Where Does Anamnestic Reason Belong?' trans. Peter Dews, in *Religion and Rationality. Essays on Reason, God and Modernity*, ed. and intro. Eduardo Mendieta (Cambridge: Polity Press, 2002), 132–3.

different standing to the biblical heritage. It is not just seen as a counterpart but as a catalyst. Being able to draw on such a history of interaction should make the public sphere more able to understand the background of religious contributions. Ricoeur's position on where to locate religious traditions is similar to Habermas: while 'institutional authority' lies with the neutral state, traditions exert influence at the 'enunciative' level.[21] What Ricoeur adds is a dynamic and praxis-oriented understanding from the internal perspective of members of these traditions. He urges Christian communities to take up, 'without any hang-ups, their part in this cofoundation in open competition with other, heterogeneous traditions, which themselves are reinvigorated and driven by their unkept promises.'[22] Thus, members of a faith community also have an internal reason to engage in the public sphere: apart from wishing to keep the democratic project oriented by its ideals of fraternity as well as liberty and equality, they owe it to their religion to restart its original promise in their own generation.

It seems to me that the differentiated responses of Habermas and Ricoeur have only gained in topicality in view of the current tide of populism across relatively secure and educated democratic countries. It certainly has causes in the loss of previous protections through globalization, the financial crisis and growing inequality in income and assets; but the erosion of intuitions of global and local solidarity that biblical monotheism fostered, as noted by Habermas, is also a factor of cultural change. At the same time, as Jürgen Werbick points out in his systematic theological discussion of 'tradition', the call for religions as 'resources' is ambivalent.[23] It has to be examined whether it is the invitation to a self-instrumentalization for purposes that are part of detrimental developments; such as, shoring up identities for work processes where employees are surveilled and micromanaged. If the goals for which Christian attitudes are to be a resource are not co-determined by this tradition, the systemic process may just use up this source and then turn to the next 'aestheticized, success-oriented' candidate.[24]

Werbick's warning is one more reason to join forces with analysts who put the human subject at the centre, and to examine the directions contemporary society is taking. Yet how should this dialogue be structured?

---

[21] Ricoeur, *Reflections on the Just*, 94.

[22] Ibid., 105.

[23] Cf. Werbick, *Den Glauben verantworten*, 823.

[24] Ibid.

(c) Which language in the public sphere?

A much-discussed question also from the theological side is whether the language of participating in public discourse should be religious, introducing faith-based evaluations directly, or whether to argue on the basis of a shared – not just an overlapping – allegiance to human dignity. In this debate, the systematic theologian Saskia Wendel has taken the latter view, not only because it draws on shared moral convictions, but also because of the difference between discourses of justification from other modes of communication. Here, an alternative returns that has already appeared in Chapter 6 in Hübenthal's response to Anzenbacher's position: does the public forum consist completely of exchanges between different worldviews?[25] *Or* can it draw on the equal competence of believers as moral agents to formulate their assessments with reference to the principle of human dignity, in the language of a deontological practical reason? How does Wendel's outline of two distinct levels and modes of communication clarify the argument, especially in situations of entrenched culture wars where each side knows in advance what the other side will defend?

Wendel is critical of an 'unfiltered, direct' transmission of faith positions in public debate on policies that require a general justification. She regards the prophetic statements of political theology to topical questions as examples of direct interventions. Understanding Christianity as a 'world programme of compassion' fits into the enunciative sphere. Christian intuitions are imparted as offers, invitations and demands. They serve to inspire and to offer heuristic sensitization. What is decisive for Wendel, however, is that the justification has to be allocated to the faculty of reason that is common to all. Concrete proposals for ways forward have to be grounded in practical reason. Instead of proclaiming their religious convictions, she wants believers to translate them into the medium of reason. Before examining her argument, it should be highlighted that this is relevant for the problem raised by Böckenförde: that the state is dependent on the 'vitality' of traditions for the mentalities that sustain democratic life. Is it a mark of 'vitality' to be willing to translate, or does it mark a position of

---

[25] Rawls calls them 'comprehensive doctrines', but while they encounter each other in the 'background culture', there is no direct exchange between them and each worldview translates on its own. I have compared his model with the approaches of Habermas and Ricoeur and their philosophical and theological discussion in *Religion and Public Reason. A Comparison of the Positions of John Rawls, Jürgen Habermas and Paul Ricoeur* (Berlin and Boston: de Gruyter, 2014).

weakness that one is forced to translate? Each of the two positions implies different assumptions about the self and the other.

Wendel's reasons against the immediate use of the texts of a faith tradition by politically active members for their evaluations are twofold. One, it strengthens an already problematic tendency in a public that is increasingly defined by identity politics and enclaves of like-minded people. What may be a confirmation for its members, is unsuitable to win over fellow citizens from other worldviews. There is a double problem with such testimonies: for non-religious participants in society who are affected and need to be consulted, they do not constitute justifications. And a second task corresponds to the external argumentation: the internal process of agreement that has to happen within a faith community on how to accentuate its core message in response to the matter in question.

This interpretive task towards the internal membership includes the need to argue convincingly for one's position in relation to the foundational texts. It poses an exegetical and hermeneutical task which cannot be replaced by applying material taken from the Bible directly to a specific situation. Wendel refers to divergent biblical foundations of statements about the refugee and asylum policies in the European Union and about same-sex marriage. An example relevant outside Europe would be the use of the Bible for and against capital punishment. By asking, 'which authority decides what is legitimate and what is not?',[26] and, 'what distinguishes justified interpretations from pure ideologies?',[27] a 'hermeneutics of suspicion' in 'critically examining one's own positions and interpretations' is encouraged.[28] Though interpretations have also to be argued for internally,[29] it is important to be able to distinguish what can be related to as evident in the *forum internum* of communities of faith, from the different requirements of the general capacity of reason:

> Ethical and political positions aim for … reciprocal justification, for the greatest possible acceptance, indeed, for universality. But in that case they require processes of justification that can in principle address all; they therefore have to renounce to explicitly religious reasons for the logics of justification … Thus, taking recourse to contents that are legitimated through a theology of revelation has to be ruled out.[30]

---

[26] Wendel, 'Religiös motiviert – autonom legitimiert – politisch engagiert', 292.
[27] Ibid., 298.
[28] Ibid., 299.
[29] Ibid., 296.
[30] Ibid., 296–7.

In public debate one cannot expect particular religious motifs such as being made in the image of God to have justificatory force. Universal validity claims have to be able to be shared by all. Distinct from such argumentation is the level of motivating reasons. They can be articulated publicly without needing translation. An example of such a reason which elucidates a religious hope for meaning is 'that the history of suffering of the victims cannot be the last word'.[31]

Thus, the position of the autonomy school with its recognition of morality as the shared platform for argumentations on policies that affect all is defended against political theologies that legitimate their proposals directly from the revealed source of scripture. For Wendel, the heuristic, motivating, integrating and relativizing contribution from the Christian perspective is important for public debate. Yet the distinction remains that the justification of obligation is achieved by practical reason, that of the horizon of meaning by faith.

By supporting the role of practical reason to argue out conflicting positions, the Christian community strengthens a capacity that is accessible to all. There are cultural and intellectual trends that undermine it, such as genetic determinism and conclusions drawn from neurological studies that abolish the philosophical question of freedom. These trends indirectly relieve people of the burden of moral justification by overplaying determining factors to an extent that they verge on eradicating the consciousness of freedom. Against this symptomatic view, Höffe had clarified that finite freedom cannot be thought independently of determining factors, but that this is not the same as being coerced.[32] There are good reasons for theological ethics to endorse the concepts of practical reason.

At the same time, the public sphere should not be deprived of the language of the Bible and theology, together with their translations which can be multiple. Wendel is right that this level of religious contributions to public debate is not appropriate for justifying a position in general terms; this needs to be done in the terms of autonomous reason, having considered results from the individual sciences for the issues at hand. It is also true, as Habermas insists in his discussion with Cardinal Ratzinger, that democratic society does not need religion to provide a foundation for recognizing the other. This is the task of practical reason. However, the diagnosis must be taken

---

[31] Ibid., 300, 297.
[32] Höffe, *Can Virtue Make Us Happy?*, 219: One does not have to 'take freedom to be action without determination, but action without compulsion.'

into account that the moral is being reduced to the legal level. The possibly one-sided, generous action demanded by the categorical imperative then becomes limited to a strict reciprocity that can no longer be distinguished from a strategic and self-serving *do ut des*. Thus, it is the consciousness of the moral call that will benefit from the counter-images and models sustained by the biblical texts also for the contemporary generation of diverse participants in political culture. These texts provide counterpoints to the flood of images, to the supposed 'icons' and emblems of success presented by the media. The task of translation would be misunderstood if it was taken to mean Rawls's model of each comprehensive doctrine translating its worldview into the shared political values of liberty and equality before even entering the area of possible overlapping consensus. Mieth's and Bloch's 'images of attitude', Tracy's and Gadamer's 'classics', Habermas's and Ricoeur's awareness of the critical and poetic power of the religious part of cultural self-understandings indicate a different course, of allowing these sources to speak.

If, as Pröpper and Hübenthal observe, a progressive self-objectification and an erosion of the consciousness of freedom can be detected, then this diagnosis becomes the most urgent site for efforts to regain scope for people's sense of agency.[33] In Part 1, the human capacity for moral reflection was identified as the basis of all the systems of ethics. The resonance of cultural productions which express this key component of the sense of self confirms that it is a faculty one can still appeal to. For example, the role of keeping one's promise, and even getting a second chance to do so, in J. R. R. Tolkien's *The Lord of the Rings* can be taken as an encouraging sign that morality is able to call on an evidence of its own. Margaret Farley takes moral experience as the site of a genuine plurality of persons: 'Almost everyone can recall experiences of their own, dramatic or mundane, of a clear moral obligation that cannot be denied, even if it can be refused ... Such diversity of consciousness ... does not ... yield relativism but it may – for many reasons – yield genuine pluralism.'[34]

The universal human capability for morality is specified by the particular traditions which make up the world's cultures. Biblical monotheism has been the key factor for individualizing this awareness into a personal call to

---

[33] Pröpper, *Evangelium und freie Vernunft*, 70–1, in a text from 1995, and elsewhere. Hübenthal, 'Groß vom Menschen denken', 392. The terms 'self-instrumentalization' and 'self-objectification' have been used by Habermas in *The Future of Human Nature*, 66, 71, 101–15.

[34] Farley, 'Framework for Moral Discernment', 139.

respond to God's prior gift of life and freedom. Having been part of its origin, theological ethics should invest its intellectual resources into sustaining its presence and future. This effort can draw on the history of effects of the biblical heritage in philosophy and literature, art and music: from the 'Who? – Me?' gesture of Caravaggio's *The Calling of Saint Matthew*,[35] to the '*factum*' of the moral law within us for Kant. At the same time, the experience of moral obligation does not have to absorb the self whose existence is approved prior to all agency and before responding to the rights and hopes of others.

The discovery of the inescapable capacity for moral autonomy can be found in a text that expresses this common human property in the poetic image of a journey. It is a fitting end after a long tour through volumes of analysis of ethical, moral and theological reflection: a poem by the Irish Nobel Prize winner for Literature, Seamus Heaney, 'From the Republic of Conscience', dedicated to Amnesty International. In three parts – arrival, impressions of the foreign land, departure – it pictures the encounter of a visitor from a particular culture with a country concretized by its customs. It is not a 'generic' human being, but one with a specific origin who discovers both a prior familiarity through a family photo, and decidedly different understandings of self, world and sky-god. Governance – the 'presumption to hold office' – is seen as a practice one has to 'atone' for. The guest is sent off with 'dual citizenship', conferred by the 'old man', and a new calling:

> He therefore desired me when I got home
> to consider myself a representative
> and to speak on their behalf in my own tongue.
>
> Their embassies, he said, were everywhere
> but operated independently
> and no ambassador would ever be relieved.[36]

---

[35] Dated 1598–1601, it is located in S. Luigi, Chiesa dei Francesi, in Rome.
[36] Seamus Heaney, 'From the Republic of Conscience', in *100 Poems* (London: Faber & Faber, 2018), 94–5.

Bibliography

Ammicht-Quinn, Regina and Elsa Tamez (eds), *The Body and Religion, Concilium* 38 (London: SCM Press, 2002).

Ammicht-Quinn, 'Whose Dignity is Inviolable? Human Beings, Machines and the Discourse of Dignity', in *The Discourse of Human Dignity, Concilium* 39, ed. Regina Ammicht-Quinn, Elsa Tamez and Maureen Junker-Kenny (London: SCM, 2003), 35–45.

Ammicht-Quinn, Regina, Monika Bobbert, Hille Haker, Marianne Heimbach-Steins, Ulrike Kostka, Dagmar Mensink, Mechthild Schmedders, Susanna Schmidt and Marlies Schneider, 'Women in the Practice of Reproductive Medicine and in Bioethical Discourse – An Intervention', in *The New Pontificate: A Time for Change?, Concilium* 42, ed. Erik Borgman, Maureen Junker-Kenny and Janet Martin Soskice (London: SCM Press, 2006), 119–36.

Ansorge, Dirk, *Gerechtigkeit und Barmherzigkeit Gottes. Die Dramatik von Vergebung und Versöhnung in bibeltheologischer, theologiegeschichtlicher und philosophiegeschichtlicher Perspektive* (Freiburg: Herder, 2009).

Ansorge, Dirk, *Kleine Geschichte der christlichen Theologie. Epochen. Denker, Weichenstellungen* (Regensburg: Pustet, 2017).

Anzenbacher, Arno, *Einführung in die Ethik* (Düsseldorf: Patmos, 1992).

Anzenbacher, Arno, *Einführung in die Philosophie* (Freiburg: Herder, 8th edn 2008).

Anzenbacher, Arno, *Christliche Sozialethik* (Paderborn: Schöningh/UTB, 1998).

Anzenbacher, Arno, 'Sozialethik als Naturrechtsethik', in *Gesellschaft begreifen – Gesellschaft gestalten. Konzeptionen christlicher Sozialethik im Dialog*, ed. Karl Gabriel, *Jahrbuch für Christliche Sozialwissenschaften*, vol. 43 (Münster: Regensberg, 2002), 14–32.

Anzenbacher, Arno, 'Menschenrechtsbegründung zwischen klassischem und neuzeitlichem Naturrecht', in *Die Begründung der Menschenrechte. Kontroversen im Spannungsfeld von positivem Recht, Naturrecht und Vernunftrecht*, ed. Margit Wasmaier-Sailer, and Matthias Hoesch (Tübingen: Mohr Siebeck, 2017), 121–33.

Apel, Karl-Otto, 'Normatively Grounding "Critical Theory" by Recourse to the Lifeworld? A Transcendental-Pragmatic Attempt to Think with Habermas Against Habermas', in *Jürgen Habermas*, vols. I–IV (Sage Masters of Modern

Thought), ed. David M. Rasmussen and James Swindal (London: Sage, 2002), vol. III, 344–78.

Aristotle, *The Nicomachean Ethics*, trans. J. A. K. Thomson, revised with notes and appendices Hugh Tredennick, intro. Jonathan Barnes (London: Penguin, 1976).

Auer, Alfons, *Autonome Moral und christlicher Glaube*, repr. of 2nd ed. 1984, with a Postscript of 1984 and an introductory essay by D. Mieth (Darmstadt: WBG, 2016).

Austin, Victor Lee, *Christian Ethics: A Guide for the Perplexed* (London: Bloomsbury T & T Clark, 2013).

Barr, James, *Fundamentalism* (London: SCM Press, 1977).

Barton, John, 'Virtue in the Bible', in *Studies in Christian Ethics* 12 (1999): 12–22.

Barton, Stephen C., 'The Epistles and Christian Ethics', in *The Cambridge Companion to Christian Ethics*, ed. Robin Gill (Cambridge: CUP, 2001), 63–73.

Baumgartner, Christoph, 'Theological Ethics without Theology: Assessing Theological-ethical Reflection of Moral Challenges Posed by Pluralism in Relation to Theology', in *Theology in a World of Specialization, Concilium* 42, ed. Erik Borgman, and Felix Wilfred (London: SCM Press, 2006), 53–64.

Beinert, Wolfgang and Francis Schüssler Fiorenza, (eds), *Handbook of Catholic Theology* (New York: Crossroad, 1995).

Beinert, Wolfgang, 'Kanon', in *Handbuch der katholischen Dogmatik*, ed. W. Beinert (Freiburg: Herder, 1987), 298–302.

Benhabib, Seyla, 'The Debate over Women and Moral Theory Revisited', in *Feminists Reading Habermas: Gendering the Subject of Discourse*, ed. and intro. Johanna Meehan (New York: Routledge, 1995), 181–203.

Bloch, Ernst, *The Principle of Hope*, 3 vols., trans. Neville Plaice, Stephen Plaice and Paul Knight (Oxford: Blackwell, 1986).

Bobbert, Monika, 'Erster Teil: Zum Proprium der christlichen Moral: systematische Ansätze angesichts neuerer Ansätze theologischer Ethik', in Bobbert, Monika and Dietmar Mieth, *Das Proprium der christlichen Ethik. Zur moralischen Perspektive der Religion* (Fribourg: Edition Exodus, 2015), 15–106.

Böckenförde, Ernst-Wolfgang, *Staat – Gesellschaft – Freiheit. Studien zur Staatstheorie und zum Verfassungsrecht* (Frankfurt: Suhrkamp, 1976).

Brand, Cordula, Jessica Heesen, Birgit Kröber, Uta Müller and Tom Pothast (eds), *Ethik in den Kulturen – Kulturen in der Ethik. Festschrift Regina Ammicht-Quinn* (Tübingen: Narr Francke Attempto Verlag, 2017).

Cahill, Lisa Sowle, *Between the Sexes* (Philadelphia: Fortress, 1985).

Cahill, Lisa Sowle, 'On Richard McCormick', in *Christian Voices in Medical Ethics*, ed. Allen Verhey and Stephen E. Lammers (Grand Rapids: Eerdmans, 1993), 78–105.

Cahill, Lisa Sowle, 'Accent on the Masculine', in Wilkins, John (ed.), *Understanding Veritatis Splendor* (London: SPCK, 1994), 52–60.

Cahill, Lisa Sowle, *Sex, Gender, and Christian Ethics* (Cambridge: Cambridge University Press, 1996).

Cahill, Lisa Sowle, 'Gender and Christian Ethics', in Robin Gill (ed.), *The Cambridge Companion to Christian Ethics* (Cambridge: CUP, 2001), 112–24.

Cahill, Lisa Sowle, *Theological Bioethics: Participation – Justice – Change* (Washington, DC: Georgetown University Press, 2005).

Cahill, Lisa Sowle, 'Genetics, Theology, Common Good', in L.S. Cahill (ed), *Genetics, Theology, and Ethics. An Interdisciplinary Conversation* (New York: Crossroad/Herder & Herder, 2005), 117–36.

Cahill, Lisa Sowle, Hille Haker and Eloi Messi Metogo (eds), *Human Nature and Natural Law, Concilium* 46 (London: SCM, 2010).

Cahill, Lisa Sowle, *Global Justice, Christology, and Christian Ethics* (Cambridge: CUP, 2013).

Cahoy, William, 'One Species or Two?' in *Modern Theology* 11 (1995): 429–54.

Cavanaugh, William, 'Killing for the Telephone Company', in *Modern Theology* 20 (2004): 243–73.

Cavanaugh, William, 'Church', in *The Blackwell Companion to Political Theology*, ed. Peter Scott and W. T. Cavanaugh (Oxford: Blackwell, 2007), 393–406.

Cavanaugh, William, *The Myth of Religious Violence* (Oxford: OUP, 2009).

Chan, Yiu Sing Lucas, James F. Keenan and Ronaldo Zacharias (eds), *The Bible and Catholic Theological Ethics* (Maryknoll, NY: Orbis, 2017).

Chan, Yiu Sing Lucas, 'Biblical Ethics: 3D', in *The Bible and Catholic Theological Ethics*, ed. Yiu Sing Lucas Chan, James F. Keenan and Ronaldo Zacharias (Maryknoll, NY: Orbis, 2017), 17–33.

Collins, John, *The Apocalyptic Imagination: An Introduction to Jewish Apocalyptic Literature* (Grand Rapids, MI: Eerdmans, 2nd edn 1998).

Curran, Charles and Richard A. McCormick (eds), *The Use of Scripture in Moral Theology (Readings in Moral Theology No. 4)* (Ramsey, NJ: Paulist Press, 1984).

Curran, Charles and Richard McCormick (eds), *Natural Law and Theology (Readings in Moral Theology No. 7)* (Mahwah, NJ: Paulist Press, 1991).

Curran, Charles and Richard McCormick (eds), *The Historical Development of Fundamental Moral Theology in the U.S. (Readings in Moral Theology No. 11)* (Mahwah, NJ: Paulist Press, 1999).

Curran, Charles and Richard McCormick (eds), 'Veritatis Splendor: A Revisionist Perspective', in *The Historical Development of Fundamental*

Moral Theology in the U.S. (Readings in Moral Theology No. 11), ed. Charles Curran and Richard McCormick (Mahwah, NJ: Paulist Press, 1999), 242–66.

Curran, Charles and Leslie Griffin (eds), *The Catholic Church, Morality, and Politics (Readings in Moral Theology No. 12)* (Mahwah, NJ: Paulist Press, 2001).

Daughton, Amy, *With and for Others: Developing Ricoeur's Ethics of Self Using Aquinas's Language of Analogy* (Studien zur theologischen Ethik vol. 146) (Fribourg i. Ue: Academic Press/Freiburg. i. Br.: Herder, 2016).

Dean, Jodi, 'Discourse in Different Voices', in *Feminists Reading Habermas: Gendering the Subject of Discourse*, ed. and intro. Johanna Meehan (New York: Routledge, 1995), 205–29.

Deidun, Tom, 'The Bible and Christian Ethics', in *Christian Ethics: An Introduction*, ed. Bernard Hoose (London: Cassell, 1998), 3–46.

De Schrijver, Georges, *Recent Theological Debates in Europe: Their Impact on Interreligious Dialogue* (Bangalore: Dharmaram Publ., 2004).

Dungs, Susanne, Review of Christa Schnabl, *Gerecht sorgen: Grundlagen einer sozialethischen Theorie der Fürsorge* (Studien zur theologischen Ethik) (Freiburg: Herder, 2005), in *Theologische Literaturzeitung* 132 (2007): 995–7.

Düwell, Marcus, 'Angewandte Ethik. Skizze eines wissenschaftlichen Profils', in *Interdisziplinäre Ethik. Grundlagen, Methoden, Bereiche, Festschrift Dietmar Mieth*, ed. Adrian Holderegger and Jean-Pierre Wils (Freiburg. i. Ue: Universitätsverlag/ Freiburg i. Br.: Herder, 2001), 165–84.

Düwell, Marcus, Jens Braarvig, Roger Brownsword and Dietmar Mieth (eds), *Cambridge Handbook of Human Dignity: Historical Traditions, Philosophical Interpretations, Legal Implementation and Contemporary Challenges* (Cambridge: CUP, 2014).

Eicher, Peter (ed.), *Neues Handbuch theologischer Grundbegriffe* (München: Kösel, 1985).

Farley, Margaret, 'A Framework for Moral Discernment', in *Catholic Theological Ethics, Past, Present, and Future: The Trento Conference*, ed. James Keenan (Maryknoll, NY: Orbis, 2011), 138–46.

Fergusson, David, *Community, Liberalism and Christian Ethics* (Cambridge: CUP, 1998).

Fitzmyer, Joseph A., *The Gospel According to Luke: Introduction, Translation, and Notes* (Garden City, NY: Doubleday, 1981, 1985).

Fliethmann, Thomas, 'Radical Orthodoxy. Zu einer neuen Bewegung in der anglo-amerikanischen Theologie', in *Herder-Korrespondenz* 56 (2002) 407–11.

Frey, Christofer, 'Konvergenz und Divergenz von Ethik und Praktischer Theologie', in *Reconsidering the Boundaries between Theological Disciplines*, ed. Michael Welker and Friedrich Schweitzer (Münster: LIT Verlag, 2005), 113–22.

Freyne, Seán, 'The Bible and Christian Theology: Inspiration, Projection, Critique?', in S. Freyne, *Texts, Contexts, and Culture: Essays on Biblical Topics* (Dublin: Veritas, 2002), 238–55.

Freyne, Seán, 'Christological debates among Johannine Christians', in *The Many Voices of the Bible, Concilium* 38, ed. Seán Freyne and Ellen van Wolde (London: SCM, 2002), 59–67.

Freyne, Seán, *Jesus, a Jewish Galilean: A New Reading of the Jesus Story* (Edinburgh: T & T Clark, 2004).

Freyne, Seán, 'The Galilean Jesus and a Contemporary Christology', in *Theological Studies* 70 (2009), 281–97.

Friedman, Marilyn, 'Jenseits von Fürsorglichkeit. Die Ent-Moralisierung der Geschlechter', in *Jenseits der Geschlechtermoral. Beiträge zur feministischen Ethik*, ed. Herta Nagl-Docekal and Herlinde Pauer-Studer (Frankfurt: Fischer, 1993), 241–66.

Gaïth, Jérôme, *La conception de la liberté chez Grégoire de Nysse. Etudes de philosophie médievale* 43 (Paris: Librairie Philosophique J. Vrin, 1953).

Gerwen, Jef Van, 'Origins of Christian Ethics', in *The Blackwell Companion to Religious Ethics*, ed. William Schweiker (Oxford: Blackwell, 2005), 204–13.

Gewirth, Alan, *The Community of Rights* (Chicago: University of Chicago Press, 1996).

Gill, Robin (ed.), *The Cambridge Companion to Christian Ethics* (Cambridge: CUP, 2001).

Gilligan, Carol, *In a Different Voice: Psychological Theory and Women's Development* (Cambridge, MA: Harvard University Press, 1982).

Greisch, Jean, 'Ethics and Lifeworlds', in *Questioning Ethics: Contemporary Debates in Philosophy*, ed. Richard Kearney and Mark Dooley (London/New York: Routledge, 1999), 44–61.

Gula, Richard, 'Natural Law Today', in *Natural Law and Theology (Readings in Moral Theology) No. 7*, ed. Charles Curran, and Richard McCormick (Mahwah, NJ: Paulist Press, 1991), 369–91.

Gustafson, James, *Theology and Christian Ethics* (Philadelphia: Pilgrim Press, 1974).

Habermas, Jürgen, *Moral Consciousness and Communicative Action*, trans. C. Lenhardt and S. Weber Nicholsen (Cambridge, MA: MIT Press, 1990).

Habermas, Jürgen, *Religion and Rationality: Essays on Reason, God and Modernity*, ed. and intro. Eduardo Mendieta (Cambridge: Polity Press, 2002).

Habermas, Jürgen, 'Israel or Athens: Where Does Anamnestic Reason Belong?' trans. Peter Dews, in *Religion and Rationality*, 129–38.

Habermas, Jürgen, *The Future of Human Nature*, trans. Hella Beister, Max Pensky and William Rehg (Cambridge: Polity Press, 2002).

Habermas, Jürgen, *Between Naturalism and Religion*, trans. Ciaran Cronin (Cambridge: Polity, 2008).

Hadot, Pierre, *Exercises spirituelles et philosophie antique* (Paris: Albin Michel, 3rd edn 1993).

Haight, Roger, *Jesus, Symbol of God* (Maryknoll, NY: Orbis, 1999).

Haker, Hille, 'Selection Through Prenatal Diagnosis and Preimplantation Diagnosis', in *Genetics in Human Reproduction*, ed. Elisabeth Hildt and Sigrid Graumann (Aldershot: Ashgate, 1999), 157–65.

Haker, Hille, *Ethik der genetischen Frühdiagnostik.Sozialethische Reflexionen zur Verantwortung am Beginn des menschlichen Lebens* (Paderborn: Mentis, 2002).

Haker, Hille, 'The Perfect Body: Biomedical Utopias', in *The Body and Religion*, *Concilium* 38, ed. Regina Ammicht-Quinn and Elsa Tamez (London: SCM, 2002), 9–18.

Haker, Hille, 'Feministische Bioethik', in *Bioethik. Eine Einführung*, ed. Marcus Düwell and Klaus Steigleder (Frankfurt: Suhrkamp, 2003), 168–83.

Haker, Hille, 'Geschlechter-Ethik der Reproduktionsmedizin. Ethik – Geschlecht – Wissenschaften', in *Ethik – Geschlecht – Wissenschaft. Der 'ethical turn' als Herausforderung für die interdisziplinären Geschlechterstudien*, ed. Ursula Konnertz, Hille Haker and Dietmar Mieth (Paderborn: Mentis, 2006), 255–87.

Haker, Hille, 'Synthetic Biology: an Emerging Debate in European Ethics', in *Ethics for Graduate Researchers*, ed. Cathriona Russell, Linda Hogan and Maureen Junker-Kenny (Oxford: Elsevier, 2013), 227–39.

Harrington, Daniel and James Keenan, *Jesus and Virtue Ethics* (Lanham, MD/ Chicago: Sheed & Ward, 2002).

Harrington, Donal, *What Is Morality? The Light Through Different Windows* (Dublin: Columba Press, 1996).

Hauerwas, Stanley, *A Community of Character* (South Bend, IN: University of Notre Dame Press, 1981).

Hauerwas, Stanley, *Vision and Virtue: Essays in Christian Ethical Reflection* (South Bend, IN: University of Notre Dame Press, 1981).

Hauerwas, Stanley, *The Peaceable Kingdom: A Primer in Christian Ethics* (South Bend, IN: University of Notre Dame Press, 1983).

Hauerwas, Stanley, *Christian Existence Today* (Durham: Labyrinth Press, 1988).

Hauerwas, Stanley, and Gregory Jones (eds), *Why Narrative?* (Grand Rapids: Eerdmans, 1989).

Hauerwas, Stanley, Murphy, Nancey and Nation, Mark (eds), *Theology Without Foundations: Religious Practice and the Future of Theological Truth* (Nashville, TN: Abingdon Press, 1994).

Hauerwas, Stanley and Samuel Wells (eds), *The Blackwell Companion to Christian Ethics* (Oxford: Blackwells, 2004).

Heaney, Seamus, *100 Poems* (London: Faber & Faber, 2018).

Heimbach-Steins, Marianne, 'Grund zur Sorge – Genderfragen im Feld der Care-Arbeit', in *Ethik in den Kulturen – Kulturen in der Ethik. Festschrift Regina Ammicht-Quinn*, ed. Cordula Brand et al. (Tübingen: Narr Francke Attempto Verlag, 2017), 231–40.

Heimbach-Steins, Marianne and Georg Steins, '"Canon and Community". On the Social-Ethical Relevance of Scripture', in *'The Soul of Theology': On the Role of Scripture in Theology*, ed. Pierre Van Hecke, Conference Proceedings, Leuven, 17–20 September 2015, 155–66.

Henrich, Dieter, 'What Is Metaphysics – What Modernity?', in *Habermas: A Critical Reader*, ed. Peter Dews (Oxford: Blackwell, 1999) [Original: 1987], 291–319.

Herman, Barbara, *Moral Literacy* (Cambridge, MA: Harvard University Press, 2008).

Höffe, Otfried (ed.), *Einführung in die utilitaristische Ethik* (Stuttgart: UTB, 1975).

Höffe, Otfried, (ed.), *John Rawls – Eine Theorie der Gerechtigkeit* (Berlin: Akademie-Verlag, 1998).

Höffe, Otfried, 'Einführung in Rawls's Theorie der Gerechtigkeit', in *John Rawls – Eine Theorie der Gerechtigkeit*, ed. Höffe (Berlin: Akademie-Verlag, 1998), 3–26.

Höffe, Otfried, *Can Virtue Make Us Happy? The Art of Living and Morality*, trans. Douglas R. McGaughey, trans. ed. Aaron Bunch (Evanston/Ill: Northwestern University Press, 2010).

Hoffmann, Paul and Volker Eid, *Jesus von Nazareth und die christliche Moral. Sittliche Perspektiven der Verkündigung Jesu* (Freiburg: Herder, 1975, 3rd. edn 1979).

Hoffmann, Veronika, *Vermittelte Offenbarung. Paul Ricoeurs Philosophie als Herausforderung der Theologie* (Mainz: Grünewald, 2007).

Holderegger, Adrian and Jean-Pierre Wils (eds), *Interdisziplinäre Ethik. Grundlagen, Methoden, Bereiche. Festschrift Dietmar Mieth* (Freiburg. i. Ue: Universitätsverlag/ Freiburg i. Br.: Herder, 2001).

Hollenbach, David, *The Common Good and Christian Ethics* (Cambridge: CUP, 2002).

Hollenbach, David, 'Human Dignity in Catholic Thought', in *Cambridge Handbook of Human Dignity*, ed. Marcus Düwell, Jens Braarvig, Roger Brownsword, and Dietmar Mieth (Cambridge: CUP, 2014), 250–59.

Honnefelder, Ludger, *Woher kommen wir? Ursprünge der Moderne im Mittelalter* (Darmstadt: WBG, 2008).

Honneth, Axel, *Das Ich im Wir. Studien zur Anerkennungstheorie* (Frankfurt: Suhrkamp, 2010).

Honneth, Axel, *Das Recht der Freiheit. Grundriss einer demokratischen Sittlichkeit* (Berlin: Suhrkamp, 2011).

Hoose, Bernard (ed.), *Christian Ethics. An Introduction* (London: Cassell, 1998).

Horster, Detlev (ed.), *Weibliche Moral – ein Mythos?* (Frankfurt: Suhrkamp, 1998).

Horster, Detlev (ed.), *Jürgen Habermas und der Papst. Glauben und Vernunft, Gerechtigkeit und Nächstenliebe im säkularen Staat* (Bielefeld: Transcript, 2006).

Hübenthal, Christoph, 'Prolegomena zur christlichen Sozialethik. Theologische Vorbereitung und anthropologische Grundlegung', in *Interdisziplinäre Ethik. Grundlagen, Methoden, Bereiche, Festschrift Dietmar Mieth*, ed. Adrian Holderegger and Jean-Pierre Wils (Freiburg i. Ue.: Universitätsverlag/ Freiburg i. Br.: Herder, 2001), 75–100.

Hübenthal, Christoph, 'Autonomie als Prinzip. Zur Neubegründung der Moralität bei Kant', in *Kant und die Theologie*, ed. Georg Essen and Magnus Striet (Darmstadt: WBG, 2005), 95–128.

Hübenthal, Christoph, 'Teleologische Ansätze', in *Handbuch Ethik*, ed. Marcus Düwell, Christoph Hübenthal and Micha Werner (Stuttgart: Weimar, 2006 2nd edn), 61–8.

Hübenthal, Christoph, 'Rechte', in *Lexikon der Ethik*, ed. Jean-Pierre Wils and Christoph Hübenthal (Paderborn: Schöningh, 2006), 314–21.

Hübenthal, Christoph, *Grundlegung der christlichen Sozialethik. Versuch eines freiheitsanalytisch-handlungsreflexiven Ansatzes* (Münster: Aschendorff, 2006).

Hübenthal, Christoph, 'Solidarität – Historische Erkundung und systematische Entfaltung', in *Solidarität und Gerechtigkeit. Die Gesellschaft von morgen gestalten*, ed. Dietmar Mieth, in cooperation with Katharina Eckstein (Stuttgart: Katholisches Bibelwerk, 2009), 62–89.

Hübenthal, Christoph, 'Groß vom Menschen denken. Sozialethik als theologische Disziplin', in *Freiheit – Natur – Religion. Studien zur Sozialethik, Festschrift Arno Anzenbacher*, ed. Christian Spieß (Paderborn: Schöningh, 2010), 377–92.

Hübenthal, Christoph, 'Moral Philosophy and the Foundation of Catholic Social Thought', in *Gewirthian Perspectives on Human Rights*, ed. Per Bauhn (New York/London: Routledge, 2016), 96–110.

Hübenthal, Christoph, 'Ethische Begründung aus dem theologischen Grund des Säkularen. Eine katholische Sicht', in *Ökumenische Ethik*, ed. Thomas Weißer (Fribourg: Academic Press/Würzburg: Echter, 2018), 45–63.

Imbach, Ruedi, *Laien in der Philosophie des Mittelalters* (Bochum: B. R. Grüner, 1989).

Insole, Christopher J., 'Against Radical Orthodoxy: The Dangers of Overcoming Political Liberalism', in *Modern Theology* 20 (2004): 213–41.

Insole, Christopher J., *The Politics of Human Frailty. A Theological Defense of Political Liberalism* (London: SCM Press, 2004).

Jasanoff, Sheila, 'In the Democracies of DNA: Ontological Uncertainty and
    Political Order in Three States', in *New Genetics and Society* 24 (2005): 139–55.
Jeanrond, Werner G. and Jennifer L. Rike (eds), *Radical Pluralism and Truth:
    David Tracy and the Hermeneutics of Religion* (New York: Crossroad, 1991).
Jones, Gareth, 'The Authority of Scripture and Christian Ethics', in *The
    Cambridge Companion to Christian Ethics*, ed. Robin Gill (Cambridge: CUP,
    2001), 16–28.
Junker-Kenny, Maureen, 'Virtues and the God Who Makes Everything New', in
    Recognising the Margins: Essays in Honour of Seán Freyne, ed. Andrew
    Mayes and Werner Jeanrond (Dublin: Columba Press, 2006), 298–320.
Junker-Kenny, Maureen, *Habermas and Theology* (London: New York: T & T
    Clark International, 2011).
Junker-Kenny, Maureen, 'Recognising Traditions of Argumentation in
    Philosophical Ethics', and 'Introduction to Section 2, Research Ethics
    Governance in the EU: The Role of Civic Debate, the Question of Limits in
    Research', in Cathriona Russell, Linda Hogan, and Maureen Junker-Kenny
    (eds), *Ethics for Graduate Researchers: A Cross-Disciplinary Approach*
    (Oxford: Elsevier, 2013), 7–26 and 51–8.
Junker-Kenny, Maureen, 'Dignity, Fragility, Singularity in Paul Ricoeur's Ethics', in
    Cambridge Handbook of Human Dignity, ed. Marcus Düwell, Jens Braarvig,
    Roger Brownsword and Dietmar Mieth (Cambridge: CUP, 2014), 286–97.
——, *Religion and Public Reason. A Comparison of the Positions of John Rawls,
    Jürgen Habermas and Paul Ricoeur* (Berlin/New York, De Gruyter, 2014).
——, 'Enunziative Autorität' der Religionen als 'Mitbegründer' (Ricoeur) und
    Übersetzer in der pluralen Öffentlichkeit', in *Die gegenwärtige Krise
    Europas. Theologische Antwortversuche (Quaestiones disputatae* 291), ed.
    Karlheinz Ruhstorfer and Martin Kirschner (Freiburg: Herder, 2018),
    83–100.
Kampling, Rainer, 'Tradition', in *Neues Handbuch theologischer Grundbegriffe*
    vol. 4, ed. Peter Eicher (München: Kösel, 1985), 221–35.
Kant, Immanuel, *Critique of Pure Reason* [1781], trans. Norman Kemp Smith
    (New York: St Martin's Press/Toronto: Macmillan, 1965).
Kant, Immanuel, *Groundwork of the Metaphysic of Morals* [1785], trans. and
    analysed by H.J. Paton (New York: Harper, 1964).
Kant, Immanuel, *Critique of Practical Reason* [1788], trans. Lewis W. Beck
    (Indianapolis: The Library of Liberal Arts/Bobbs Merrill, 1980).
Kant, Immanuel, *Religion within the Limits of Reason Alone* [1793], trans.
    Theodore M. Greene and Hoyt H. Hudson (New York: Harper Torchbooks,
    1960).
Kant, Immanuel, *Perpetual Peace* [1795], in *On History*, ed. Lewis White Beck
    (Indianapolis/New York: The Library of Liberal Arts/Bobbs Merrill, 1963),
    85–135.

Kant, Immanuel, *The Doctrine of Virtue: Part II of the Metaphysic of Morals* [1797], trans. Mary J. Gregor. Foreword H. J. Paton (New York: Harper Torchbooks, 1964).

Kasper, Walter, *Jesus the Christ*, trans. V. Green (London: Burns & Oates/New York: Paulist Press, 1976).

Kasper, Walter, 'Die Wissenschaftspraxis der Theologie', in *Handbuch der Fundamentaltheologie vol. 4, Traktat Theologische Erkenntnislehre*, ed. Walter Kern, Hermann J. Pottmeyer and Max Seckler (Freiburg: Herder, 1988), 242–77.

Keenan, James, 'Virtue Ethics' in *Christian Ethics: An Introduction*, ed. Bernard Hoose (London: Cassell, 1998), 84–94.

Keenan, James, (ed.), *Catholic Theological Ethics in the World Church: The Plenary Papers from the First Cross-cultural Conference on Catholic Theological Ethics* (New York/London: Continuum, 2007).

Keenan, James, (ed.), *Catholic Theological Ethics, Past, Present, and Future: The Trento Conference* (Maryknoll, NY: Orbis, 2011).

Kobusch, Theo, *Christliche Philosophie. Die Entdeckung der Subjektivität* (Darmstadt: WBG, 2006).

Kohlberg, Lawrence, *Stages in the Development of Moral Thought and Action* (New York: Holt, Rinehart & Winston, 1969).

Kohlberg, Lawrence, *Essays on Moral Development*, vols. 1 and 2 (San Francisco: Harper & Row, 1981, 1984).

Latourelle, René and Fisichella, Rino (eds), *Dictionary of Fundamental Theology* (New York: Crossroad, 1994).

Leclerc, Gérard, *Histoire de l'autorité. L'assignation des énoncés culturels et de la généalogie de la croyance* (Paris: Presses universitaires de France, 1986).

Lenk, Hans (ed.), *Comparative and Intercultural Philosophy* (Berlin/Münster: LIT, 2009).

Lewin, David and Todd Mei (eds), *From Ricoeur to Action. The Socio-Political Significance of Paul Ricoeur's Thinking* (Continuum Studies in Continental Philosophy) (London: Bloomsbury, 2012).

Lewin, David, 'Ricoeur and the Capability of Modern Technology', in *From Ricoeur to Action: The Socio-Political Significance of Paul Ricoeur's Thinking*, ed. David Lewin and Todd Mei (London: Bloomsbury, 2012), 54–71.

Long, Fiachra and Siobhán Dowling Long (eds), *Reading the Sacred Scriptures: From Oral Tradition to Written Documents and Their Reception* (Abingdon: Routledge, 2017).

Long, Fiachra, 'The Hermeneutic Task', in *Reading the Sacred Scriptures: From Oral Tradition to Written Documents and Their Reception*, ed. Fiachra Long and Siobhán Dowling Long (Abingdon: Routledge, 2017), 1–24.

Lovin, Robin W., *An Introduction to Christian Ethics: Goals, Duties, and Virtues* (Nashville: Abingdon Press, 2011).

Mack, Elke, *Gerechtigkeit und gutes Leben. Christliche Ethik im politischen Diskurs* (Paderborn: Schöningh, 2002).

MacNamara, J. Vincent, *Faith and Ethics. Recent Roman Catholicism* (Dublin: Gill & MacMillan/Washington, DC: Georgetown University Press, 1985).

MacNamara, J. Vincent, *The Truth in Love: Reflections on Christian Morality* (Dublin: Gill & Macmillan, 1988).

McCormick, Richard, 'Theology in the Public Forum', in *The Catholic Church, Morality, and Politics (Readings in Moral Theology No. 12)*, ed. Charles Curran and Leslie Griffin (Mahwah, NJ: Paulist Press, 2001), 110–30.

Mayes, Andrew and Jeanrond, Werner (eds), *Recognising the Margins: Essays in Honour of Seán Freyne* (Dublin: Columba Press, 2006).

Mealey, Ann Marie, 'Reinterpreting the *Glaubensethik*/Autonomy Debate Through the Work of Paul Ricoeur', in *Paul Ricoeur: Poetics and Religion*, ed. Joseph Verheyden, Theo L. Hettema and Pieter Vandecasteele (Leuven: Peeters, 2011), 371–91.

Meehan, Johanna (ed.), *Feminists Reading Habermas: Gendering the Subject of Discourse* (New York: Routledge, 1995).

Meeks, Wayne, *The Moral World of the First Christians* (London: SPCK, 1986).

Meeks, Wayne, *The Origins of Christian Morality: The First Two Centuries* (New Haven, CT/London: Yale University Press, 1993).

Meeks, Wayne, 'The Christian Beginnings and Christian Ethics: The Hermeneutical Challenge', in *Bulletin European Theology* 9 (1998): 171–81.

Metz, Johann Baptist, *Theology of the World*, trans. William Glen-Doepel (New York: Herder & Herder, 1969).

Metz, Johann Baptist, *Zeit der Orden? Zur Mystik und Politik der Nachfolge* (Freiburg: Herder, 1977).

Metz, Johann Baptist, *Faith in History and Society*, trans. David Smith (New York: Crossroad, 1980).

Metz, Johann Baptist, *A Passion for God: The Mystical-Political Dimension of Christianity*, trans., ed. and intro. J. Mathew Ashley (Mahwah, NJ.: Paulist Press, 1998).

Mieth, Corinna, 'The Double Foundation of Human Rights in Human Nature', in *Human Rights and Human Nature*, ed. Marion Albers, Thomas Hoffmann, and Jörn Reinhardt (Ius Gentium: Comparative Perspectives on Law and Justice 35) (Dordrecht: Springer, 2014), 11–22.

Mieth, Dietmar, 'Autonomy of Ethics – Neutrality of the Gospel?' in *Is Being Human a Criterion of Being Christian?*, *Concilium* 18 (Edinburgh: T & T Clark, 1982), 32–9.

Mieth, Dietmar, *Moral und Erfahrung* (Freiburg i. Ue.: Universitätsverlag and Freiburg i. Br.: Herder, 3rd edn 1982).

Mieth, Dietmar, *Die neuen Tugenden* (Düsseldorf: Patmos, 1984).

Mieth, Dietmar, 'Autonomy or Liberation – Two Paradigms of Christian Ethics?', in *The Ethics of Liberation – The Liberation of Ethics, Concilium* 20, ed. Dietmar Mieth and Jacques Pohier (Edinburgh: T & T Clark, 1984), 87–93.

Mieth, Dietmar, 'Continuity and Change in Value Orientation', in *Changing Values and Virtues, Concilium* 23, ed. Dietmar Mieth and Jacques Pohier (Edinburgh: T. & T. Clark, 1987), 47–59.

Mieth, Dietmar, 'Gewissen', in *Grundbegriffe der christlichen Ethik*, ed. Jean-Pierre Wils and Dietmar Mieth (Paderborn: Schöningh/UTB, 1992), 225–42.

Mieth, Dietmar, 'Norm', in *Grundbegriffe der christlichen Ethik*, ed. Jean-Pierre Wils and Dietmar Mieth, 243–53.

Mieth, Dietmar, 'Theologie und Ethik/Das unterscheidend Christliche', in *Grundbegriffe der christlichen Ethik*, ed. Jean-Pierre Wils and Dietmar Mieth, 209–24.

Mieth, Dietmar, 'Statt einer Einleitung: Ist die Katholische Soziallehre christlich?', and 'Statt eines Schlusswortes: Centesimus annus: Christliche Sozialethik im Anspruch der Zukunft', in Dietmar Mieth (ed.), *Christliche Sozialethik im Anspruch der Zukunft. Tübinger Beträge zur Katholischen Soziallehre* (Freiburg i. Ue: Universitätsverlag/Freiburg i. Br.: Herder, 1992), 7–12, and 175–83.

Mieth, Dietmar, *Moral und Erfahrung II. Entfaltung einer theologisch-ethischen Hermeneutik* (Freiburg i. Ue.: Universitätsverlag and Freiburg i. Br: Herder, 1998).

Mieth, Dietmar, 'Bioethics, Biopolitics, Theology' in Maureen Junker-Kenny (ed.), *Designing Life? Genetics, Procreation and Ethics* (Aldershot: Ashgate, 1999), 6–22.

Mieth, Dietmar, 'Kulturethik', in *Angewandte Ethik und Religion*, ed. Thomas Laubach (Tübingen: A. Francke/UTB, 2003), 293–308.

Mieth, Dietmar, (ed.), in cooperation with Katharina Eckstein, *Solidarität und Gerechtigkeit. Die Gesellschaft von morgen gestalten* (Stuttgart: Katholisches Bibelwerk, 2009).

Mieth, Dietmar, 'Human Dignity in Late Medieval Conflicts', in *Cambridge Handbook of Human Dignity*, 74–84.

Mieth, Dietmar, 'Zweiter Teil: Ethik, Moral und Religion', in Bobbert, Monika and Dietmar Mieth, *Das Proprium der christlichen Ethik. Zur moralischen Perspektive der Religion* (Fribourg: Edition Exodus, 2015), 109–288.

Mieth, Dietmar, 'Moralische Autonomie – Selbstbestimmung und Selbstverpflichtung nach Alfons Auer', in Auer, *Autonome Moral*, I–XXXIX.

Mill, John Stuart, *Utilitarianism, Liberty, Representative Government. Selections from Auguste Comte and Positivism*, ed. H. B. Acton (London: J. M. Dent & Sons, 1972).

Möhring-Hesse, Matthias, 'Sozialethik als Naturrechtsethik – oder lieber nicht? Im Gespräch mit Arno Anzenbacher', in *Freiheit – Natur – Religion. Studien zur Sozialethik*, ed. C. Spieß, (Paderborn: Schöningh, 2010), 299–327.

Moltmann, Jürgen, *Sonne der Gerechtigkeit* (Gütersloh: Gütersloher Verlagshaus, 2008).

Müller, Klaus and Magnus Striet (eds), *Dogma und Denkform. Strittiges in der Grundlegung von Offenbarungsbegriff und Gottesgedanke* (Regensburg: Pustet, 2005).

Nagl-Docekal, Herta, 'Feministische Ethik oder eine Theorie weiblicher Moral?', in *Weibliche Moral – ein Mythos?*, ed. Detlev Horster (Frankfurt: Suhrkamp, 1998), 42–72.

Nagl-Docekal, Herta, 'Ein Postscriptum zum Begriff Gerechtigkeitsethik', in *Weibliche Moral – ein Mythos?*, ed. Detlev Horster, 142–53.

Nagl-Docekal, Herta, *Feminist Philosophy*, trans. Katharina Vester (Boulder, CO: Westview Press, 2004) [1999].

Nagl-Docekal, Herta, '"Many Forms of Non-Public Reason"? Religious Diversity in Liberal Democracies', in *Comparative and Intercultural Philosophy*, ed. Hans Lenk (Berlin/Münster: LIT, 2009), 79–92.

Nagl-Docekal, Herta, 'Issues of Gender in Catholicism. How the Current Debate Could Benefit from a Philosophical Approach', in *Church and People: Disjunctions in a Secular Age*, ed. Charles Taylor, José Casanova and George F. McLean (Washington, DC: The Council for Research in Values and Philosophy, 2012), 155–87.

Nagl-Docekal, Herta, *Innere Freiheit. Grenzen der nachmetaphyischen Moralkonzeptionen (Deutsche Zeitschrift für Philosophie Sonderband 36)* (Berlin/Boston: De Gruyter, 2014).

Nagl-Docekal, Herta and Pauer-Studer, Herlinde (eds), *Jenseits der Geschlechtermoral. Beiträge zur feministischen Ethik* (Frankfurt: Fischer, 1993).

Nagl-Docekal, Herta and Klinger, Cornelia (eds), *Continental Philosophy in Feminist Perspective. Re-reading the Canon in German* (University Park, PA: University of Pennsylvania University Press, 2000).

Orth, Stefan and Peter Reifenberg (eds), *Facettenreiche Anthropologie* (Freiburg/München: Alber, 2004).

O'Neill, Onora, *Bounds of Justice* (Cambridge: CUP, 2000).

Pfotenhauer, S. M., C. F. Jones, K. Saha and S. Jasanoff, 'Learning from Fukushima', in *Issues in Science & Technology* 28 (2012): 79–84.

Pope, Stephen, 'Reason and Natural Law', in *Human Nature and Natural Law, Concilium* 46, ed. Lisa S. Cahill, Hille Haker and Eloi Messi Metogo (London: SCM Press, 2010), 148–67.

Porter, Jean, *The Recovery of Virtue: The Relevance of Aquinas for Christian Ethics* (London: SPCK, 1994).

Porter, Jean, *Moral Action and Christian Ethics* (Cambridge: CUP, 1995).

Porter, Jean, *Natural and Divine Law. Reclaiming the Tradition for Christian Ethics* (Grand Rapids, MI: Eerdmans, 1999).

Porter, Jean, 'Virtue', in *The Oxford Handbook of Theological Ethics*, ed. Gilbert Meilaender and William Werpehowski (Oxford: OUP, 2005), 205–19.

Pottmeyer, Hermann J., 'Tradition', in *Dictionary of Fundamental Theology*, ed. René Latourelle and Rino Fisichella (New York: Crossroad, 1994), 1119–26.

Power, David N., 'Eucharist', in *Systematic Theology: Roman Catholic Perspectives*, ed. Francis Schüssler Fiorenza and John P. Galvin (Minneapolis: Fortress Press, 1991), 261–88.

Pröpper, Thomas, *Der Jesus der Philosophen und der Jesus des Glaubens. Ein theologisches Gespräch mit Jaspers – Bloch – Kolakowski – Gardavsky – Machovec – Fromm – Ben-Chorin* (Mainz: Grünewald, 1976).

Pröpper, Thomas, *Erlösungsglaube und Freiheitsgeschichte. Eine Skizze zur Soteriologie* (München: Kösel, 3rd edn 1991).

Pröpper, Thomas, *Evangelium und freie Vernunft* (Freiburg: Herder, 2001).

Pröpper, Thomas, *Theologische Anthropologie*, vols 1 and 2 (Freiburg: Herder, 2011).

Rahner, Hugo (ed.), *Die Pfarre. Von der Theologie zur Praxis* (Freiburg: Herder, 1956).

Rahner, Karl, 'Zur Theologie der Pfarre', in *Die Pfarre. Von der Theologie zur Praxis*, ed. Hugo Rahner (Freiburg: Herder, 1956), 27–39.

Ricoeur, *History and Truth*, trans. and intro. Charles Kelbley (Evanston: Northwestern University, 1965).

Ricoeur, *The Conflict of Interpretations*, ed. Don Ihde (Evanston, IL: Northwestern University, 1974).

Ricoeur, 'Hope as a Structure of Philosophical Systems' [1970], in *Figuring the Sacred. Religion, Narrative, and Imagination*, ed. Mark I. Wallace, trans. D. Pellauer (Minneapolis: Fortress, 1995), 203–16.

Ricoeur, *Hermeneutics and the Human Sciences*, ed. and trans. John B. Thompson (Cambridge: CUP, 1981).

Ricoeur, *Time and Narrative*, 3 vols., trans. Kathleen Blamey and David Pellauer (Chicago: University of Chicago Press, 1984–1988).

Ricoeur, 'Love and Justice', in *Radical Pluralism and Truth. David Tracy and the Hermeneutics of Religion*, ed. Werner G. Jeanrond and Jennifer L. Rike (New York: Crossroad, 1991), 187–202.

Ricoeur, *Oneself as Another*, trans. Kathleen Blamey (Chicago: University of Chicago Press, 1992).

'Les religions, la violence et la paix', Entretien Hans Kung-Paul Ricoeur autour du 'Manifeste pour une ethique planetaire' (ed. du Cerf), ARTE 5 April 1996, Redaction: Laurent Andres, cf. www.fondsricoeur.fr, under ,texts on line' (last accessed 6 January 2019), and in *Sens. Revue de l'amitié judéo-chrétienne de France* 5 (1998): 211–30.

——, *The Just*, trans. David Pellauer (Chicago: University of Chicago Press, 2000).

——, 'Ethics and Human Capability: A Response', in *Paul Ricoeur and Contemporary Moral Thought*, ed. John Wall, William Schweiker and David Hall (London/New York: Routledge, 2002), 279–90.

——, *Reflections on the Just,* trans. David Pellauer (Chicago: University of Chicago Press, 2007).

——, *The Course of Recognition*, trans. David Pellauer (Cambridge, MA: Harvard University Press, 2005).

Ross, Susan, 'Christian Anthropology and Gender Essentialism', in *A Time for Change? Open Questions, Concilium* 42, ed. Erik Borgman, M. Junker-Kenny and Janet Martin Soskice (London: SCM, 2006), 43–50.

Russell, Cathriona, Linda Hogan and Maureen Junker-Kenny (eds), *Ethics for Graduate Researchers: A Cross-Disciplinary Approach* (Oxford: Elsevier, 2013).

Saiving, Valerie, 'The Human Situation: A Feminine View', in *Journal of Religion* 40 (1960): 100–12.

Schill, Andreas, *Theologische Prinzipienlehre. Lehrbuch der Apologetik*, 2nd edn revised by Oskar Witz (Paderborn: Schöningh, 1903).

Schillebeeckx, Edward, *Jesus. An Experiment in Christology*, trans. Hubert Hoskins (New York: Seabury Press, 1979).

Schillebeeckx, Edward, *Christ. The Experience of Jesus as Lord*, trans. John Bowden (New York: Seabury Press, 1980).

Schleiermacher, Friedrich D. E., *The Christian Faith* (2nd edn 1830/31), trans. and ed. H. R. Mackintosh and J. S. Stewart (Edinburgh: T & T Clark, 1986).

Schnabl, Christa, *Gerecht sorgen: Grundlagen einer sozialethischen Theorie der Fürsorge* (Studien zur theologischen Ethik) (Freiburg: Herder, 2005).

Schnabl, Christa, 'Vulnerability, Reciprocity, and Familial-Care Relations: A Socioethical Contribution, in *Catholic Theological Ethics, Past, Present, and Future: The Trento Conference*, ed. James Keenan (Maryknoll, NY: Orbis, 2011), 224–34.

Schnädelbach, Herbert, *Zur Rehabilitierung des animal rationale. Vorträge und Abhandlungen 2* (Frankfurt: Suhrkamp, 1992).

Schneider, Birgit, '*Wer Gott dient, wird nicht krumm.' Feministische Ethik im Dialog mit Karol Wojtyla und Dietmar Mieth* (Mainz: Grünewald, 1997).

Schockenhoff, Eberhard, *Natural Law and Human Dignity. Universal Ethics in an Historical World*, trans. Brian McNeil (Washington, DC: CUA Press, 2003).

Schreiter, Robert, *Constructing Local Theologies* (Maryknoll, NY: Orbis, 1985).

Schulz, Walter, *Philosophie in der veränderten Welt* (Pfullingen: Neske, 1972).

Schulz, Walter, *Grundprobleme der Ethik* (Pfullingen: Neske, 1989).

Schweiker, William (ed.), *The Blackwell Companion to Religious Ethics* (Oxford: Blackwell, 2005).

Scott, Peter and William T. Cavanaugh (eds), *The Blackwell Companion to Political Theology* (Oxford: Blackwell, 2007).

Siep, Ludwig, 'Natural Law and Bioethics', trans. J. G. Cumming, in *Human Nature and Natural Law, Concilium* 46, ed. Lisa S. Cahill, Hille Haker and Eloi Messi Metogo (London: SCM, 2010), 44–67.

Siker, Jeffrey S., 'Stanley Hauerwas: The Community Story of Israel and Jesus', in J. S. Siker (ed.), *Scripture and Ethics. Twentieth Century Portraits* (New York and Oxford: OUP, 1997), 97–125. 237–48.

Spieß, Christian (ed.), *Freiheit – Natur – Religion. Studien zur Sozialethik, Festschrift Arno Anzenbacher* (Paderborn: Schöningh, 2010).

Spohn, William, *Go and Do Likewise: Jesus and Ethics* (New York: Continuum, 1999).

Striet, Magnus (ed.), *Gestorben für wen? Zur Diskussion um das 'pro multis'* (Freiburg: Herder, 2007).

Striet, Magnus (ed.), 'Nur für viele oder doch für alle? Das Problem der Allerlösung und die Hoffnung der betenden Kirche', in *Gestorben für wen? Zur Diskussion um das 'pro multis'*, ed. Magnus Striet (Freiburg: Herder, 2007), 81–92.

Taylor, Charles, José Casanova and George F. McLean (eds), *Church and People: Disjunctions in a Secular Age* (Washington, DC: The Council for Research in Values and Philosophy, 2012).

Thomasset, Alain, 'The Virtue of Hospitality According to the Bible and the Challenge of Migration', in *The Bible and Catholic Theological Ethics*, ed. Yiu Sing Lucas Chan, James F. Keenan and Ronaldo Zacharias (Maryknoll, NY: Orbis, 2017), 34–44.

Tierney, Brian, *The Crisis of Church and State 1050-1300* (Englewood Cliff, NJ: Prentice-Hall, 1964).

Tierney, Brian, *The Idea of Natural Rights: Studies on Natural Rights, Natural Law and Church Law 1150-1625* (Atlanta: Scholars Press, 1997).

Tracy, David, *Blessed Rage for Order: The New Pluralism in Theology* (New York: Seabury Press, 1975).

Tracy, David, 'Theology, Critical Social Theory, and the Public Realm', in Don S. Browning and Francis Schüssler Fiorenza (eds), *Habermas, Modernity, and Public Theology* (New York: Crossroad, 1992), 19–42.

Tracy, David, 'Three Kinds of Publicness in Public Theology', in *International Journal of Public Theology* 8 (2014): 330–4.

Tracy, David, 'Religion in the Public Realm: Three forms of publicness', in *At the Limits of the Secular: Reflections on Faith and Public Life*, ed. Willliam A. Barbieri (Grand Rapids, MI: Eerdmans, 2014), 31–50.

Traina, Cristina L. H., *Feminist Ethics and Natural Law. The End of the Anathemas* (Washington, DC: Georgetown University Press, 1999).

Verhey, Allen and Stephen E. Lammers (eds), *Christian Voices in Medical Ethics* (Grand Rapids, MI: Eerdmans, 1993).

Veritatis Splendor, Encyclical of Pope John Paul II (London: Cath. Truth Society, 1993).

Verstraeten, Johan, 'Re-Thinking Catholic Social Thought as Tradition', in *Catholic Social Thought – Twilight or Renaissance?*, ed. J.S. Boswell, F.P. McHugh and J. Verstraeten (Leuven: Peeters, 2000), 59–77.

Verstraeten, Johan, 'Re-thinking the Economy, a Matter of Love or Justice? The Case of the Compendium of the Social Doctrine of the Church and the Encyclical *Caritas in Veritate*', in *Concilium* 47, *The Economy and Religion*, ed. Luis Carlos Susin and Erik Borgman (London: SCM Press, 2011), 92–102.

Walde, B., 'Inspiration', in *Lexikon für Theologie und Kirche*, vol. 5 (Freiburg: Herder, 1st edn 1933), 423–29.

Wall, John, William Schweiker and David Hall (eds), *Paul Ricoeur and Contemporary Moral Thought* (London/New York: Routledge, 2002).

Welker, Michael and Friedrich Schweitzer (eds), *Reconsidering the Boundaries between Theological Disciplines* (Münster: LIT Verlag, 2005).

Wells, Samuel, 'How Common Worship Forms Social Character', in *Studies in Christian Ethics* (Special Issue Liturgy and Ethics) 15 (2002): 66–74.

Wendel, Saskia, *Affektiv und inkarniert. Ansätze deutscher Mystik als subjekttheoretische Herausforderung* (Regensburg: Pustet, 2002).

Wendel, Saskia, 'Religiös motiviert – autonom legitimiert – politisch engagiert. Zur Zukunftsfähigkeit politischer Theologie angesichts der Debatte um den öffentlichen Status religiöser Überzeugungen', in *Religion – Öffentlichkeit – Moderne. Transdisziplinäre Perspektiven*, ed. Judith Könemann and S. Wendel (Bielefeld: Transcript, 2016), 298–306.

Werbick, Jürgen (ed.), *Offenbarungsanspruch und fundamentalistische Versuchung* (Freiburg: Herder, 1991).

Werbick, Jürgen (ed.), 'Einleitung', in *Offenbarungsanspruch und fundamentalistische Versuchung*, ed. Jürgen Werbick (Freiburg: Herder, 1991), 11–35.

Werbick, Jürgen (ed.), *Den Glauben verantworten. Eine Fundamentaltheologie* (Freiburg: Herder, 2000).

Werbick, Jürgen (ed.), 'Umkehren? – Umgekehrt werden! Was P. Ricoeurs Bibelhermeneutik der Fundamentaltheologie zu denken gibt', in *Facettenreiche Anthropologie* , ed. Stefan Orth and Peter Reifenberg (Freiburg/München: Alber, 2004), 115–36.

Wilkins, John (ed.), *Understanding Veritatis Splendor* (London: SPCK, 1994).

Wils, Jean-Pierre and Dietmar Mieth, 'Tugend', in *Grundbegriffe der christlichen Ethik*, ed. J.-P. Wils and D. Mieth (Paderborn: Schöningh/UTB, 1992), 182–98.

Wogaman, J. Philip, *Christian Ethics: A Historical Introduction* (Louisville: Westminster/John Knox, 1993, 2nd enlarged edn 2011).

Zimmermann, Ruben and Jan G. van der Watt, in cooperation with Susanne Luther (eds), *Moral Language in the New Testament*, WUNT 296 (Tübingen: Mohr Siebeck, 2010).

Index